Broadcast Announcing

Broadcast Announcing

WILLIAM L. HAGERMAN

University of Southwestern Louisiana

PRENTICE HALL, Englewood Cliffs, New Jersey 07632

Library of Congress Cataloging-in-Publication Data

HAGERMAN, WILLIAM L.
   Broadcast announcing/William L. Hagerman.
     p. cm.
   Includes index.
   ISBN 0-13-036872-5
   1. Radio announcing. 2. Television announcing. I. Title.
  PN1990.9.A54H3 1993
  808.5—dc20   92-28940
                            CIP

Acquisitions editor: Steve Dalphin
Copy editor: Eleanor Walter
Prepress buyer: Kelly Behr
Manufacturing buyer: Mary Ann Gloriande
Cover design: Rich Dombrowski
Editorial assistant: Caffie Risher

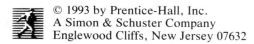

© 1993 by Prentice-Hall, Inc.
A Simon & Schuster Company
Englewood Cliffs, New Jersey 07632

Printed in the United States of America

10 9 8 7 6 5 4 3 2 1

ISBN 0-13-036872-5

PRENTICE-HALL INTERNATIONAL (UK) LIMITED, *London*
PRENTICE-HALL OF AUSTRALIA PTY. LIMITED, *Sydney*
PRENTICE-HALL CANADA INC., *Toronto*
PRENTICE-HALL HISPANOAMERICANA, S.A., *Mexico*
PRENTICE-HALL OF INDIA PRIVATE LIMITED, *New Delhi*
PRENTICE-HALL OF JAPAN, INC., *Tokyo*
SIMON & SCHUSTER ASIA PTE. LTD., *Singapore*
EDITORA PRENTICE-HALL DO BRASIL, LTDA., *Rio de Janeiro*

Contents

2   THE ANNOUNCER PREPARES   27

3   UNDERSTANDING COMMUNICATION   43

4   THE FAVORED NEWS SOURCE   66

7   THE THEATRE AND BROADCASTING   149

8   INTERVIEWING   177

9   THE SPORTSCASTER   199

10 THE AUDIO AND VIDEO STUDIOS   227

11 RADIO FORMATS   261

12   A LOOK AHEAD   **294**

Broadcast Vocabulary Word Lists

Preface

This book is the result of some 20 years of teaching broadcasting courses. In my years as a beginning instructor in broadcasting, I headed a program at a small college in Nebraska. It was a good program. We did a lot of things early on that many good programs did not adopt until later, or somehow have never gotten the opportunity to do at all. However, one memory still haunts me. The beginning radio production course emphasized the mechanics of the electronics: how to cue a record, microphone pickup patterns, backtiming, and the like. Copy reading usually came as part of another exercise, which emphasized other skills or techniques. The generalized approach of such courses as "Fundamentals of Speech" and "Oral Interpretation" were supposed to give students the oral skills to perform as broadcasters.

After graduation, one of our best students academically got a full-time job at the local radio station with my highest recommendations. It was a catastrophe and embarrassing for all concerned. The lad could not read copy without stumbling over his own words. Since then I have resolved that where I had any control, students graduating in broadcasting would take an announcing class in which they learned how to competently read broadcast copy.

One does not learn to sing by studying music theory. One must practice singing. The same is true with announcing. Dedicated practice is required to become a good announcer.

Some instructors may not find it expedient to assign one or more hours a week of cassette reading for students to complete, as is suggested in the exercises at the end of each chapter. Dedicated students can on their own, however, practice material found at the end of each chapter and develop their broadcasting skills, paying close attention to such things as avoiding voice patterns and practicing good voice placement.

As this book took form, my students were most helpful in testing and evaluating it. Without their help this book never could have happened.

ACKNOWLEDGMENTS

In fact, without the help of many individuals this book could not have come into being. I wish to thank the following for their assistance:

Prentice-Hall College Field Representative Edith Hall, who "discovered" the in-process manuscript, Executive Editor Steve Dalphin, whose nurturing brought the book to its final form, and Rob DeGeorge, who kept things on schedule.

The reviewers who provided new insights and offered constructive criticism. They are: Janet R. Kenney at Murray State University, Bob Buckalew at the University of Texas–Austin, and Don Singleton at Salisbury State University.

I also wish to thank:

U.S.L. Communication Department Head, Dr. Robert Simmons, who offered continuing encouragement.

KLFY-TV Vice President for News, Maria Placer, and KRVS-FM Manager Dave Spizale, who permitted complete access to their facilities for photographic purposes.

To U.S.L. Television Engineer, James Moore, for his evaluation of the chapter on audio and video studios.

To then Graduate Assistant, Stephen Foster, for his untiring efforts in taking pictures and processing film for the book; also to Jeremy Schiro for photographical assistance.

William L. Hagerman

Broadcast Announcing

1

Announcing
Techniques

OBJECTIVES
Upon completion of this chapter the student should be able to:

1. Explain the origins of the term *announcer.*
2. Explain challenges faced by the present-day announcer.
3. List four attitudes recommended for announcers and explain the importance of each.
4. Describe yoga relaxation techniques useful to announcers.
5. List and explain four ways to overcome "mike fright."
6. Explain to whom an announcer is responsible and how these responsibilities should be carried out.
7. List the four main structures and functions that produce the voice.
8. Name five physical elements of the voice mechanism and describe how they may be used to help properly place the voice in announcing.
9. List seven benefits of diaphragmatic breathing.
10. Describe improper breathing techniques announcers should try to avoid, and two other (often proper) techniques that might be overdone.
11. Point out how listening can be used to improve announcing skills.
12. Describe three important factors that help provide announcer credibility.
13. Indicate ways in which the language changes geographically and historically.
14. Explain how the body may be used in announcing for radio and for television.
15. Properly pronounce the listed commonly mispronounced words.

PLAYING THE ANNOUNCER

> Speak the speech, I pray you, as I pronounced it to you, trippingly on the tongue; but if you mouth it as many of your players do, I had as lief the town-crier spoke my lines.[1]
>
> —*William Shakespeare*

Shakespeare apparently had little regard for the announcers of his day: the town-criers rated naught but disdain. It was the players (the actors) who received instruction. Perhaps if Hamlet had made his speech instead to the announcers of the time (the town-criers), these town-criers would have been as effective as today's announcers. This book is to help today's town-criers—today's announcers—communicate effectively.

ANNOUNCER DEFINED

Looking at the Latin root for the word "announce," we find it has evolved from *ad annuntiare,* to announce, which was in turn derived from *nuntius,* the word for messenger. An "announcer," then, in the earlier sense of the word, was one who carried a message and perhaps declared it to an awaiting group. The messenger

Figure 1–1 An early "announcer."

[1] William Shakespeare, *Hamlet,* Act III, Sc. ii.

who brought news of the battle of Thermopylae was an early announcer. (Much as the early messengers may have been punished or even killed because they were blamed for the bad news they bore, today's announcers are at times disdained if the message is continuously bad news.) Other pre-radio announcers might have declared an edict of the king in the public square, proclaimed the arrival of the performers in the Roman gladiator ring, or made religious declarations to an assembled multitude.

Scripture readers and other church "announcers" helped sustain the culture. Early preliterate cultures had "announcers" who memorized the poetry, history, and traditions of the culture to pass them on to the people and the next generation.

With the advent of the phonetic alphabet, learning changed from memorizing to reading. (Plato is credited with organizing information alphabetically.) During the Dark Ages the church sustained knowledge of writing and reading. Priests can be assumed to have read aloud to people in a manner similar to that of broadcast announcers today. Still later, announcers on trains and in train stations heralded the coming of the transportation revolution.

Like these earlier announcers, the stadium announcer of athletic events today is addressing an assembled crowd as a group, much as early radio announcers did. However, today's good radio announcers are interpersonal communicators rather than announcers to the many.

The twentieth century has thus added a new meaning for announcer. Not only does *announcer* mean one who officially proclaims, but it now has a second meaning: one who communicates via one of the electronic mass media, often in the form of interpersonal communication.

AN INTELLECTUAL CHALLENGE

Skilled professional announcers are constantly engaged in intellectual exercises. They must be forever on the alert to understand what is happening in the environment—both in the immediate world about them and on the wider national and international scenes. By being interested in what is happening, announcers can make their interpretation of the news, presentation of commercials, and even delivery of music commentary meaningful and relevant.

Announcers face the challenge of providing materials of interest to the listener in a manner that is both provocative and insightful. The way a phrase is interpreted can often mean the difference between a listener's comprehension and misunderstanding.

In many instances announcers choose the material to be presented. Disc jockeys (dee-jays) who carefully prepare their material can be not only entertaining but purveyors of valuable information as well. Of course, in many circumstances announcers present what is prepared for them. Here, as well, professional announcers should be able to use their extensive knowledge to provide skillful interpretation and broad understanding.

HELPING OTHERS UNDERSTAND

Broadcast personnel are often expected to furnish a view of the environment for the illiterate and for those who choose not to read. It has been argued that the electronic media make people lazy and make reading appear unnecessary to them. Arguing the point will not solve this problem. But recognition of the problem puts a continued and almost overwhelming responsibility on electronic media personnel to provide needed information for their listeners in a form that these listeners find relevant. Responsible announcers provide important information to allow their audiences to express themselves individually, through their spokespersons, and at the ballot box.

ATTITUDES OF THE ANNOUNCER

Announcers need to display confidence to achieve credibility. A lack of confidence can sometimes lead to nervous and uncontrolled actions, which must be overcome by the announcer. Announcers need to take pride and demonstrate enthusiasm in what they do to ensure success. Announcing also entails attitudes of grave responsibility.

Confidence

The wealth of information at their command and their understanding of the world about them should give announcers self-assurance. Broadcasters' styles of delivery should let them converse with members of the audience as individuals, unintimidated by anyone they think might be listening. To be effective, announcers need to be conversational in presentation and readily understandable in the manner in which they project ideas. A confident delivery can go to extremes, however. Announcers may be so overconfident in manner that they appear to their audiences as egotistical and almost unbearable. When announcers find that they are *always* right and other programmers do *not* really understand how best to attract an audience, it is time for them to step back and evaluate themselves. Has the announcer become arrogant? As in any endeavor, success in announcing can go to one's head. Haughty self-importance is to be avoided at all costs. With the adulation announcers often receive, it is important for them to remember how repugnant arrogance can be.

Mike Fright

In contrast to overconfidence is underconfidence, which can lead to "mike fright," and which can be so intense as to limit an announcer's ability to communicate effectively. Relaxation is one key to an effective performance. A relaxed (but controlled) posture helps. The body should be erect whether sitting or standing, yet as free of tenseness as possible, allowing air to flow freely from the lungs. It is often helpful to consciously relax the shoulders by shrugging, the arms by swinging, and the hands by shaking limply at the wrist. Yoga-like exercises are suggested for body relaxation. Yoga's "lotus" position entails folding your legs under you as you sit with your back erect, head and rib cage up. In most instances announcers will not be in an environment where they can assume the lotus position without calling attention to their actions. They can, however, sit in a chair and consciously yet quietly relax their entire being. One exercise that readily helps relaxation without calling attention to itself can often be practiced before an announcing stint.

> Start by thinking of your toes. Consciously relax them and feel them relax. Do the same with your feet, then your ankles. Proceed by relaxing your calves, knees, and thighs, one by one. Continue the relaxation process with your hips, your abdomen, and your chest. The shoulders (as suggested earlier) seem to be particularly important in the relaxation process. When relaxing your neck, roll your head around and tilt it back and forth. Think about relaxing your jaw as you gently move it side to side. You have now relaxed your whole body. If you can remain relaxed in this position, while you project the sound "ohm-m-m" quietly to yourself, you should feel renewed.

The apologies that beginning announcers make for their mistakes can be more distracting than the mistakes themselves. Apprehension about the possibility of making a mistake—even though none is apparent to the listener—can rob beginning announcers of their effectiveness. How can this apprehension be overcome?

1. Beginning announcers need a firm determination to succeed. They must be fully committed and determined that nothing will keep them from achieving their goals.
2. It is important that the beginning announcer prepare carefully the material that is to be presented. Knowing that one has the material well in hand builds confidence and contributes to relaxation.
3. Learning how to relax is often a key to overcoming microphone apprehension. In addition to determination, preparation, and relaxation, the thing that best overcomes nervousness before the microphone is practice.
4. Constant practice and experience are vital. As one's performance becomes routine, apprehension subsides. Perhaps it is best to retain a bit of "mike fright," because this adrenaline rush can be used to keep a fine edge on one's performance and keep announcers alert to pitfalls that can impede their professional presentation.
5. Energy comes from an attitude of excitement and a belief in the importance of the material being presented. An announcer is expected to generate energy on an almost continuous basis. Energy is required in advertising (Chapter 6), news (Chapter 4), and each of the various broadcasting formats (Chapters 9 and 11).

Responsibility

It is important to recognize the responsibility that one has as an announcer. Announcers have an obligation to the station owners and management, to the listeners, to the advertisers (on a commercial station), and to themselves. It is indeed a serious charge. Announcers can enhance or destroy a station's money-making potential. A single rash action by one announcer can tarnish a station's image. Announcers represent not only themselves but also the advertisers and the station management with every statement they make, with every record they play. Advertisers' messages need to get top priority: they must be delivered with enthusiasm and conviction, on time, and in a manner designed to increase the advertisers' sales. Statements that offend a minority of the audience (even if they are not listening at the time) can reflect on the advertiser and the station. Advertisers have been known to remove their advertising from a station that made pronouncements deemed sexually improper, sacrilegious, or offensive to a portion of the audience. It is the duty of the announcer to project an image consistent with the employing organization at all times.

Announcers also have the responsibility for the maintenance of expensive equipment. In many instances on a night or weekend shift, a single person may be responsible for the operation of an entire radio station.

As noted earlier, the announcer's obligation to the audience cannot be overemphasized. In most cases announcers are expected to provide information and entertainment with a positive attitude about the programming, the station, and the community that comes from pride in their work. Likewise, the station is obligated to operate in "the public interest, convenience and necessity."[2] So, while the owners may be interested primarily in making a profit, serving the public well and making a profit often go hand in hand. Advertisers pay significant sums to get their messages to as many persons as possible. Therefore, providing the public with what they expect and want on a particular station is the obligation of broadcast personnel. Doing the best possible job at providing broadcast service benefits the announcer as well with a secure job, experience for the future, recognition from listeners, and sometimes even with fan loyalty.

Broadcast announcing does indeed require positive and responsible attitudes and a willingness to meet the intellectual challenge.

USING THE VOICE

In order to do the outstanding job expected of announcers by themselves, by their employers, by their advertisers, and by their audiences, it is important to control the voice. Foremost in consideration are breathing, voice placement, articulation, and tone. Though voice teachers do not necessarily agree on how to best produce the most desirable voice quality, most agree upon the physical parts the student has to work with. Let's take a look at the equipment we will use to try to produce a pleasant, expressive, and credible voice.

The Physical Structure

Theorists of voice as a rule acknowledge that the main structures and functions that produce the voice are:

[2] Communications Act of 1934.

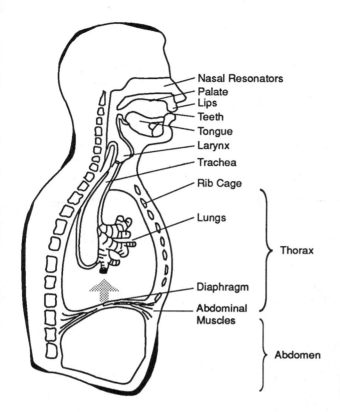

Nasal Resonators
Palate
Lips
Teeth
Tongue
Larynx
Trachea
Rib Cage
Lungs
Thorax
Diaphragm
Abdominal
Muscles
Abdomen

Figure 1-2 The base of the lungs lies on the diaphragm.

1. All parts concerned with the breath: the Motor Power;
2. All parts concerned with the vibrator: the Generator of Sound;
3. All parts concerned with the resonance cavities: the Amplifier of Sound.[3]

Most voice teachers likewise acknowledge a fourth structure: All parts concerned with listening: the Feedback.

The diaphragm is the membrane separating the abdomen and the thorax. The abdomen is roughly the lower third of the body cavity and the thorax fills the upper two-thirds. The muscles of the upper thorax control what is called *thoracic breathing. Abdominal* or *diaphragmatic breathing* is controlled primarily by the muscles of the abdomen. Since the lungs tend to be more or less cone shaped with the base lying on the diaphragm, there is greater capacity for air at the base of the lungs than at the top.

Abdominal breathing.

[3] Henry N. Jacobi, *Building Your Best Voice* (Englewood Cliffs, N.J.: Prentice Hall, 1982), p. 115.

Thoracic Breathing

Look in a mirror if you have one handy. Watch yourself as you take a deep breath. Did you raise your shoulders as you inhaled? If you did, you have just demonstrated thoracic breathing. Thoracic breathing is what most of us do most of the time. Instead of using the greater lung capacity at the base of the cone, we are trying to force air into the limited, narrower space of the upper lungs.

Diaphragmatic Breathing

Diaphragmatic breathing, or expansion of the abdomen and the rib cage as one inhales, allows for greater quantities of air to be captured in the lungs than does shallow thoracic breathing. On inhalation the rib cage should expand out and sideways as the upper abdominal muscles similarly expand. Airflow as the breath is exhaled can then be controlled by the diaphragm, the muscle wall that separates the abdomen and the thorax. Diaphragmatic breathing is the breathing technique used by singers, actors, and trained announcers.

A highly developed diaphragm may hinder effective breath control. Learn to breathe by practicing diaphragmatic breathing rather than doing sit-ups, lifts, or other diaphragmatic exercises not directly related to voice production.[4]

To demonstrate the naturalness of diaphragmatic breathing, get down on your hands and knees. Inhale, allowing gravity to help expand your lower rib cage and stomach muscles. Pressure on your shoulders from placing part of your body weight on your arms should restrain shoulder movement as a result of taking a deep breath. Next, contract your lower ribs and tighten your upper abdomen, forcing the air out. You have now demonstrated "natural" diaphragmatic breathing. Unfortunately, as we stand or sit erect, we often have to think consciously about the process in order to invoke diaphragmatic breathing and to realize its benefits. With extended practice, use of the diaphragm for breath support becomes habit.

Comparing Breathing Types

Thoracic exhalation tends to be rapid and uncontrolled, while proper diaphragmatic airflow can be controlled by the use of the abdominal muscles adjacent to the diaphragm. Better voice projection can result from the use of the added capacity and control at the base of the lungs. With abdominal breathing there is less wasted airflow, because abdominal muscles can control the flow when speaking stops. It is generally agreed that thoracic breathing also leads to a higher pitch and often to nasality because neck muscles are tight. Tenseness of the vocal chords may be the result of the general anxiety of performance, or it may be the result of one's habitual speaking style. Diaphragmatic breathing allows more relaxation of the larynx (voice box or vocal chords) and therefore a lower pitch

[4] Jacobi, p. 136.

[handwritten: will not pick up Diaphragmatic]

and generally a more pleasant voice. Diaphragmatic inhalation is less noticeable and less apt to be picked up by a sensitive microphone. Noisy breathing or breathiness may sound sexy for a short time, but it very rapidly becomes distracting. Further, the relaxed larynx and diaphragmatic breathing allow extended speaking without hoarseness. Obviously, diaphragmatic breathing is worth striving for.

Diaphragmatic Techniques

[handwritten: Place Tone Articulation]

How does one achieve this breathing style? Remember how when taking a deep breath, while sitting or standing, your shoulders may have gone up as you inhaled using thoracic breathing? Try again. This time, while sitting or standing erect, consciously expand your rib cage right and left and your upper abdomen as you inhale, keeping your shoulders back and down. Now exhale, forcing your abdomen in and pulling your ribs together. Hold your hand on your ribs and abdomen to help you get the feel of expansion and contraction as you breathe. If you mentally picture your breath as coming from your diaphragm as you speak, it soon becomes an almost automatic action as you are speaking, especially in a situation where you are "on mike."

One of the objectives of proper breathing is breath support and control of the taking of breaths. Announcers should refrain from taking overly large breaths, as too much air may crowd the breathing passages and create tension in the breath control muscles. Generally the announcer's tone is improved by a relaxed, controlled flow of air. Breaths should never be taken in the middle of sentences or phrases in such a way that the flow of an idea is interrupted. Constantly, replenishing the air supply at commas, periods, and other appropriate points in the copy, prevents the announcer from gasping for breath or breathing at an inappropriate point.

Breathing through the nose moistens and warms the air taken in, which is, of course, desirable. There are times, however, when this may not supply an adequate quantity of air, so breathing through the mouth is necessary. (Taking too much air too rapidly through the nose can result in a sniffling sound, which would be picked up by most mikes).

"The purpose of vocal support is to produce an even, vibrant tone flow and to sustain vocal phrases, full length with ease."[5]

Voice Placement

In the "golden age of radio" the announcer was expected to have a beautiful, deep voice and project mellifluous tones with a formal correctness that was always "perfect." Network radio announcers at one time were expected to be so perfect and so formal that they even wore tuxedos for evening performances. While a deep bass voice is no longer required for announcing and formality is

[5] Jacobi, p. 143.

generally shunned, it is still desirable to use your full pitch range with emphasis on the natural lower register of your speaking voice to avoid grating on listeners' nerves. Always try to avoid tenseness of the larynx by relaxing your whole body. Never achieve loudness by shrieking or project nasality by placing your voice in your head. Instead, think your voice "down," and feel it coming from your diaphragm. One reason why women's voices were unacceptable on radio for many years in anything but dramatic parts was the feeling that a higher pitch was less pleasant to listen to for an extended period of time.

Most persons learn to talk by imitating the speech of their mothers. Most mothers speak with untrained voices and certainly have higher pitch to their voices than fathers do, for example. Most adolescents leave childhood with voices pitched higher than ideal for non-irritating communication. Some voices even have a nasal quality or a breathiness that is much less pleasant than the quality achieved with proper voice placement.

Probably the best way to overcome the problem of incorrect voice placement (i.e., a voice probably pitched higher than really "natural," or a voice with an unpleasant nasal quality) is to use diaphragmatic breathing and think your voice "down," constantly thinking of the diaphragm as the point of origin for the voice. This process may seem somewhat illogical, since you know that the voice comes from the larynx. Yet the support for the voice and the controlled flow of air does come from the diaphragm, and thinking the voice "down" does work for many students. Constant practice using this technique is amazingly effective for both men and women. Remind yourself, "Think my voice down; think of my voice coming from my abdomen. Use my diaphragm for support."

Obviously, like any technique, this can be overdone. Don't strain for a low voice. Don't become monotone, using only your lower register. You still want a conversational variation of pitch. The main objective is to use your lower register and make use of the "natural" resonance of your voice. Some announcers seem to have two voices: the one they use when they are on the air or "on mike," and the one they use when they are doing anything else. The on-the-air voice may seem somewhat unnatural to people who converse regularly with them, but to those in the radio audience, that is the only voice they have heard from this particular announcer. To them, this *is* the person's "natural" voice.

Tone Production

The parts of the speech mechanism combine to create the tone that is heard as one speaks. The column of air directed from the lungs by pressure from the diaphragm causes the vibration of the vocal chords (larynx). This sound then is directed into the resonant cavities of the chest, throat, and head.

Upper and lower resonating sources provide a variety of contrasts and a wide selection of possibilities from which to draw, in modifying, magnifying and adorning tone. The combination of these will vary as pitch, volume and color of tone vary—and must be allowed to do so. . . . The task is to channel the tides of the sound to best individual advantage in order to produce a free, rich, round tone.[6]

Resonating chambers in the head initially give students a false sense of voice quality. As they become more adept at listening, however, and practice with a tape recorder, they can learn and commit to memory what it takes to produce the free, rich, round tone for which they are striving.

All parts of the physical system work together to create the sounds that are produced. Often individuals will not realize the importance of resonating chambers until they have head cold and find some of their resonating chambers blocked. The importance of the larynx is emphasized when the speaker is disabled by laryngitis. Asthma or other breathing disorders call attention to the importance of a controlled, vigorous breath.

One of the most natural, relaxed tones is produced when one laughs. Here is an example of vibrant, bubbly, flexible, bouyant, natural tone. It is not necessarily the most desirable tone an individual can produce, but it can serve as a basis for vocal improvement if studied carefully. The broadcast voice is the tone produced by the breath, vibrator, and resonators as articulated by the lips, tongue, palate, and other related physical aspects of the mouth.

Articulation

Articulation is a term that refers to *the movements of lips, tongue, jaw, and soft palate to form speech sounds*. Articulation is what changes vocal sound into recognizable speech. Good articulation means producing sounds that are clear and distinct without being overly precise or affected.[7]

The most common articulation problems are

1. the *slurring* of words together ("Did you eat?" becomes "jeet?");
2. the *omission* of ending sounds ("Informing is communicating," becomes "Informin' is communicatin' "); and
3. the *substitution* of one sound for another ("With the South" becomes "wit du Sout").

When children are learning to speak, they are learning so much so fast that child learning experts continue to be amazed. It's no wonder then that eager parents often learn to comprehend the slurred speech of "mush-mouthed" articulation and may even unconsciously encourage such performance by learning to understand what the child is trying to say. I'm sure you've heard doting relatives talk baby talk to a budding scion. Not surprisingly, we often find remnants of this "gobbledegook" in the speech of adults. Many of us have lazy speech articula-

[6] Jacobi, p. 162.
[7] Anita Taylor et al., *Communicating,* 4th ed. (Englewood Cliffs, N.J.: Prentice Hall, 1986), pp. 342, 343.

tors—lips, tongue, or jaws particularly. These articulators need to be used to provide clearly defined, correct sounds and properly emphasized syllables.

Lazy speech habits can be overcome by opening the mouth and moving the lower jaw vigorously, and by elaborately exercising the tongue and lips in an exaggerated manner. Initially those with lazy speech organs may find these exercises to be excessive contortions. Not unlike thinking of the voice as coming from the abdomen, however, exercising the speech organs will make the speaker conscious of the use of these tools, and the resulting careful articulation can be a decided improvement.

A word of caution: as pointed out earlier, almost anything can be overdone—including articulation. For students who find they have mushy articulation, the practice of exaggerated preciseness in articulation can help them speak more clearly, but overarticulation is also to be avoided. When most students were learning to read, their elementary teacher probably expected them to clearly pronounce each word and to precisely articulate each syllable. There may even be a tendency now for these students to give each syllable equal emphasis when they read. Of course this is not conversational. Clear and concise *conversational* speech should be the announcer's aim.

Using Articles

Another holdover from learning to read in elementary school is the way students pronounce articles when they read aloud. (Articles are "a," "an," and "the.") Being careful to give equal value to all syllables, students may overemphasize articles when reading. Articles are of secondary or tertiary importance in most sentences. The indefinite article "a" (or "an") indicates one of several, while the definite article "the" refers to a specific person, place, or thing.

People usually use the weak forms of articles in conversation. In other words, for the article "a," instead of the strong form "ay" in conversation usually one says "uh." For "the," instead of the strong form "thee," one says "t/hu" (a voiced "th" sound and the unaccented vowel sound "uh").

The rule in singing, which also works in conversation, is the use of the weak form of "a" ("uh") or "the" (with the "uh" sound) before words beginning with a consonant. "The" pronounced "thee" is properly used before words beginning with a vowel. Of course instead of "a," "an" is properly used before words beginning with a vowel sound when the indefinite article is intended.

The only other times that the strong forms of articles are used is when the article is used in place of "one." This usually follows a statement in which a choice is offered. For example:

Of the several boys present, he is the (*can be pronounced thee*) boy that was selected.
She found she could select only a (*ay*) question.

Using the strong form of an article at all times sounds extremely stilted, though you will find the use of the weak form of "the" every time also seems unnatural. Be prepared to look for nouns beginning with vowel sounds where you can use the strong form of "the." The use of the proper article emphasis has much to do with making the speaker or reader sound conversational.

Peer Influence

In addition to parental imitation in learning the speech process, people are also influenced by others in their social circles. Speech habits and voice patterns common in certain geographical areas often become part of one's speech. Faddishness may also influence one's speech patterns and expressions. An example of this is the "valley girl" popularized expression "y'know," often used when a person cannot immediately think of something to say. Certain verbal crutches are almost universal and include the interjection of "uh" or "and-uh" to fill the space between thoughts. While the occasional use of a verbal crutch may lend to the speaker's apparent informality or spontaneity, the interjection of meaningless expressions generally is to be avoided.

USING THE EAR

Do you remember the first time you heard a recording of your voice? Was it disappointing? You have since learned that the way your voice sounds to you as you are speaking is much more pleasant to listen to than your voice after it has been recorded and played back. Your head has marvelous resonating chambers that make the sounds you emit from your mouth much more resonant and softened to your own ears than to those of others. If you speak from the back of your mouth and use diaphragmatic breathing, much of the resonance can be "captured" by the microphone. You need to listen to your voice as recorded and as you speak—especially when you announce.

Listening to Yourself

To develop a voice that communicates clearly, announcers must listen as they speak. Most people speak almost automatically, paying little attention to how sounds are created or what they sound like. In order to correct mistakes people must first become conscious of making them. Practice with a tape recorder. Listen to yourself on tape. Try to make the changes suggested by your instructor. Then listen to yourself in everyday conversation as well as when you are practicing as an announcer. Some times a best friend or roommate can be alerted to help you listen for specific errors in everyday speech. When you are conscious of the mistakes you are making, you can correct them repeatedly until you no longer need to be intensely aware of the sound of what you are saying, because it will "automatically" come out right.

In addition to listening to voice quality and voice placement, you need to listen for correct *pronunciation* (word sounds and accents) and *enunciation* (precise articulation), as well as rate, pauses, and variation of pitch, which are discussed more completely in Chapter 2. If you have some obvious grammatical errors that appear in normal conversation and will be inherent in your ad libbing, these should be corrected too.

Listening to Others

Proper pronunciation is probably most easily learned by listening to correct pronunciation and imitating those sounds. For this reason students should take every chance possible to listen to credible network news announcers. Most network news announcers try religiously to use correct pronunciation.

Foreign names and terms most often cause confusion. Trying to translate sounds from another language into English, which does not have these particular sounds, sound sequences, or manner of accenting, can sometimes result in several variations of the same non-English terms, especially when a new term or name suddenly hits the news. Usually within about a week, a consensus will be arrived at by the wire services and national newscasters. Listening once, then, is not enough. In order to be fully aware of terms in the news, one needs to listen regularly to be fully aware of changes as they occur.

Nor should an announcer in an unfamiliar geographic area neglect local newscasts. The names of families vary in different locales. There is also variation across the country in the way different places names are pronounced by the local residents—and the local pronunciation is accepted as correct.

Different spellings may elicit the same pronunciation, or names that look similar may be pronounced quite differently. The family name Hebert (''ay' bair'' in southern Louisiana) usually becomes pronounced ''hee' burt'' by the same family in other parts of the country.

The oldest municipality in Texas, Nacogdoches, and the oldest settlement in Louisiana, Natchitoches, seem to have similar names. The Texas town is pronounced ''nak u doh' chus.'' The Louisiana town: ''nak' u dish.''

The Willamette (wil lam' ut) River in Oregon is pronounced differently than the similarly spelled Wilmette (wil met') River in Illinois. It is properly the state of Arkansas (ar' kan saw), but the Arkansas (ar kan' zus) River.

Across the country Spanish, French, Native American, and many other languages have had their influences on place names—names and spellings that often tend to defy any phonetic rules of pronunciation we may have learned. A good gazetteer or atlas will reveal most proper pronunciations, but smaller subdivisions, such as Scio (sigh' oh), Oregon, may not be in most listings.

International names transplanted to the United States often come out with different pronunciations: for example, Cairo (kay' roh), Illinois, but Cairo (kigh' roh), Egypt; Edinburg (ed' in burg), Texas, but Edinburgh (ed' in bur oh), Scotland.

The only way to be sure of proper pronunciation of place names may be to ask a native of the area. Of course, you may not even realize you are incorrect except by listening to knowledgeable local newscasters or in conversation with local residents.

CREDIBILITY

A good announcer has a pleasant voice, articulates clearly, and has credibility gained through properly using the language and having a sufficient variation in his or her presentation to maintain attention and interest. Credibility and authority come from good command of the language: correct grammar and proper pronunciation. You are expected to have learned grammar in English class, but proper use of the written language is not enough. Although the wire service copy and the materials copywriters prepare for you are probably grammatically correct, the writers cannot pronounce words for you. Proper names or foreign terms may be represented by phonetics, but it is usually up to the announcer to know the correct pronunciation of most of the words that appear in copy. For this reason, lists of often mispronounced words, taken mostly from news and news discussion programs, are presented at the end of each chapter. Mastery of these words will go far toward acquainting you with words that otherwise might give you trouble. The word list paragraphs are designed solely to give you practice using these words. The paragraphs are intended to be neither realistic nor logical; their *Alice in Wonderland* quality provides a presentational challenge. Many students have found them to be fun as well as rewarding in helping to master pronunciation.

Job Application

When you are applying for a job—almost any job—you are judged on the way you use the language. In an interview for an announcing position, it should be obvious that your pronunciation and use of the language are supremely important.

Black government office workers in Washington, D.C., had found they were not getting the job advancement to which they felt entitled because of ability and seniority. It became clear to them that their black dialect was hindering their advancement. Often the supervisors were not consciously prejudiced, but the image projected by an individual who does not speak standard American English—who pronounces words with regionalism or ethnicity—can be deemed to be less intelligent. Classes in the pronunciation of standard American English for government workers in Washington, D.C., seem to have helped many people learn to speak without ethnic speech patterns, to be better accepted by the wider society, and to get desired job advancements.

Arbitrary Standards

As is often the case, people perceive others based on arbitrary standards set by society. This may not be a fair way to do things, but unfortunately that's the way the system works. One of these arbitrary standards is the way people use the language, including the way they pronounce words. Some mispronunciations are regional; some are ethnic; some are generational; yet others, educational. Some mispronunciations are just plain laziness on the part of the speaker.

Check yourself and correctly pronounce the list of words that follows. Note that the correct pronunciation rhymes with the word in the second column. If your pronunciation sounds like the rhyme word in the third column, you are mispronouncing the word.

BROADCAST VOCABULARY WORD LIST   Unit 1-A

COMMONLY MISPRONOUNCED WORDS

Word	*Phonetics or Rhyme Word*	*Incorrect Rhyme or Phonetics*
across	toss	tossed
again	pen	pin
am	jam	gem
and	sand	send
any	penny	skinny
asked	masked	taxed
ask	task	tax
been	thin	den
begin	thin	den
bury	dairy	worry
can	fan	thin
catch	match	fetch
cent	vent	hint
chic	sheik	lick
corps	more	corpse
creek	weak	wick
for	or	car
friend	bend	den
genuine	one	wine
get	bet	bit
golf	Rudolph	cough or gulf
gross	dose	toss
guess	less	kiss
hundred	grid	thundered
if	stiff	Jeff
instead	bed	bid
just	must	mist
last	past	pass
length	strength	tenth
little	whittle	still
many	penny	mini
maybe	baby	webby
men	ten	tin
milk	silk	elk
most	toast	dose
next	vexed	necks
Oregon	gun	gone

Word	Phonetics or Rhyme Word	Incorrect Rhyme or Phonetics
our	power	are
pen	ten	tin
picture	pik'chur	pitcher
plague	vague	beg
poem	poh' um	home
poor	lure	pour
pretty	witty	dirty or Betty
real	steal	still
recognize	re' kug nighz	re' ku nighz
rinse	prince	tense
roof	proof	rough
since	prince	tense
soot	foot	boot
south	mouth	out
success	suk-ses'	sus-ses
such	much	fetch
suite	sweet	suit
sure	your	fur
sword (no "w")	board	ward
tell	bell	bill
their	air	near
them	hem	hum or him
think	pink	enk
W	double-yew	dub u yew
wash	josh	harsh
water	otter	order
went	sent	lint
when	pen	pin
worst	first	nurse

Look It Up

Your credibility as a reliable source of information depends on correct pronunciation. If you are in doubt about a word in copy and you are too embarrassed to ask someone, check a dictionary. In many cases you will find that more than one pronunciation is acceptable, often because words change through usage or through the strong influence of television.

A Living, Changing Language

Not many years ago speech teachers tried to get their students to carefully pronounce each "r" in February (feb' rew air ee). Many folks left out the first "r" (feb' yew air ee), but this was not really accepted as correct until the avuncular Walter Cronkite used the pronunciation with only the final "r" sound. As the most popular newscaster of his time and the "most trusted man" in America, Walter Cronkite had great credibility and his pronunciation of February became the standard.

A similar type of pronunciation change was brought about primarily through television commercials. At a time within the memory of many people, the word *luxury* was pronounced so that the "x" had the obvious and recommended "ks" or "ksh" sound. Somehow, someone, somewhere on Madison Avenue got the idea that the "g" sound was much sexier than "ksh." So, the glamorous models with limpid eyes in the shampoo and auto ads were saying "lug′ zhur ee." You will find "lug′ zhur ree" in modern dictionaries as correct along with "luk′ shur ee."

Advertising can change attitudes on products—and on the language. When a new pronunciation becomes acceptable, the old one is not discarded immediately or at all. Many cling to and insist on the purity of such words as "February" and "luxury."

Interestingly, some words have changed in the past half-century in the opposite way as well: i.e., from a non-phonetic pronunciation to one more in keeping with the way in which the words are spelled. "Caramel" was formerly correct as "kair′ u mel." "Caramel" is now pronounced "kar′ a mul" or even "kar′ mul."

The only pronunciation listing in the *Merriam-Webster Collegiate Dictionary* in 1942 for "forehead" rhymed with "horrid." In all probability you pronounce it "for′ hed," and may not have even heard the "for′ id" pronunciation, depending on where you live.

Don't get the idea that if you mispronounce a word on radio or TV, the world will change its acceptance of what is correct. Though you may some day be as famous as Walter Cronkite, chances are you will not be able to influence the language as Cronkite did. It is important that you learn to conform to the accepted pronunciation of standard American English if you plan to function with credibility in the worlds of business or broadcasting.

USING THE BODY

The mind and the voice are essential parts of the announcing activity. The body can also be important both on radio and television, not only as a resonating chamber but also as used by an actor to intensify meaning.

On Radio

You cannot see a radio announcer. So what good are body movements on radio? Often body movements can help an announcer project an idea with emphasis or clout that he or she might not otherwise be able to muster. Clenching your fist as you wish to make a point can tense not only your hand but your whole body—including your vocal mechanisms. Perhaps pointing or using other gestures will stress a point you wish to make. Pounding on the table may be an even stronger tool for emphasis. How about putting a smile in your voice? Certainly the smile on your lips can be heard in your voice. When breathing was discussed earlier, it was pointed out that posture is important in providing the best support for your voice. Abdominal muscles cramped from being hunched over deprive you of space for air and control of those muscles. Proper use of the body is important to the radio announcer and to the announcer on television as well.

On Television

On television the audience may see the gestures and other movements of the announcer. But bodily movement in television may actually be less important for some announcers than it is in radio. Gestures on radio help announcers add emphasis to what is being said to make their point. On television the movements must be more restrained. You are a close-up guest in families' homes. Your movements can be seen clearly, unlike on radio or in a large theatre, where the actor needs to make broad gestures to be sure his actions are seen in the second balcony. We will look more carefully at bodily movement on television in the section on television announcing.

Announcing for the electronic media is an art that takes the full application and concentration of the body, the mind, the voice, the mouth, and the ear. It looks easy when performed by experts, as well it should. Like preparation for sports or dance, proper announcing preparation can take years, yet as with these other skills announcing should appear quite effortless and in many cases almost casual.

EXERCISES

1. Be prepared to correctly pronounce the list of commonly mispronounced words in this chapter in class or on a written quiz.
2. Read onto an audio cassette the news items that follow. Listen to yourself critically. Concentrate on voice placement and proper pronunciation. Keep repeating the news items, striving for perfection until you have filled a one-hour tape. Hand in the tape for credit and evaluation by your instructor. Obviously, the instructor cannot listen to all of each student's tape. Random samplings of your work and the last few minutes of the tape will be used for evaluations.
3. Review the objectives at the beginning of the chapter and see if you have achieved these objectives. Since these objectives often are the basis for testing, you may want to write out key ideas for future reference and study.
4. Stand and inhale, expanding your rib cage and diaphragm. Place your hand above your diaphragm to show you are using the correct lung expansion as you inhale. Say the alphabet, breathing in before each letter and forcing air out using the diaphragm. Exaggerate the use of the diaphragm as you pronounce each letter.
5. Inhale as in exercise 4, but project the letters A through L without taking a breath. Then, do L through Z in the same way. Can you project the entire alphabet in one breath? Why might the last section of this exercise not be appropriate?
6. Articulation can be practiced using tongue twisters. You will often find that the word list paragraphs at the end of each chapter have a tongue twister quality and need to be

practiced with clarity of articulation in mind. Here are a few others which you may find challenging:

a. She sells sea shells down by the sea shore with sentiment for the sediment that spells success for the Samaritan.

b. Bob bobbled the ball while the bawdy biblical braggart, Bubbles, babbled like a baboon that had imbibed in Babylon.

c. The therapist thought the mouth of the South would be asked to think of this and that as the thespian thundered.

d. Hang the picture of the pitcher by the poor public portico and pout not as you pour out the puppy's puree.

e. The purple people eater put the puppy and puppet in the picture with the pitcher.

f. Lie low and lend lentils to the lascivious, lethargic lawyer.

g. Where and why will Willie want the whole whale to wallow?

h. The white wheelwright whittled while we whispered and whiffed the whortleberry.

i. The champion will challenge the chairman at the chalet by the chapel on the chaparral.

BROADCAST VOCABULARY   Unit I-B

SYMBOLS FOR PHONETIC TRANSCRIPTION USING REVISED WIRE SERVICE PHONETICS

a	bat	hw	white	oh	boat	sh		push	zh	vision
ay	cape	i	if	oi	oil	th		thin		
aw	raw	igh	ice	oo	book	t/h		that		
ch	beach	j	just	ew	fool	ur		burn		
e	ebb	ng	sing	y	yes	u		up		
ee	seat	o	box	ow	out	u (unaccented)	above			

WORDS TO TRANSCRIBE

Word	Transcription	Definition
adjective		a word that points out or describes a noun
escape		to get away
asked		questioned
bureaucracy		administration of government through non-elected officials
Malathion		an insecticide trade name
pseudonym		fictitious name of an author
poor		lacking assets
pour		to dispense liquid
picture		a visual reproduction
pitcher		a container for liquid

Word	Transcription	Definition
aesthetic		relating to a sense of beauty
my name		first, middle, and last

Note: A correct transcription of these words may be found at the end of this chapter.

v0465int--

r c AP-DIVERSIONS:HOMEENTERT   04-14   0330
∧ AP-DIVERSIONS: HOME ENTERTAINMENT

  by Chuck Rice

falling sound
stable sd. —
stress

TWO-WAY T-V, AND ANATOMY OF A VIDEOTAPE SHELL. THOSE STORIES NEXT ON: DIVERSIONS.

--BREAK--

MARY WAS SKEPTICAL. SHE DIDN'T THINK THE ELECTRONIC DEVICE TECHNICIANS INSTALLED ON HER T-V, BACK IN MARCH, WOULD ALLOW HER TO COMMUNICATE WITH HER SET. SHE DIDN'T BELIEVE THE INTERACTIVE SYSTEM WOULD LET HER CHOOSE HER OWN MOVIES, PLAY GAMES AND SELECT CAMERA ANGLES FOR SPORTING EVENTS.

AFTER A FEW HOURS, MARY, THAT'S NOT HER REAL NAME, REALIZED SHE WAS WRONG. SHE SAYS THE SYSTEM MAKES YOU FEEL LIKE YOU'RE PART OF A TEAM. MARY SAYS SHE HAD A CHOICE AND FELT INDEPENDENT—AS IF YOU'RE WATCHING WHAT YOU TRULY WANT TO SEE.

MARY IS ONE OF 300 PEOPLE IN THE SPRINGFIELD, MASSACHUSETTS, AREA TAKING PART IN A TEST OF NEW INTERACTIVE T-V SYSTEM. THIS SYSTEM, UNLIKE OTHERS, IS MORE SOPHISTICATED AND LETS THE VIEWER MAKE ALL SORTS OF CHOICES.

FOR INSTANCE, LATER ON THIS MONTH DURING A GOLF TOURNAMENT BROADCAST, INTERACTIVE VIEWERS WILL BE ABLE TO PLAY DIRECTOR. THEY'LL PICK FROM SEVERAL DIFFERENT CAMERA

ANGLES--AND BE ABLE TO ACTUALLY FOLLOW THEIR FAVORITE GOLFERS AROUND ON THE COURSE.

AS ONE CABLE T-V OFFICIAL PUTS IT, THE SYSTEM GETS THE COUCH POTATOES UP OFF THE COUCH.

ALL OF A SUDDEN THE MOVIE YOU'RE WATCHING ON VIDEOTAPE TURNS TO STATIC. BAD SIGN. YOU PRESS EJECT AND YOU GET AN ARMFUL OF TAPE. IF YOU'RE LUCKY, YOU CAN WIND IT BACK INTO THE SHELL. IF THE TAPE'S BROKEN—YOU MIGHT BE ABLE TO FIND BOTH ENDS AND SPLICE. THAT'S IF YOU'RE LUCKY.

IF ONE END OF THE TAPE HAS DISAPPEARED INTO THE TAPE SHELL—YOU'LL HAVE TO OPERATE.

YOU DON'T HAVE TO BE A SURGEON, BUT STEADY FINGERS COME IN HANDY WHEN YOU OPEN UP THE TAPE SHELL. SOME SHELLS HAVE SCREWS HOLDING THEM TOGETHER—WHICH MAKES THE INCISION EASIER. OTHERS, HOWEVER, WILL HAVE TO BE CRACKED OPEN. THAT'S DIFFICULT, BECAUSE THERE'S A GOOD CHANCE THE INNARDS WILL FLY EVERY WHICH WAY—MAKING IT TOUGH TO KNOW WHERE ALL THE PARTS GO.

O-K, SO YOU FINALLY GOT THE SHELL APART. YOU SHOULD BE ABLE TO QUICKLY SPOT THE END OF THE TAPE. YOU WANT TO THREAD IT BACK THROUGH THE ROLLERS. USE A PIECE OF ADHESIVE SPLICING TAPE AND THEN PUT THE SHELL BACK TOGETHER.

IF YOU'RE ALL THUMBS—YOU CAN ALWAYS LET A PRO REPAIR YOUR TAPE—BE PREPARED TO PAY AT LEAST FIVE BUCKS.
AP-NP-04-14-90 0844CDT< +

v04681al--

ro AP-THE NATION'S WEATHER-TAK   04-14   0181
∧ AP - THE NATION'S WEATHER - TAKE 3

. . . .NATIONAL FORECAST. . . . .

WIDELY SCATTERED RAIN SHOWERS WILL CONTINUE TODAY ACROSS WASHINGTON TO THE NORTHERN ROCKIES, WHILE VERY WARM TEMPERATURES WILL CONTINUE OVER THE SOUTHWEST DESERTS. THERE WILL BE A SLIGHT CHANCE OF SOME AFTERNOON THUNDERSTORMS OVER THE SIERRA NEVADA.

EXPECT A FEW RAIN AND SNOW SHOWERS NEAR THE CANADIAN BORDER FROM NORTH DAKOTA TO UPPER MICHIGAN. SCATTERED RAIN SHOWERS AND EMBEDDED THUNDERSTORMS WILL BE OVER THE EASTERN AND SOUTHERN GREAT LAKES REGION, SOUTHWARD THROUGH THE MISSISSIPPI VALLEY AND TO THE GULF COAST. SOME THUNDERSTORMS ACROSS EASTERN TEXAS AND INTO LOUISIANA COULD APPROACH SEVERE LIMITS WITH GUSTY WINDS, HAIL AND HEAVY RAINS.

ALSO, WIDELY SCATTERED SHOWERS WILL BE POSSIBLE TODAY NEAR THE SOUTHEAST COAST. SOME OF THIS MOISTURE WILL SLIDE INTO NEW ENGLAND BY THIS AFTERNOON AND EVENING AND MAY PRODUCE SOME SHOWER ACTIVITY THERE.

GUSTY NORTHWESTERLY WINDS ACROSS PORTIONS OF WYOMING WILL BE DECREASING THROUGHOUT THE DAY. HOWEVER, WINDS TO 50 MPH ARE POSSIBLE FOR A TIME THROUGH THE MORNING HOURS.

. . . .FILED BY WEATHERBANK, INC.

AP-NP-04-14-90 0845CDT< +

v0387int

r d AP-7THNEWSWATCH   04-14   0409
/\AP-7TH NEWSWATCH<

by Karen Bauer

/\

HERE IS THE LATEST NEWS FROM THE ASSOCIATED PRESS:

/\

LITHUANIA SAYS IT WON'T KNUCKLE UNDER TO MOSCOW'S
DEMAND THAT IT CHANGE ITS MIND ABOUT INDEPENDENCE—OR
SUFFER ECONOMIC SANCTIONS. THE REPUBLIC PRESIDENT, VYTAUTAS
LANDSBERGIS (VIGH-TAW'-TUS LAWNDS'-BUR-GIS), SAYS "WE
EXPECTED WORSE." HE SAYS HE ASSUMES THAT FOR NOW THE SOVIET
UNION WON'T RESORT TO OTHER MEASURES, SUCH AS A VIOLENT
MILITARY CRACKDOWN.

/\

BUT PRESIDENT BUSH IS URGING GORBACHEV NOT TO CARRY OUT
THE THREATENED SANCTIONS. BUSH ISSUED A PLEA TO THE SOVIET
LEADER TO SOLVE HIS DIFFERENCES WITH THE BALTIC REPUBLIC
THROUGH DISCUSSIONS RATHER THAN COERCION. IN BERMUDA
YESTERDAY FOR MEETINGS WITH BRITISH PRIME MINISTER
MARGARET THATCHER, BUSH SAID NOW IS NO TIME FOR ESCALATION.

/\

A GROUP OF RENEGADE SOLDIERS IN THE PHILIPPINES HAS
DELIVERED A WRITTEN THREAT TO THE BRITISH EMBASSY IN MANILA.
AN OPEN LETTER SAYS THE YOUNG OFFICERS UNION PLANS TO ATTACK
ALLEGED BRITISH MERCENARIES TRAINING PRESIDENT CORAZON
AQUINO'S (KOR'-U-ZON AW-KEE'-NOHZ) SECURITY GUARD. THE GROUP
SAYS IT KNOWS WHERE THE SO-CALLED MERCENARIES ARE, AND WARNS
THE BRITISH EMBASSY TO ORDER THEM OUT OR FACE "DRASTIC
ACTION."

∧

IT WAS A LITTLE SHAKY LAST NIGHT IN PARTS OF WASHINGTON
STATE AND BRITISH COLUMBIA. SEISMOLOGISTS SAY AN EARTHQUAKE
MEASURING FIVE-POINT-ONE ON THE RICHTER SCALE SHATTERED
SOME WINDOWS, BUT DIDN'T CAUSE ANY MAJOR DAMAGE.

∧

IN CALIFORNIA, AGRICULTURE OFFICIALS HAVE SCHEDULED A
MONDAY MEETING TO TRY TO DECIDE HOW TO RESPOND TO DISCOVERIES
OF THREE CROP-DESTROYING MEDFLIES. ONE FLY WAS FOUND IN
RIVERSIDE COUNTY, PROMPTING A QUARANTINE ON COMMERCIALLY
GROWN CROPS THERE. ANOTHER WAS DISCOVERED IN SUBURBAN
WALNUT, AN AREA THAT HASN'T BEEN SPRAYED WITH THE
CONTROVERSIAL PESTICIDE MALATHION. OFFICIALS ARE WORRIED
ABOUT THE ECONOMIC IMPACT OF A SERIOUS INFESTATION.

∧

LOGGERS IN OREGON SAY THEY'RE FIGHTING A PROPOSED
LOGGING BAN THEY SAY COULD HAVE THE ECONOMIC IMPACT OF THE
GREAT DEPRESSION. THOUSANDS RALLIED IN DOWNTOWN PORTLAND
YESTERDAY TO PROTEST THE MOVEMENT TO CUT BACK ON LOGGING
PRODUCTION—IN ORDER TO SAVE THE SPOTTED OWL.
ENVIRONMENTALISTS SAY THE OLD GROWTH TIMBER MUST BE
PROTECTED TO SAVE THE OWL FROM EXTINCTION.

∧

BIG MAC IS ON THE ATTACK. AN ATTORNEY FOR MCDONALD'S IS
WARNING NEWSPAPERS THAT REPRINTING AN ADVERTISEMENT
CLAIMING THE RESTAURANT'S FOOD IS TOO FATTY COULD RESULT IN A
LAWSUIT. THE ORIGINAL AD WAS PLACED IN MAJOR NEWSPAPERS BY

NEBRASKA INDUSTRIALIST PHIL SOKOLOF. HE CHARGES THAT
MCDONALD'S FOOD HAS TOO MUCH FAT. AND HE SAYS HE WILL CONTINUE
HIS BATTLE.

        /\

        NEW YORK HOTEL QUEEN AND CONVICTED TAX EVADER LEONA
HELMSLEY STILL SAYS SHE'S INNOCENT—AND SHE WENT ON
SYNDICATED T-V TO TRY TO PROVE IT. UNDER THE WATCH OF CAMERAS
FROM THE SHOW "A CURRENT AFFAIR," HELMSLEY WROTE OUT A CHECK
TO THE I-R-S FOR 42 (M) MILLION, 65-THOUSAND DOLLARS. SHE SAYS
THAT SHOWS SHE PAYS HER TAXES.

CORRECT TRANSCRIPTION of the words in vocabulary unit 1-B

ad' jek tiv, es kayp', askt', byew rok' ru see,
mal u thigh' on, sew' doh nim, pewr', por', pik' chur,
es the' tik

2
The Announcer Prepares

OBJECTIVES
Upon completion of this chapter the student should be able to:

1. Describe three phonetics pronunciation systems.
2. Describe the use of five commonly used copy marking symbols.
3. Explain three ways to use the voice to increase emphasis of ideas in broadcast copy.
4. Give an example of scholarly influence on broadcast pronunciation.
5. Describe four important announcing elements of which the beginning announcer should be aware.
6. Describe differences between wire service phonetics and *revised* wire service phonetics.
7. List three benefits of revised wire service phonetics.
8. Transcribe words into revised wire service phonetics using the supplied phonetics chart for reference.
9. Define the words in the broadcast vocabulary word lists when used in a sentence.

COPY TECHNIQUES

"Learning by doing" is one of the important precepts of education. Learn to announce by announcing. Learn to read aloud by reading aloud. "Practice makes perfect." *Clichés* are phrases that have been overused, often for good reason. They are aphorisms that have repeatedly proven to relate a truth. Practicing oral reading for announcing creates confidence and perfects style *if the person doing the practice is practicing correctly*. However, practicing bad habits can reinforce and perpetuate those bad habits. As previously suggested, one element of successful practice is listening to oneself.

Maybe after 20 or 30 years of professional experience you will have enough ability that you can expect to do a good job of presenting copy without lengthy preparation. It is interesting to note, however, that most professional announcers know that they need to mark copy, check pronunciation, and constantly keep abreast of what scholars and other authorities have to say about language changes.

MARKING COPY

Announcer preparation is paramount for success. One of the primary means of effective preparation is marking copy. Most announcers probably have their own ways of marking broadcasting copy. Certainly there is no one correct way. There are, however, certain techniques such as underlining, slashes, and overlining that have proven helpful for different announcers, and you may wish to add them to your own methodology. In addition, certain punctuation marks such as parentheses and quotation marks have traditional oral reading style implications. These may be inserted where they are not already in the text.

A marking system must meet at least four criteria. It needs to:

1. be easy to interpret,
2. be consistent,
3. be flexible, and
4. include more than just emphasis markings.

Evaluate the following techniques with these criteria in mind.

Underlining for Emphasis

Underlining is the one standard that probably everyone uses for emphasis of written materials, whether it is broadcast copy or not. When you write a letter, you probably underline things you want to stress. In a thesis or paper the writer may underline passages for emphasis or use italics. Similarly, the titles of books are easily discernible because of italics or underlining in the written paper. Underlining then means not only that this material is important, but if the underlining is under a group of words, it probably also means that these words are all part of the same thought or idea.

The Constitution of the United States <u>guarantees</u> the right of free speech.

Carrying the simple single line under a word or phrase one step further, the marker of copy can <u>use two lines to indicate even greater intended intensity or emphasis</u>.

The <u>Constitution of the United States</u> <u>guarantees</u> the <u>right</u> of free speech.

Emphasis can be gained in announcing in several ways. Most people think that increased emphasis means saying a word or phrase louder. Where loudness may work well in the theatre or in a lecture hall, it is less effective in radio and television because of the limitations of the broadcasting system. Extreme loudness may cause distortion or be clipped by an automatic limiter, which does not allow the full range of intensities that can be perceived by the human ear.

think emphasis means saying things louder.

Obviously, loudness is one form of emphasis, but it is certainly not the only one. Variation of pitch and tone can also call attention to an idea. Reducing the pace dramatically is probably one of the techniques best adapted by most announcers.

Slashes for Pauses

Slashes can be used to indicate pauses, pace, and phrasing. As the continuous line can include a phrase that is to be emphasized, so too can slashes delineate words that need to be grouped together. A single slash can indicate a pause. <u>Slashes/between each word in series/can suggests/a slower pace</u>. Two slashes after a word can be used to note a longer pause, as at the end of an idea, or where an extended pause may be desirable for extreme emphasis.

The /Constitution of the United States //guarantees// the /right/ of/ free/ speech.

Prevent flexing in the middle of the sentence.

Listen to Paul Harvey's radio commentary. How does he emphasize ideas?

Overlining to Indicate Pitch

Underlining is putting a line under the copy to be emphasized. Overlining is putting a line over the copy to be considered. Overlining is often necessary when students have a tendency to raise their voices at the beginning or in the middle of a sentence or idea and drop their voices at the end of sentences or thoughts. Though this is the most common voice pattern, it is not the only one. Students should listen carefully to themselves to be sure they do not have a pitch or pace voice pattern.

Putting a line with an upward swing above material may be done to tell the reader to raise the pitch of his or her voice to call attention to an idea or to

Figure 2–1 Paul Harvey emphasizes ideas by varying his speech.

gain variety, especially where a voice pattern may be creating problems. If the end of the line has a tail up, the ending inflection is up. If the end of the line has a tail down, the reader's voice is directed in a downward inflection. The student should be seeking to communicate through variety, which comes from understanding. Inflection patterns are not necessarily limited only to the ends of the lines.

A voice pattern may include excessive downward inflections.

To break this habit, mark your copy with an upward pattern and follow the symbols

inserted.

Since there may be an inclination to pause at the ends of lines—especially with poetry or poetry-like material—it may be helpful to insert an arrow above the last few words of a line to indicate that there should *not* be a pause at a line's end.

Arrows over copy at the end of lines may be used to

indicate that the announcer should *not* pause.

Quotation Marks for Tone

Tone of voice emphasis can be indicated by the use of quotation marks. Depending on the content, quotation marks can be used to suggest to the reader that a voice change is intended. Quotation marks may suggest sarcasm, sexual innuendo, and other intonations with specific implications from elation to depression. The person marking a script may want to indicate the attitude to be taken. Quotation marks are related directly to the specific content of the material, so it is essential that the announcer be thinking about the meaning of what is being used. Look at this example, which suggests a meaning different from the literal meaning of the word *accident:*

The so-called "accident" happened earlier.

Parentheses for De-emphasis

An idea that is Redundant.

A *parenthesis* or *parenthetical expression* is a comment that is inserted into a sentence to qualify a statement, to provide an explanation, or to indicate a grouping (as in mathematical expressions). Since the parenthesis already has these meanings, it is logical to use parenthesis marks to mean much the same kinds of things when they are used to mark copy. Parentheses are often inserted by a copy marker to indicate ideas that are redundant or repetitive and so can be de-emphasized.

When a sentence contains an *appositive,* a word that explains the preceding noun, a pair of parentheses will help the reader remember to change the emphasis for this phrases as it is read. For example, consider:

Mary Ann, (a beautiful and charming young lady), led all others.

One means of de-emphasis is speeding up that particular phrase. Another is to lower the pitch.

Any phrase or clause that is inserted into a sentence to explain or qualify an idea may be hurried over, particularly when it is *redundant*, repeating an already known concept.

The old man climbed the rugged mountain, (though he knew the incline was long and steep).

Ellipses, Dashes, Hyphens

An Acronym should be pronounced a word.

Some other conventions of copywriting are also worth considering. You will not find semicolons or colons used in most properly written broadcast copy. Instead, the tradition is to use an ellipsis (series of three periods with spaces between them) or a dash (two hyphens with no space between) to indicate a break longer than a comma but shorter than a period. Single hyphens connecting words indicate that the words connected represent a single concept; e.g., mail-train, outside-seat, etc. Single hyphens between letters indicate that each letter is to be pronounced by name, as in U-S-A. If the letters are to be pronounced as a word (an *acronym*), the capital letters are written without spaces or hyphens, as with

NASA. All of these concepts need to be kept in mind when you are reading material prepared for broadcast and can logically be used to further mark your copy.

Crossing Out

In editing material for time, it may be necessary to eliminate paragraphs, sentences, or words. If it is an optional cut, based on estimated time, you may want to draw a single line through material so that it can be reinserted if your estimates are wrong. For making corrections of wording or spelling, however, it is important that the marking out be absolute. The line drawn through deleted material needs to be so obliterating that you are not tempted to think about the previous construction and can read only the correct copy.

One trick many local newscasters use when reading wire copy is to refer to some minor foreign leaders by title only, thus eliminating the often hard-to-pronounce names of those foreign officials who have not gained international stature and will probably never be heard of again by most of the listeners. These names should also be completely marked through so that you the newscaster will not hesitate, suggesting to the listener that something has been left out.

Clarity is essential in the communication of ideas. Another newscaster trick is to avoid contractions with "not" in them. It is not possible to emphasize the "nt" sound in "don't" or "isn't." So it is recommended that the announcer rewrite these contractions as "do not" and "is not." This way the word "not" can be emphasized and there is less chance of misunderstanding. This is an exception to another rule: use contractions to make your material sound conversational. Contractions generally do make your copy sound less formal, and can be substituted in some scripts where contractions have not been written in. Most people use many contractions when they speak.

Note the following box, "Important Announcing Elements to Watch For." Can you provide logical copy marking to help overcome some of these problems? These are the types of comments most often made by an evaluator listening to the performance of beginning announcers. Be prepared to provide examples of these ideas in class.

LEARNING CORRECT PRONUNCIATION

There are two basic ways of learning correct pronunciation: by listening and by reading phonetic transcriptions. But, before learning a pronunciation, the student needs to be sure he or she is learning the correct pronunciation. Who determines what pronunciation is correct?

SCHOLARLY INFLUENCE

Foreign language scholars often influence our pronunciation of foreign terms. In recent years the accepted correct pronunciation of Chinese has changed as scholars reevaluate the transpronunciation process. The capital of China for many years

---

IMPORTANT ANNOUNCING ELEMENTS TO WATCH FOR

PHRASING: Grouping words together into phrases or ideas, but avoid a repetitious rhythm or pitch pattern.

TRANSITIONS: Between new stories or sections of most copy:

1. Change pitch.
2. Change pace.
3. Pause before proceeding.

EMPHASIZING KEY IDEAS:

1. Pause before and after important words.
2. Emphasize "not" and other words that change meanings.
3. Emphasize the main verb when it shows action.
4. De-emphasize unimportant articles, helper verbs, prepositions, and redundant concepts.

PRONUNCIATION: Spell out difficult words or names phonetically when marking copy.

A PRONOUNCING RULE OF THUMB

A two syllable **verb** that is spelled the same as a **noun**:
   accent the verb on the second syllable

A two syllable **noun** that is spelled the same as a **verb**
   accent the noun on the first syllable

Examples: record (verb)—ree kord´
                record (noun)—rek´ urd

Note: A rule-of-thumb is an approximation that is often right. Several other examples of this "rule" are to be found in subsequent vocabulary word lists.

In Russia - only Pronounciation.

Some words spelling has changed along Peiking. / Beijing.
with the Pronounciation.

was spelled "Peiking" and pronounced pee king´. Now we are told the proper translation of the Chinese capital into English is "Beijing," pronounced bay jing´. The "p" has become "b" and the "k" has become "j." The Chinese (unlike the Soviets) have not changed the name of a major city. It is merely that the "correct" anglicized pronunciation has changed. Scholars have changed their minds, as well as the minds of network announcers, as to what is correct.

As previously suggested, local place names are determined by local usage. Cairo, the town in Illinois, is pronounced kay´ roh. In Egypt, of course, the city with the same name is pronounced kigh´ roh.

People's names are correctly pronounced the way they themselves pronounce them. Though the presidents Roosevelt (Theodore and Franklin) were cousins, they are said to have pronounced their names differently. Old-timers have told us that the correct pronunciations are:

Theodore ROHZ' VELT

and

Franklin ROH' ZU VELT.

President Reagan (ray' gun) had a cabinet member named regan (ree' gun). Correctly pronouncing national and international names, and especially names of people in a person's hometown, is extremely important for an announcer's credibility.

Listening to network news presentations is one of the best ways to learn the current, acceptable pronunciation of national and international names and foreign terms.

PHONETIC ALPHABETS

Do you know there are just 44 sounds in the English language—44? When you learn these 44 sounds (called phonics), you can read and spell almost everything.[1]

There are essentially three systems of transcription for changing printed symbols into pronounced sounds. These are the International Phonetic Alphabet (IPA), dictionary diacritical markings, and the AP-UPI broadcast phonetic system.

The International Phonetic Alphabet

Scholars have devised a system that allows interpretation of the sounds of all major languages using letters and specialized symbols. The system is so exact that it allows even subtle nuances of difference. The IPA incorporates symbols for sounds that are not even used in American English. Learning to speak a foreign language would seem to be made much easier by using this system, though this has not proven to be a popular approach to teaching in U.S. universities' foreign language departments. One of the primary problems with this system for broadcasters is the inclusion of unique symbols that are not found on most typewriters or on American teletype machines. In addition, some of the letters are used as symbols that most Americans do not normally associate with these particular letters. In order to use this system, the student or newscaster must learn a new alphabet of sounds.

[1] Radio commercial for *Hooked on Phonics* (Mutual Broadcasting System, August 1991), run-of-schedule.

Dictionary Markings

What about dictionary diacritical markings? These can usually be figured out from the explanation chart at the bottom of the page in most dictionaries. But many dictionary compilers have created new systems to meet their own idea of how phonics should work. Thus, no two dictionaries by different publishers can be expected to be the same. Also, again we have the problem of unavailability of the symbols on most typewriters or on news teletype machines.

Wire Service Phonetics

At radio and television stations the most common way of transcribing the correct pronunciations is that used by the Associated Press (AP) and the United Press International (UPI). Both news services provide pronunciation guides via their teletype networks on a regular basis.

It seems probable that the AP-UPI system evolved from a need for a simple pronunciation system. Because it evolved, rather than being carefully planned, the system is inconsistent and at times confusing. If you learned phonics when you were learning to read, you learned that certain letters had specific sounds. Various combinations of letters also were usually pronounced in the same way. But since the English language (especially as spoken in the United States) developed in a melting pot of nationalities and languages, trying to pronounce a word based on its spelling can at times prove frustrating.

The AP-UPI system has several points in its favor.

1. It is currently being used by the industry.
2. It is possible to reproduce on a standard typewriter.
3. It can be transmitted via news teletype machines.
4. It is fairly easy to comprehend in most cases without lengthy study.

With all of these things going for it, there seems little question that the AP-UPI method should be understood by broadcasting students. But if standards were to be set up as to logic and consistency, the AP-UPI sytem has some shortcomings.

SYSTEMS CRITERIA

In order for a system to be immediately recognizable by any reader and for it to be adhered to:

1. Standard phonetic sounds as learned by students should be pronounced as they commonly appear in the language, and
2. consistent use of letters for sounds is essential, especially where one or more consonants are added to a vowel to modify its basic pronunciation.

(Handwritten margin notes:)
it isn't conventional." because it isn't clear how is to begin with. For example—there are no typewriters that I
don't Know how many sounds are in the English language, but learning these groupings of sounds will enable you to
If the IPA system, but learning any number possibility speak
This system can be used. standard Type writer
w/ a standard Type writer
Fairly Easy

Since the currently used AP-UPI phonetics do not fully conform to these criteria, a revised wire service phonetics system is suggested.

REVISED WIRE SERVICE PHONETICS

Consonant sounds would be much the same as those used in the IPA or AP-UPI systems, with the exception of the addition of "t/h" used to transcribe the voiced "th" sound as in *this* (t/his) or *that* (t/hat). The use of "th" without a slash remains the soft "th" sound as in *think* or *thought*.

Most of the lack of uniformity in the AP-UPI system comes with vowels. In elementary school students are taught the short "a" as in *cat*, short "e" as in *wed*, the short "i" as in *fit*, short "o" as in *got*, and short "u" as in *nut*. There would seem to be no need to change some of these rules as the currently used system does by adding an "h" to many vowels for the short vowel sound.

BEING CONSISTENT

Not only is the added "h" not needed, the redundant "h" is not used in a consistent manner by the AP-UPI system. Added to the "a," the "h" produces an "au" sound as in *father*. (This may be difficult at times to distinguish from the broad "a" in *saw*.)

Added to an "e" or "i," the additional "h" (as used in the AP-UPI system) indicates the short form of the vowel as in *set* (seht) or *sit* (siht). With the "h" added to an "o," the reader is expected to pronounce the long form of the vowel as in *boat* (boht).

Stranger still, the "h" (and "g") added to "u" produces a sound terminated with an "f" sound as in *trough,* according to some authorities.[2] In the *NBC Pronunciation Handbook,*[3] trough is transcribed *trawf.*

Revised Systems

The revised wire service phonetics system used in this book does not use the redundant "h" for the pronunciation of the short form of the vowel. The "h" following a vowel is eliminated except after the "o." The vowel followed by an "h" becomes a long "o."

In common usage the "o-w" sound is also often pronounced as a long "o" as in *know, flow,* and *row* (Know the flow when you row). But this use has been precluded by the more common "o-w" sound as used in "*How now, brown cow?*" "Oh" can be easily recalled as the long "o" sound, since "oh" is by itself always pronounced as the long form of the vowel. For the "ough" sound as in

---

[2] Arthur Wimer and Dale Brix, *Handbook for Radio and TV News Editing and Writing,* 4th ed. (Dubuque, Iowa: Wm. C. Brown Co., 1975), p. 38.

[3] James F. Bender, rev. by Thomas Lee Crowell, Jr., *NBC Handbook of Pronunciation* (New York: Thomas Y. Crowell Co., 1964), p. 375.

trough, the revised system uses "of," which includes the short "o" and the "f" sounds. The word would be transcribed "trof." ("Trawf" would also be correct.) The word *of* would, of course, be transcribed "uv."

Other changes from the current AP-UPI system include single letters for the short sounds of vowels. "Au" is used for the "a" sound in *father* (faut/her). "Igh" is the only three-letter sound. Yet the logic is apparent when you look at the words *might, sight, fright, flight,* etc. The double "o" is sometimes confusing. Using "ew," as in *stew, flew, crew,* and *new,* for the sound in *stoop* (stewp), allows use of "oo" for vowel sound in *foot* (foot) or *book* (book). "U" followed by an "r" takes on the sound of the vowel-consonant combination in *burn.* The revised phonetics changes are few but they bring logic to the system.

Revised System Benefits

Basically there are three reasons why the proposed revised wire service phonetics have been chosen for this text.

1. Revised wire service phonetics are easily learned with little or no special instruction, giving students valuable time for other vocabulary studies.
2. The system is adaptable to the standard typewriter and to the standard teletype machine and computer keyboard.
3. The revised system allows accurate representation of the sound of American English words and names in the manner generally accepted as correct in the United States.

Who's Correct?

While it is probably true that wire service phonetics usage only approximates the pronunciation of foreign terms, most announcers are not capable of making the "correct" sounds of many foreign languages—nor is the audience particularly upset if foreign names or foreign terms are not said perfectly. Perhaps the most important aspects are that there be consistency among the pronunciation of various announcers when terms or names are anglicized or Americanized and that the announcer pronounces them with confidence and authority.

Very seldom is it possible to have absolutely correct pronunciation on which all authorities agree because of differences and preferences of individuals, changing usage, regionalisms, and the presence of the electronic media. Check any two dictionaries. Even these "absolute" authorities have trouble agreeing on the fine points of syllabication and pronunciation, especially of foreign names and words. Changing foreign words to American sounds will always be an approximation.

SYSTEM EFFICIENCY

With the information explosion it is important that students not be overburdened with learning unnecessary skills or relearning basic skills concepts. By adopting revised wire service phonetics, students should have an easy way to vocalize and transcribe words being added to their vocabularies. When you are in doubt about how to transcribe a word, you may refer to the following examples.

REVISED WIRE SERVICE PHONETICS[4]

A SOUNDS
A	cat
AY	fade
AI	fair
AU	fat/her
AW	saw
U	(unaccented)
	above, arena

E SOUNDS
E	wed
EE	treat
EW	stew
U	(unaccented)
	effect, after
YEW	news
UR	earn, term

O SOUNDS
O	top
OH	dope
OI	boy, boil
OO	book
EW	stoop
OW	cow
UR	favor, minor

I SOUNDS
I	fit
IGH	trite
U	(unaccented)
	tapir
UR	gird, stir

U SOUNDS
U	pup
YEW	educate
UR	burn

Y SOUNDS
Y	yellow
IGH	why
EE	lately
I	bicycle

C SOUNDS
CH	cheap
S	preface
K	cool

G SOUNDS
G	good
J	gentle
F	enough

J SOUNDS
J	jam
ZH	rajah

N SOUNDS
N	phone
NG	ring
NY	news

P SOUNDS
P	put
F	phase

S SOUNDS
S	sled
SH	sheep
Z	news
ZH	vision

Q SOUNDS
KW	quick
K	raquet

T SOUNDS
T	trip
TH	think
T/H	other

W SOUNDS
W	way
HW	when

X SOUNDS
Z	Xerox
KS	next

Z SOUNDS
Z	Zoo
ZH	azure

SINGLE-SOUND LETTERS
B, D, F, H, K, L, M, R, V

For your information, the following chart compares the vowel sounds of the standard AP-UPI system with the revised system. Consonants remain essentially the same.

[4] William L. Hagerman, ''Revised Wire Service Phonetics,'' *Feedback,* XXII, 2 (1980), pp. 22–24. *Feedback* is a publication of the Broadcast Education Association.

COMPARISON OF UPI-AP PHONETICS WITH REVISED WIRE SERVICE PHONETICS

AP-UPI		Revised		Example Word
a		a		cat
ay	*cheese*	ay	*chEEZ*	fade
ai		ai		fair
ah		au		father
aw	*Tray*	aw	*Tray*	saw
eh		e		wed
ee		ee	*B*	feet
ew	*Ban*	ew		stew
ih		i		fill
eye	*door*	igh		night
ah		o		top
oh		oh		dope
oo	*chips*	ew		stoop
u		oo		book
ugh		of		trough
ow		ow		cow
uh		u		pup
ew		yew		mule
er		ur		burn
u		oo		put

EXERCISES

Different students require different emphasis in their practice readings. Since each student is different, your instructor may give you individual assessments in class or in evaluating your tapes from Chapter 1. It is recommended that students practice correcting only one of the types of errors noted in their evaluations. Concentration is usually better directed at only one problem at a time. State at the beginning of your tape the focus of your presentation.

1. Mark the triple-spaced copy provided at the end of this chapter as recommended with underlining, overlining, slashes, parentheses, and quotation marks, etc. Can you think of any additional markings that might be useful in helping you read copy?

2. Obtain some wire copy and mark it for emphasis as suggested in exercise 1.

3. Follow the instructions for studying word lists in Chapter 1. Test yourself and be prepared to pronounce the words correctly and write the correct phonetic transcriptions when tested. You should also be prepared to define each word when it is presented in a sentence. You may be called upon to use each word in a sentence in class.

At the end of each chapter is a paragraph using the words in that chapter. The paragraphs do not necessarily make complete sense. They are drills for pronouncing the words and developing other announcing skills. It is suggested that each of these paragraphs be read onto your cassette tape until you have done your best.

4. Read your marked copy from exercises 1 and 2 onto your cassette tape to be handed in for evaluation. Be sure to hand in your marked copy with your cassette.

Procedure to follow for reading onto your cassette tape: Read your marked copy once onto your cassette. Listen and evaluate it, then read it again, correcting errors you have found. Continue reading until you have done the best job you possibly can, or until you have read for a full hour. If you feel you have done your best before completion of an hour's reading, get additional news copy to read for the balance of your hour-long tape, or use the news copy at the end of Chapter 1 if you feel you can improve on its presentation.

5. Bring your marked copy to class. Pick your best 60 seconds to be read "live" in class.

6. Be sure the assigned material (best you can do, one last time) is at the end of your tape since your instructor will pay particular attention to the last five minutes of the tape.

BROADCAST VOCABULARY WORD LIST   Unit 2

Lay a piece of paper across this page so that it exposes only the word to be pronounced. Write your phonetics without looking at the "preferred" transcription. Then check to see if you are correct. Note: Some vowel sounds tend to be interchangeable. Syllabication may vary slightly and still be correct. Be sure you mark the primary accent.

1. Catholicism (n)—the faith, system, and practice of the Catholic church

   _____   *ku   thol'   u   siz   um*

2. celibacy (n)—the state of being unmarried, especially in accordance with religious

         beliefs

   _____   *sel'   u   bu   see*

3. papacy (n)—the office, jurisdiction, or dignity of the Pope

   _____   *pay'   pu   see*

4. papal nuncio (n)—permanent representative of the Pope in a foreign capital

   _____   *pay'   pul   nun'   see   oh*

5. sacrilegious (adj)—that which violates anything sacred

   _____   *sak   ru   lij'   us*

6. basilica (n)—an oblong building, usually for church ceremonies

   _____   *bu   sil'   i   ku*

7. charismatic (n)—emotionally expressive Protestant or Catholic group whose members

         speak in "unknown tongues."

   _____   *ku   riz   ma'   tik*

8. rabbi (n)—spiritual leader of a Jewish congregation

   _____   *ra'   bigh*

9. synod (n)—an assembly of ecclesiastics or other church delegates

_____   *sin'   ud*

10. synagogue (n)—a Jewish house of worship

_____   *sin'   u   gog*

11. prelate (n)—a clergyman of high order, such as a bishop

_____   *prel'   ut*

12. requiem (n)—the mass celebrated for the repose of the souls of the dead

_____   *rek'   wee   um*

13. anachronism (n)—an error in chronology or time sequence

_____   *u   nak'   ru   niz   um*

14. sacrosanct (adj)—held holy beyond challenge

_____   *sak'   roh   sangt*

15. ascetic (n)—a person who practices extreme self-denial for religious reasons

_____   *u   set'   ik*

16. synchronize (v)—to cause to occur at the same time or to agree in time

_____   *sing'   kru   nighz* or

                                 sink' ru nighz

17. hospice (n)—a home for persons facing death; an organization that takes care of the

      dying

_____   *hos'   pus*

18. ayatollah (n)—Moslem religious leader

_____   *igh   u   toh'   lu*

19. deity (n)—a god or goddess

_____   *dee'   u   tee*

20. diocesan (adj)—having to do with the diocese

_____   *digh   os'   i   sun*

21. pontiff (n)—the Pope or bishop

_____   *pon'   tif*

WORD LIST COPY FOR PARAGRAPH 1:
Mark for Maximum Interest.

When you ask for a synonym for quality, when you want an adjective that describes dependability, when you want to escape from the mundane and enter the sacrosanct realm of a living heritage, you can approach the federal bureaucracy and find the Forest Service.

These foresters do not present a poor picture of neglect. They are rather like a pitcher on the mound pouring strikes over the plate almost every time.

Protecting the environment, personnel of the Forest Service have asked that you not use a pseudonym, but that you use your real name, that you have the courage to come right out and tell the world that you support environmental preservation.

WORD LIST PARAGRAPH   Word List 2

Catholicism can be expected to reflect its traditional grandeur this month when the papacy will be presented before a synod of prelates in the U-S. Citizens of Iowa are being invited to papal audiences. The sacrilegious may see a grandiose display of splendor, an anachronism analogous to the biblical golden calf, while charismatics and other believers in the faith can be expected to see the sacrifices of an asetic pope and priestly celibacy as holy self-denial. The ayatollah, who sees himself as a deity, must reside in the diocesan hospice with the condemned rabbi. Perpetual bigotry may seem inherent in church and synagogue, but who can say that a requiem for religion is at hand?

3

Understanding Communication

OBJECTIVES
Upon completion of this chapter the student should be able to:

1. Define communication, list and place seven communication elements on a communication model, and explain why the announcer needs to understand elements of the communication models.

2. Distinguish between the elements of interpersonal communication and mass communication.

3. Explain the three possible perspectives of mass communication transactions.

4. Give two reasons why mass communication may not effectively transmit messages, and explain three objective-setting techniques to improve transmission.

5. Indicate the four ways in which mass media feedback can show that a message is being received.

6. Describe Keltner's five binding elements (as related in the chapter) and explain how they apply to broadcast announcing.

7. List and explain nine functions of mass communication.

8. Point out how mass media can be said to be dysfunctional, and give examples.

9. Transcribe and define in context the vocabulary words on the chapter's word lists.

COMMUNICATION EXPLAINED

> Radio is . . . the most personal, intimate medium there is for both the participants and the listener.[1]
>
> —*Larry King*

All of us communicate with others regularly. Communicating is something that we take for granted, like seeing, hearing, eating, and breathing. Though we go through the physical actions without conscious effort, we often give little thought to the communication *process*. A little effort can make your communication more effective both in interpersonal and in mass communication interactions. A look at the process can help one understand communication transactions and make communication efforts more effective.

COMMUNICATION DEFINED

We often think of communication as meaning an exchange of messages. To communicate (the verb) comes from the Latin *communicare:* "to make common; to make known." This term might seem to refer to mass communication. Mass communication does make information widely known. Indeed, communication with masses of people does make certain messages "common knowledge." On the other hand, "knowledge in common" might have a slightly different connotation. It suggests that two people have the same understanding of certain information, in spite of the fact that no two persons can have exactly the same concept of anything. Each of us has differing experiences from which to view the world and, of course, different understanding of messages we send or receive.

More modern dictionary definitions include:

to communicate: to impart knowledge of, make known.

communication: the imparting or interchange of thoughts, opinions, or information.[2]

mass communication: communication directed at many people through the use of technology.

A Communication Model

One way in which communication can be explained is graphically, with a communication model. Somewhat like a road map, the communication model shows where the action begins, where it ends, and how the communication reached its receiver. It is important to have an understanding of these model concepts so

[1] Larry King and Emily Joffe, *Larry King* (New York: Simon & Schuster, 1982), p. 63.
[2] *The Random House Dictionary of the English Language,* unabridged ed. (New York: Random House, 1967).

that when a breakdown occurs, informed analysis can reveal what may need to be changed.

Communication basically entails several elements: a source, a message, a channel, and a receiver. These appear in a given social situation and may be enhanced or distorted by feedback, noise, or filters in the system. This can be illustrated with a simple communication model.

An Interpersonal Model

One point repeatedly reinforced in this book is that most good broadcast announcing is communication to individuals, one at a time. For this reason it is important that we consider some of the concepts of interpersonal communication. We see that a model similar to the first one can be used to explain the interpersonal communication process. The voice becomes a transducer, changing thoughts to audible sound, and the receiver's ear another, converting audible sound to impulses to the brain, as shown in the top section of the mass communication model on p. 48.

Berlo's Model

Another model takes somewhat different form and considers each of the basic elements in many possible forms. Each component of this model (SOURCE, MESSAGE, etc.) utilizes some or all of those elements listed below it in affecting the communication process.

SOURCE	MESSAGE	CHANNEL	RECEIVER
Communication skills	Elements	Seeing	Communication skills
Attitudes	Structure	Hearing	Attitudes
Knowledge	Content	Touching	Knowledge
Social system	Treatment	Smelling	Social system
Culture	Code	Tasting	Culture

Berlo's Communication Model[3]

This model gives a different perspective. It spells out in words the components of four of the basic communication building blocks. Under the heading SOURCE is considered communication skills. Do we speak the same language, or do we both understand Morse code? For communication to take place on the verbal level we need common verbal skills. Likewise, for each of the other channels, we need to know sign language, or be able to understand semaphore flag information,

[3] David K. Berlo, *The Process of Communication* (New York: Holt, Rinehart & Winston, 1960, p. 72.

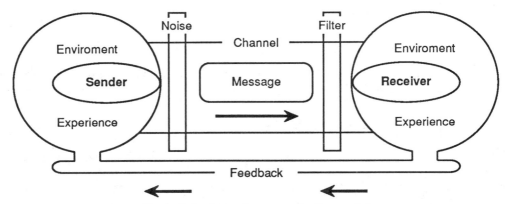

Figure 3–1 A simple communication model.

or—perhaps more subtly—interpret a smile, a touch of the hand, the odor of food cooking, or the taste of fine wine.

While *attitude, knowledge,* the *social system,* and the *culture* often interrelate, each is a specific concept to be considered in relation to the source. One's attitude may differ from those of others with similar knowledge in the same social system and culture. All people have had unique experiences resulting in a completely different attitude, or perhaps one that is only slightly different. Similarly, people reading this text will recall different aspects of the material presented. When you think about it, you realize that information and knowledge are not necessarily the same. *Information* usually just refers to basic facts. *Knowledge* often implies understanding and perhaps wisdom. The social system has much to do with one's beliefs and willingness to believe certain kinds of ideas. A person who had grown up in the Soviet social system had little in the way of Western economics and private enterprise to relate to when the Russians first tried to institute capitalistic elements into their social system. Some of the most revered traditions in some parts of the world are seen as worth going to war over in order that they be perpetuated. In other cultures, these same practices may be frowned upon or even illegal. Compare the U.S. Bill of Rights with what is seen as acceptable in other cultures.

In looking at *elements* of messages being transmitted, the *channels* through which they pass need to be considered, as do the *structure, content, treatment,* and *code* of the messages themselves. The *elements* chosen to be used or highlighted are, in and of themselves, part of the meaning of the message being transmitted. If the medium used is speech, we might ask, is the speaker using big words or an unusual vocabulary? Does the receiver fully understand the "code"? Is the speaker implying more than the basic information designated by the words themselves? What might the implication be?

The *structure* or organization of material, such as with Aristotle's "beginning, middle, and end," certainly is an important aspect of mass communication.

Does the beginning attract attention, attract an audience, have an emotional impact? Does the middle explain fully what is needed to be known? Does one idea lead logically to the next? Does the listener continue to be intrigued? How about the ending: Does it leave a feeling of resolution, or is the listener left hanging?

Content—what is said, written, or otherwise encoded—is usually what is assumed to be the primary consideration when receiving or sending a message. As Marshall McLuhan so succinctly called to communicators' attention: "The medium is [or may be] the message."[4] His idea was that the means by which a message is transmitted often obscures the message itself and can even alter that message.

The *treatment* of the message has much to say about its importance, its validity, and its sincerity. Is it enclosed in a gold-embossed envelope, or is it scribbled on a scrap from the corner of a note pad? Is it proclaimed from the mountaintops, or is it confidentially whispered in a secluded rendezvous? The treatment may be seen in the code or the channel.

Of course the *code* may be the language in which the message is written or spoken or sung. The code may be understood only by a football fan or only by a serious musician. Obviously, a message can be expected to have meaning (or at least nuances) beyond any words transmitted.

The message channel is more than words or music or other sounds. A message can be *seen* on the television screen, in a newspaper or magazine, or in the posture of a speaker. Nor is a message only seen or *heard*. The body's largest sense organ is the skin. *Touching* can be one of the most intimate of message media, and one of the most violent. Consider the caress of a lover or the forceful fist of a mugger.

What does it mean when you *smell* gas, or when the aroma of fresh bread permeates the air? To quote Pillsbury: "Nothin' says lovin' like somethin' from the oven." This may go for *taste* as well. Isn't everyone supposed to love the taste of mom's home cooking? Well, at least that was the case a generation ago when mom was the bread maker instead of a bread winner. Or, still on tasting, a bad taste in the mouth may be a message from your stomach that you're going to be sick. (This is intrapersonal communication.)

The *source* and *receiver* components of Berlo's model are much the same as in other models, yet this model recognizes that each person has a different level of ability and understanding, and that senders (sources) need to be seen within the context of the situation in which they exist. It can also be interpreted to mean that both the source and the receiver need to understand the existing communication techniques and conditions to the greatest extent possible to be sure the message is fully and correctly comprehended.

This model does not work as well for mass communication when the channel options of interpersonal communications are considered. Hearing and seeing are the ultimate channels of communication in the mass media.

A slightly different model has been proposed for mass communication. Probably the key differences are the kinds of noise and the types of feedback in

[4] Marshall McLuhan, *Understanding Media* (New York: McGraw-Hill, 1964) p. 2.

the system. *Noise* may be seen as the various forms of competition for the attention of the audience member: other commercials, other programs, other media. These can all be considered noise if they distract from the intended message of the source.

The source may be more than one entity. Corporations or political candidates may hire advertising or public relations agencies to package their messages. The radio or television transmitter serves as one transducer, radio waves as the channel, and the broadcast receiver as the other transducer. The receiver is an audience member, who may or may not be the same person as the consumer. The so-called two-step flow theory suggests that if the persons receiving the message are opinion leaders, they may influence others to use the product or service through either example or other persuasive means.[5]

Feedback for the electronic mass media is primarily in two forms: media survey reports and product sales. Direct response in the form of fan mail or telephone calls to a radio or television talk show are feedback, but they may or may not be reliable indicators of listenership. Essentially communication remains a source-message-channel-receiver-feedback-source loop, as shown in the following mass communication model.

MASS COMMUNICATION PERSPECTIVES

The performers on radio or television project their messages to the audience from one of three perspectives: objective, subjective, or presentational.

The *objective perspective* is the traditional approach used in theatre. A room with the fourth wall removed is an example. The audience is eavesdropping

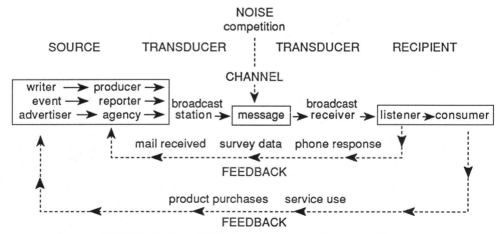

Figure 3–2 A model for mass communication transactions.

[5] Elihu Katz, "The Two-Step Flow of Communication: An Up-to-Date Report on a Hypothesis," *Public Opinion Quarterly*, 21 (1957).

on what is going on and is involved vicariously, but is not really part of the action. The audience stands back and watches the proceedings as an omniscient observer.

The *subjective perspective* is used less often, and is usually used only intermittently. In this mode the camera sees through the eyes of one of the characters—usually the protagonist. For example, the audience sees a character enter a new environment. The camera then momentarily switches to the character's point of view, surveying the new scene through the eyes of the character before switching back to an objective perspective. Subjective perspective occurs in radio when characters narrate from their own point of view. The audience's perception can be said to be subjective whenever the audience "sees" through the eyes of the protagonist.

The *presentational perspective* is the mode with which an announcer is most concerned. In this situation the speaker addresses the audience directly. We see this in "asides" in Shakespearean and other plays, where a character speaks directly to the audience. When a speaker addresses a large assembled audience, as in an auditorium, this is presentational. A similar presentational mode was used in early broadcasting. Today the good announcer is presentational in approach, but no longer talks to "all you folks out in radioland." Except when actually before an assembled audience, today's announcers address each individual listener.

The *best* way to get an idea across and to hold a media audience—to *communicate* with radio or television listeners—is on an *interpersonal* basis. It is the most effective manner of communication used in electronic media. Announcers, advertisers' spokespersons, and audio or video dee-jays should, in most instances, address listeners individually. The newscaster speaks to the audience member directly. Interpersonal communication is the mode of the announcer speaking directly to each individual audience member.

SOCIAL BONDS

Communication is a reciprocal bond among people. It is the very essence of a society. The speech act, once said, is lost forever (except as it may be recorded on tape or in print). It is essentially transitory, living only in the memory of the listener. For this reason speech must be as effective as possible. Only then will it be remembered or result in the satisfaction of, or action by, the listener. It may be even more difficult to get a point across in the electronic media than in normal interpersonal relationships, because much of the radio or television audience is concentrating on something else. This also means that advertisers want to repeat messages as many times as practical to be sure that their message penetrates.

Effective broadcast announcing is not communication with a great impersonal mass of humanity. Rather, it is a person talking interpersonally about important aspects of life to one listener at a time.

As pointed out earlier, communication consists of two different interpersonal actions: sending and receiving. Each is a learned skill, and often it is easier to receive a message than to send one. When learning a foreign language, it is usually easier to be the receiver. When taking a test, it is usually easier to match materials that are given or to select from a group of possible answers than to fill in the blank by recalling words or ideas. It is easier to recognize concepts than to remember and restate them. While the listening process is easier than the sending mode, the physical sending of a message that can be heard does not necessarily mean that listening is taking place. Hearing is not necessarily the same as listening, and listening is not necessarily the same as understanding.

SETTING OBJECTIVES

In order to effectively deliver an idea to the intended receiver, it is important to know the objective to be achieved. Objectives can be general or specific.

Broad general objectives are those goals that all levels of broadcasting seem to strive for. It would be much simpler if all levels of the communication hierarchy had the same goals, but such is not the case. Each level has its own agenda. A hierarchy of broad general goals looks something like this:

LISTENER	to be entertained to understand the world to learn new ideas
BROADCAST STATION	to attract listeners to serve the public interest, convenience, and necessity
ADVERTISER	to indoctrinate to sell merchandise or services
ANNOUNCER	to create rapport, understanding, and trust

Hierarchy of Broadcasting's General Goals

Specific goals spell out exactly what is to be achieved by a broadcast. The listener expects to be entertained by a specific kind of music or be made aware of certain types of information. If this is not achieved, the objective is not met. The station tries to attract a particular type of listener by programming easy listening or presenting informed local newscasts. An advertiser's general objective may be to familiarize the audience with the conveniences and styling of the new Pontiac; the advertiser's specific goal may be to sell 100 Pontiacs in February. The announcer's general objective may be to gain the confidence and good will of an audience by programming what the audience wants to hear; an announcer's specific objective may be to attract new listeners with contests or giveaways.

There are at least three techniques that can be applied to goal or objective achievement.

1. The speaker needs to properly select the *vocabulary*—the words and phrases to be used—based on user need and comprehension level.
2. The source must select the *manner* in which the message is to be delivered to best achieve the intended goal.
3. Speakers need to be able to analyze audience *feedback,* the apparent effectiveness of their messages as they are making their presentation. The ultimate analysis of effectiveness of the mass media communicator, of course, may be at the sales counter or in the voting booth.

The content of the message is directly related to the objectives, as are the selection and arrangement of words and phrases. Of course the listeners' needs and understanding level must also be of foremost importance. Those who are responsible for construction of the announcer's message must be fully aware of the audience's needs and wants, as well as likes and dislikes, whether it is news, advertising, or other information being transmitted. Organization of the message needs to be obvious, not only to the sender but to the receiver as well. Is the main point of the message clear? Do the subordinate concepts logically relate to the primary idea? If feedback indicates that a message is improperly organized for comprehension by a particular receiver, reorganization may be necessary to make the message meaningful and need-fulfilling.

The manner of message delivery, be it sincere or flippant, is essential for the proper meaning to be understood. Many statements can readily be changed to a question by a mere inflection of the voice. A sad message with a peppy delivery may thoroughly confuse the intended receiver. The way a message is delivered is critical to understanding.

Having an objective for message transmission means that the sender can determine whether or not the intended message was received. Sometimes this can be done by checking the receiver's comprehension. At other times the receiver's actions can be seen to be a direct result of the message transmissions. As pointed out earlier, with advertising the consumer may purchase the product or pull the recommended lever in the voting booth. With news or talk shows, listener response to their congressional representatives or government agencies may result.

The stimulation generated by radio talk show hosts is said to have forced Congress to vote down a proposed pay increase in 1989 by evoking negative response from listeners directly to members of Congress. At other times, the effectiveness of the electronic mass media can be shown by the reports of rating services such as Arbitron and Nielsen. As has often been said of setting objectives, if you don't know where you're going, how will you know when you get there?

BINDING ELEMENTS

Keltner has pointed out that there are certain elements that are common to all speech transactions. He calls these *binding elements.* They can be listed as (1) engagement, (2) self-awareness, (3) sensitivity to others, (4) a desire to communicate, and (5) the translation of others' needs into effective speech communication.[6]

Engagement

The first element on Keltner's list is that of *engagement,* or involvement and commitment. This might be compared to the "attention step" of many formulas for writing advertising and speeches. If your intended audience is not attracted, if they don't want to listen, everything else is lost. When the radio or TV set is turned on, the listener-viewer expects certain satisfactions as a result of the announcer's efforts. Announcers are expected to display a certain energy level resulting from their commitment to entertaining the listener, their dedication to the cause being espoused, or their belief in the information being transmitted.

If announcers are listless or bored with the materials they are presenting, they can be sure that their listeners will be equally bored and will look elsewhere for the satisfaction they are seeking. One element of engagement usually missing in mass media is the immediate response of the audience. This is one reason why some programs are performed before a studio audience. Talk show hosts, of course, respond to guests and callers as well as the delayed feedback of the rating services. If you've seen the TV show *Midnight Caller,* you may recall that this talk show host bounces ideas off his producer as well as getting reactions from his phone-in guests. On programs such as the *Today Show* (where there is no studio audience), other members of the cast and even the camera and other production staff members react to the weatherman's antics or to other cast members and guests. Broadcast talent needs to engage an audience (real or imagined) to be effective.

Self-Awareness

Keltner's second binding element is *self-awareness. Intrapersonal* communication involves talking to oneself. This is an essential part of thinking and of the human communication process of learning about ourselves. Many people are unaware of who they really are. The "who-they-are" changes as they gain greater skill, knowledge, and maturity in their careers and personal relationships.

Imagine yourself as a college professor. Now see yourself as a circus barker. What are the differences in the way you speak, respond to people, dress, or even use your hands? Each of these actions is a means of communication as

[6] John Keltner, *Elements of Interpersonal Communication* (Belmont, Calif.: Wadsworth Publishing Co., 1973), pp. 23–29. Though Keltner differentiates eight of these elements, they have been consolidated into five for purposes of simplification in this text.

well as an indication of how you understand the role you are playing, how much you understand the way in which your world is constructed, and how you fit in.

How do you feel about your social responsibilities and the problems of other members of society? Do you belong in a particular environment? What should your reactions be to a given social situation according to the standards of your church, the government, your parents, or a radio or TV station management? Are they the same? If not, how do they differ? Which would you choose? Is your reaction the same as that of other members of the mass media, or of the audience—or do you *have* a conscious reaction? Have you thought the problem through, or have you avoided the issue, unwilling to get involved?

We all have biases and preconceived notions of right and wrong, good and bad, important and trivial. Few of us are willing to change our ways once we think we have a successful formula. Yet change is essential, and it is important that we be willing to reconsider some of our most ingrained beliefs. One way to cope with our own bigotry is with humor. We need to be able to laugh at ourselves, to see how ridiculous some of our own ways of doing things can become.

All organisms are essentially selfish and look at events from their own points of view. The act of being "human," however, requires that we look at events and concepts from the points of view of others as well, that we place ourselves in others' situations; that we reach—and touch—as many other kinds of people as we can to help us understand ourselves and our own emotions. Before you make a statement to be heard by a friend, by a broadcast audience, or by your boss, you may want to consider the implications of what you are about to say in light of intrapersonal communication . . . weighing the pros and cons of your approach in your own mind.

It is important to realize that we do have certain limitations. We are human beings, and can never be perfect. Trying to understand oneself is essential to being able to cope with one's limitations and to be able to use one's talents to the utmost.

Sensitivity to Others

Binding element number three is *sensitivity to others*. Sensitivity to others first requires sensitivity to self, as suggested in binding element number two. But it also requires you to be interested in people, to pay attention to them, and to empathize with them (trying to put yourself in the position of others in relation to various aspects of life). To understand others, we must be interested in others and become involved in interactions with others.

To be able to understand what others feel about us, to be able to react to this—becoming neither egotistical nor completely crestfallen—can help each of us improve our communication skills. A big problem, however, is perception. Is the message we are receiving the intended message? Is the message that is intended valid? Communication is a constant challenge to interpret incoming messages and to try to evaluate their relationship to other perceptions.

How can radio and TV announcers understand how others feel about them? How can they become involved with others? In addition to those instances referred to above where an audience or a respondent (as in a talk show) is involved, an announcer is well served by a memory of interaction with the types of persons that the rating service or the station management sees to be its prime target audience. Remembering contacts made through appearances before audiences can be most helpful to the announcer who has no studio audience or other immediate feedback. Concern for the members of the audience needs to be real, and it must come from an understanding of the concerns and hopes of the demographic group at whom the programming is aimed. Biases may act as screens to understanding how other people live or what their feelings or attitudes may be. We often have preconceived notions that are hard to overcome unless we pay close attention to what is actually happening. It is essential that we closely monitor our perceptions, being careful not to perceive what we *want* to perceive or what we *think* we *should be* receiving.

The Desire to Communicate

Another binding element is a strong *desire to communicate*. The desire to communicate has little to do with *reading* copy. Communication entails "telling" about the material in the copy, presenting the material in such a way as to get the ideas across; the ideas have been processed by the mind of the announcer and are being expressed as ideas rather than words. Announcers have a responsibility to "want" to communicate. Since this is a two-way process, it also includes paying attention to the response of the receiver—real or imagined.

Effective communication requires an understanding of others' feelings and desires. It also requires a broad background of understanding, not only of people and their emotional makeup, but also of current events, which helps gauge society's acceptance of what one's reactions might be. In broadcasting a hasty, unconsidered response can be catastrophic in ratings, in lawsuits, and in job retention. Mass media can vastly multiply an improper response that in interpersonal communication (with a single individual) might pass almost unnoticed.

Translation to Communication

Those physical aspects of the speech act that have been discussed in earlier chapters—voice placement, articulation, and pronunciation—are essential to message expression in most cases. Yet speech needs to have *meaning,* meaning that comes from the thoughts and perceptions of that human being doing the communicating.

> The language of speech is not the language of writing. The language of speech involves the total person physically, emotionally, and socially; the language of writing does not. The ability to organize the messages and the translations that we have created, the ability to extract the substance or our feelings and put that substance into the messages we are creating, depend upon our ability to use the language of speech and on our skills in the mechanics of speech behavior.[7]

[7] Keltner, *Interpersonal Communication*, p. 33.

FUNCTIONS OF THE MASS MEDIA

Keltner has suggested that interpersonal communication has three possible functions: utilitarian, aesthetic, and therapeutic.[8] Since we see announcing via the mass media as a modification of the interpersonal process, these functions may also be said to apply to the mass media.

What was probably one of the first and the most important mass media functional analyses was done by Harold Lasswell, who originally saw mass media functions as being three in number:

1. *surveillance of the environment* (the reporting function);
2. *the correlation of parts of society responding to the environment* (commentary, interpretation, and prescription); and
3. *the transmission of the social heritage from one generation to the next* (the education function).[9]

These are essentially *utilitarian* functions. Using Keltner's interpersonal insights as well as further discussions by involved media personnel and scholars, the following utilitarian functions might be added:

4. *servicing the economic system* (the media entrepreneurs and advertisers may well see this function as primary; the *economic function* as acknowledged by Brown, Brown, and Rivers[10] certainly includes advertising, which relates directly also to the persuasion function as discussed by Tan[11], and
5. *prestige conferral* (when looking through the eyes of the public relations practitioner, this is a primary function).

If we continue with the Keltner concepts, there might be two *aesthetic* functions listed: one might be called just:

6. the *satisfaction-of-the-aesthetic function* (appreciation of the beautiful), which can be seen in

7. the *entertainment function* (which is probably the primary function as far as most persons are concerned).[12]

[8] Ibid., p. 35.

[9] Harold Lasswell, "The Structure and Function of Communication in Society," *The Communication of Ideas,* L. Bryson, ed. (New York: Harper & Brothers, 1948), pp. 37–51.

[10] Charlene J. Brown, et al., *The Media and the People* (New York: Holt, Rinehart & Winston, 1978), p. 167.

[11] Alexis Tan, *Mass Communication Theories and Research,* 2nd ed. (New York: Macmillan Publishing Company, 1986), p. 71.

[12] Charles R. Wright, *Mass Communication: A Sociological Perspective* (New York: Random House, 1959), pp. 22–23.

As broadly therapeutic functions, two can be listed:

8. *companionship* (as the population ages, and talk radio increases, this is becoming a much more important consideration); and
9. *morale boosting* (which is an important function that is primarily therapeutic, especially in time of national military, economic, or political crisis. The morale-boosting function may take the form of praise of the status quo, of an evolving plan, or of the system generating the message. Or it may take a negative tack, denigrating the opposition in the form of propaganda).

Utilitarian Function

The electronic media certainly are utilitarian. They transmit vital information surveying the environment in the form of news, advertising, documentaries, interviews, and various other forms of drama—real and imagined. In a sense, all television is educational.

Advertisers and station owners see mass media functions differently. The owner of a commercial station sees making a profit as a primary broadcast function.

Advertising not only surveys the environment for the consumer (showing what is available), it also stimulates the economy, creating demand for products that consumers often do not need—and might even be better off without. Advertising also serves as the commercial broadcaster's primary source of income and profit.

The world as seen by many mass media consumers is largely a creation of the media: what many people know about police procedures is derived from police dramas on TV. Similarly, the concepts of New York or San Francisco are largely "mediated realities"[13] for those who have never been there. In other words, our image and understanding of a place or thing is often the result of what we have seen on television or been exposed to in other mass media. Soap operas have been shown to be used as models for solving viewers' own problems. In general, the mass media show people how they are expected to act within the bounds of society. For many, "soaps" are a primary means of transmission of the culture.

One of the sometimes unintentional functions of the electronic media is prestige conferral. The very fact that individuals appear on the tube or on radio seems to automatically make them important. Circumstances may be such that the media find certain people interesting or newsworthy often because they are in a particular location at a particular time. Public relations practitioners try to take advantage of this by getting their clients to be at the right place at the right time. News anchors and reporters often are made to look as credible as possible by their stations or network through promotional efforts, including putting the newsperson on the scene where major events are happening.

Aesthetic Function

The aesthetic sense pertains to the feeling for, understanding of, or love for the beautiful. Radio and TV are aesthetic forms of expression when important

---

[13] Dan Nimmo and James E. Combs, *Mediated Political Realties* (New York: Longman, 1983), pp. 5–6.

drama or music is presented. Even some advertising can be said to have an aesthetic appeal. Are music videos aesthetically pleasing? Perhaps this depends on your definition of beauty, but certainly many effects used in videos are intended to have aesthetic appeal and are viewed by many as a contemporary art form.

Broadcasting can help educate about what is understood as classical beauty or what modern artists may feel is beautiful. Many people seem to think that educational TV is not supposed to be entertaining, but, of course, it is not necessary to forgo the medium's entertainment function to educate. Like so many of life's pleasures, much aesthetic appreciation and understanding are learned. The media continuously transmit the culture, from opera to rock, from Shakespeare to Cosby. To many listeners the primary function of the electronic media is entertainment; most other functions are incidental.

Therapeutic Function

The therapeutic value of radio and television varies to a great extent based upon the audience member receiving the programming. Probably the main healing value is as a *respite,* a restful break in the day-to-day routine. Helping the listener to forget the cares of an otherwise mundane existence is an important function of broadcasting entertainment.

Some religious broadcasters are profit-making organizations. Some are nonprofit. All attempt to provide a spiritual uplift for listeners. Certainly their programming often falls into the therapeutic category. The previously referred to companionship function can also be categorized as therapeutic. Perhaps the morale-building function should also be considered a type of therapy. The sportscaster who roots for the home team is building morale, local pride, and community spirit. In time of war it has been the broadcaster's function to build morale on the home front, to stir patriotism, and to support the war effort. Essentially the media are expected to be a positive force in boosting the morale of the audience—psychologically therapeutic.

All-night talk shows help fill hours of nonsomnolence with mediated communication in which listeners may participate and gain a media-conferred status. Obviously, one of the major utilitarian functions of the electronic media is companionship, especially for older people who may live alone.

MASS MEDIA DYSFUNCTIONS

Most of the media functions discussed have tended to be positive or neutral. It is also appropriate to point out that communication can be *dysfunctional* (creating a negative effect on the audience or society). Critics often claim that advertising has the effect of creating demand for products that may be harmful to the purchaser, perhaps to the economy, and often to the environment. For example, Congress has banned the advertising of tobacco products in the electronic media. Whether an effect is positive or negative may depend on your point of view.

Announcers need to be aware of the overall importance and influence of the media as reflected in the functions of radio and television. Some of the more extreme and violent materials may increase fear and apprehension, especially among older audience members[14], making the materials dysfunctional rather than therapeutic or utilitarian. When Hitler used radio to back his war machine, it may have been functional for his cause at the moment, yet it certainly was dysfunctional in the long run for Germany and for the world as a whole. Many of the functions of the electronic media are functional in one sense or for one group, yet dysfunctional at another time, at another place, or for another group.

Communication functions are taken for granted by most of us. Yet often interpersonal communication and mass communication have multiple functions beyond what is intended by the source or (in the case of mass media) by the medium itself.

EXERCISES

1. Review the objectives at the beginning of the chapter. Be sure that you can explain each objective's concepts.
2. Study the word lists at the end of this chapter. Learn the words so that you can pronounce them correctly, write out the revised wire-service phonetics, and define the words when they are used in a sentence. Note in word list 3-B the application of a pronunciation rule: when a two-syllable word can be both a noun and a verb, the noun form can be expected to be accented on the first syllable, while the verb is usually correctly accented on the second syllable.
3. Mark the copy provided with the word lists for the most interesting reading style you can provide.
4. After marking the word list copy, read the word list paragraphs onto your cassette tape until you have done them to the best of your ability. Be sure that the final versions of these paragraphs are at the end of the tape. You may add wire copy as part of your cassette reading when you have perfected the provided paragraphs.
5. Read an additional hour of wire copy in five-minute newscasts until you have done these for a total of one hour on your second tape.
6. Bring your wire copy and marked paragraphs to class to read aloud.

VOCABULARY WORD LIST   Unit 3-A

1. preface (n)—introduction, as of a book or speech

   _____   *pref' us*

2. preemption (n)—the right of claiming before or in preference

   _____   *pree   emp'   shun*

[14] George Gerbner, et al., "The Gerbner Violence Profile," *Journal of Broadcasting,* 21 (Summer), pp. 280–286.

3. predicate (on) (v)—to base or establish (a concept)

_____   *pre' di kayt*

4. predicate (n)—part of the clause that explains the subject

_____   *pre' di kit*

5. precipitation (n)—falling products of condensation in the atmosphere

_____   *pree sip u tay' shun*

6. precept (n)—a rule or principle imposing a standard of action or conduct

_____   *pree' sept*

7. precedent (n)—a preceding situation that may serve as an example or justification in subsequent cases

_____   *pres' i dunt*

8. archipelago (n)—a large body of water with many islands, or a group of small islands

_____   *ar ku pel' i goh*

9. presentation (n)—the act of offering for acceptance or approval

_____   *prez in tay' shun*

10. presage (n)—something that portends or foreshadows a future event

_____   *pres' ij*

11. preventative/preventive (adj)—a drug or measure for preventing disease

_____   *pri ven' tu tiv or pri ven' tiv*

12. prevalent (adj)—of wide extent or occurrence

_____   *prev' u lunt*

13. presumption (n)—the act of assuming or supposing

_____   *pri zump' shun*

14. posthumous (adj)—arising, occurring, or continuing after death

_____   *pos' chew mus*

15. anonymity (n)—not having a name or having no recorded name

_____   *an u nim' u tee*

16. bestial (adj)—having qualities of a beast

_____   *bes' chul*

17. analogous (adj)—similar or comparable

_____   *u   nal'   u   gus*

18. chicanery (n)—trickery, use of deception

_____   *shi   kayn'   ur   ee*

19. clandestine (adj)—done secretly or under cover

_____   *klan   des'   tun*

20. comely (adj)—having a pleasing appearance

_____   *kum'   lee*

21. preferable (adj)—worthy to be first choice; more desirable

_____   *pref'   ur   u   bul*

VOCABULARY WORD LIST   Unit 3-B

1. accept (v)—to receive with consent; to be favorably disposed toward

_____   *ak   sept'*

2. except (prep)—leaving out; with the exception of

_____   *ek   sept'*

3. excerpt (n)—a selected passage; quotation; extract

_____   *ek'   serpt*

4. excerpt (v)—to select from a book, play, or similar source

_____   *ek   serpt'*

5. executive (n)—a person who carries out or manages affairs; the branch of government
with the duty to put laws into effect

_____   *eg   zek'   yew   tiv*

6. executor (n)—the administrator of a will, or a person appointed to execute a will

_____   *eg   zek'   yew   tor*

7. executer (n)—a person who carries out or executes plans, laws, etc.

_____   *eks'   u   kyew   tur*

8. exemplary (adj)—serving as an example; being a good model or pattern; serving as a
warning; a typical example

_____   *eks   zem'   pli   ree*

9. exigency (n)—a situation demanding immediate action or attention

_____   *eks'   siz   jen   see*

10. exorbitant (adj)—exceeding what is customary, proper, or reasonable; very excessive

_____   *eks   or'   bi   tunt*

11. experiment (n)—a test or trial to find out something

_____   *eks   per'   i   ment*

12. expert (adj)—very skillful; knowing a great deal about some special thing

_____   *eks   purt'   or   eks'   purt*

13. extradite (v)—to give or deliver (a fugitive or prisoner) to another legal authority for

     trial or punishment

_____   *eks'   tru   dight*

14. extraordinary (adj)—beyond what is usual; very remarkable

_____   *eks   tror'   di   nair   ee*

15. exuberant (adj)—very abundant; overflowing; lavish; profuse in growth

_____   *eks   zew'   bur   unt*

16. exacerbate (v)—to increase severity of; aggravate

_____   *eg   zas'   ur   bayt*

17. Exchequer (n)—British revenue collection department of government

_____   *eks   chek'   ur*

18. excise (n)—tax on goods or license fee paid

_____   *ek'   sighz*

19. excise (v)—to remove by cutting, as in surgery, or the removal of passages from a text

_____   *ik   sighz'*

20. exorcise (v)—to free from evil spirits

_____   *ek'   sor   sighz*

WORD LIST PARAGRAPHS   Unit 3-A

The pseudopreventative was merely a prelude to the posthumous announcement of the
prevalent disease. To presume a presage of death would be preferable to the alternative

precept. His presumption had been predicated on the basis of precedent, yet this had-
precluded any precipitation. The presentation of a miracle drug could now only be the
preface to a period of misery. The precipitation that fell as snow was a prelude to the
posthumous presentation of the award for bravery. The audience might presume that a
precedent had been set earlier with the preemption of the band concert, but such was not
the case. Even this presage would only exacerbate the situation. But the precedent of
reverence for the dead was prevalent, and predicted that the ceremony would be held as
scheduled. This was preferable to delay. Would the shaman exorcise the evil spirit? Only
a major disaster could serve as a preventative. . . .

ANNOUNCING PARAGRAPH   Unit 3-B

The executive thought room rates exorbitant, but as executer of convention planning, he exacerbated the exigency with his prevarication. He said the Exchequer
would collect the excessive excise taxes if the executor failed to excise portions
of the will.

The executor, in fulfilling the experiment stipulated by the will, found it
necessary to serve as expert to the assembling groups except on Sundays or
holidays. Whether his counsel was expert or exemplary seemed irrelevant. He
was exuberant beyond most mortal men. This extraordinary trait alone satisfied
the will's specifications and forced the state to extradite him to collect its inheri-
tance tax. With such confusion, how could one quibble over hotel rates?

v34711nto-

r d AP-6THNEWSWATCH-TAKE2   04-13   0290
/\

THE COMPANY THAT SELLS CHICKEN OF THE SEA TUNA SAYS IT'S
ASKING ITS CONTRACT VESSELS TO MOVE THEIR TUNA HARVESTING
AWAY FROM AREAS OF THE PACIFIC WHERE DOLPHINS MIGHT BE
ENDANGERED. VAN KAMP SEAFOOD AND BUMBLE BEE SEAFOODS ARE
FOLLOWING THE STARKIST SEAFOOD COMPANY IN ANNOUNCING THEY

WILL NO LONGER BUY TUNA CAUGHT IN NETS THAT ALSO SNAG DOLPHINS. THE POLICY IS AIMED AT NET FISHING IN THE EASTERN PACIFIC OCEAN, WHERE TUNA AND DOLPHIN SWIM TOGETHER. A STARKIST SPOKESMAN PREDICTS THE CHANGE WILL COST CONSUMERS ONLY A "COUPLE OF MORE CENTS" PER CAN. BUT A SPOKESMAN FOR THE AMERICAN TUNABOAT ASSOCIATION SAYS THE POLICY COULD PUT U-S BOATS "OUT OF BUSINESS."

/\

A NEW STUDY SUGGESTS COLLEGE COSTS IN THE 1990'S WON'T INCREASE AS MUCH AS THEY DID IN THE PAST DECADE. RESEARCH CONSULTANT ARTHUR HATUPMAN SAYS TUITION AND FEES ROSE SLIGHTLY LESS THAN TEN PERCENT A YEAR FROM 1980 TO 1987. HE SAYS INSTITUTIONS CHOSE TO MATCH THOSE INCREASES, RATHER THAN RISK HARM TO THE QUALITY OF PROGRAMS. BUT HATUPMAN SAYS COLLEGES AND UNIVERSITIES SHOULD NOT CONTINUE THAT PRACTICE IN THE 1990'S—BECAUSE TUITION PRICED TOO HIGH WILL TURN AWAY APPLICANTS. THE STUDY WAS CONDUCTED FOR THE AMERICAN COUNCIL ON EDUCATION AND THE COLLEGE BOARD.

/\

THE LATEST WORD ON INFLATION AT THE WHOLESALE LEVEL IS DUE FROM THE GOVERNMENT TODAY. THE LABOR DEPARTMENT IS TO RELEASE ITS PRODUCER PRICE INDEX FOR MARCH. OVERALL WHOLESALE PRICES WERE WAY UP IN JANUARY, BUT STAYED EVEN IN FEBRUARY.

/\

SAN FRANCISCO MAYOR ART AGNOS IS BLASTING THE FEDERAL EMERGENCY MANAGEMENT AGENCY FOR ITS HANDLING OF AID AFTER LAST OCTOBER'S EARTHQUAKE. THE QUAKE CAUSED (M) MILLIONS OF DOLLARS IN DAMAGE, LEAVING MANY BAY AREA RESIDENTS HOMELESS. AGNOS YESTERDAY TOLD CONGRESS THAT "FEMA" BEHAVED

AS IF IT WERE "PROTECTING THE PUBLIC TREASURY" AGAINST THE
HOMELESS. AGNOS SAYS THE GOVERNMENT SHOULD ALLOCATE MORE
FUNDS TO HELP REBUILD AFFORDABLE HOUSING AND PROVIDE MORE
RENTAL ASSISTANCE VOUCHERS UNTIL UNITS ARE REBUILT.

/\

v35041ntg-

r d AP-6THNEWSWATCH-TAKE3   04-13   0282
/\

     SOME FILIPINO CHRISTIANS HAVE BEEN OBSERVING GOOD FRIDAY
BY BEING NAILED TO CROSSES. POLICE SAY AT LEAST TWO DOZEN PEOPLE
IN SEVERAL PHILIPPINE COMMUNITIES HAVE BEEN CRUCIFIED. OTHER
FORMS OF PENITENCE ARE ALSO BEING SEEN IN THE PHILIPPINES
TODAY. IN ONE TOWN, MEN WITH CLOTHS COVERING THEIR FACES
WHIPPED THEIR BACKS WITH WOODEN STICKS IN A RITUAL MEANT TO
"WASH" AWAY THEIR SINS.
/\

     THE F-B-I IS ASKING LOTS OF QUESTIONS OF RESIDENTS IN VEGA
BAJA (VAY'-GUH BAH'-HAH), PUERTO RICO. SOME OF THEM RECENTLY
FOUND (M) MILLIONS OF DOLLARS BURIED IN STEEL DRUMS IN A
FARMER'S FIELD. U-S ATTORNEY DANIEL LOPEZ SAYS OFFICIALS
BECAME SUSPICIOUS WHEN RESIDENTS BEGAN BUYING LUXURY ITEMS
WITH "GREAT SUMS" OF CASH. HE SAYS AUTHORITIES FOUND ONE DRUM
THAT STILL CONTAINED MORE THAN ONE (M) MILLION DOLLARS—BUT
SEVERAL OTHERS WERE FOUND EMPTY. IT'S BELIEVED THE CASH WAS
STASHED BY DRUG TRAFFICKERS.
/\

     HIS NEW JOB HELPED GEORGE BUSH AND HIS WIFE BARBARA PUSH
UP THEIR INCOME—AND TAXES—LAST YEAR. A COPY OF THE FIRST
COUPLE'S JOINT 1989 FEDERAL INCOME TAX RETURN SHOWS THEY
REPORTED INCOME OF JUST UNDER 457-THOUSAND DOLLARS—
COMPARED TO 287-THOUSAND DOLLARS IN 1988. AND THEY PAID A

LITTLE MORE THAN 101-THOUSAND DOLLARS IN 1987, AND 62-THOUSAND DOLLARS THE YEAR BEFORE. THE HIGHER INCOME IS DUE TO BUSH'S INVESTMENTS AND HIS BETTER PAY AS PRESIDENT—200-THOUSAND DOLLARS ANNUALLY, UP 85-THOUSAND DOLLARS FROM HIS PAY AS VICE-PRESIDENT.

/\

PRESIDENT REAGAN NOW HAS WHAT HE CALLS AN "UNNATURAL, AND UGLY" SLAB OF THE BERLIN WALL, WHICH WILL BE INSTALLED AT THE RONALD REAGAN PRESIDENTIAL LIBRARY IN SIMI (SEE' MEE) VALLEY, CALIFORNIA. THE NINE-FOOT TALL, THREE-FOOT WIDE CHUNK WAS DONATED BY THE BERLIN WALL COMMEMORATIVE GROUP. REAGAN SAYS IT'LL SERVE AS A REMINDER OF "WHAT HAPPENS WHEN DICTATORS STRIP THE PEOPLE OF THEIR FREEDOM."

AP-NP-04-13-90 0554CDT(+

4

The Favored News Source

Upon completion of this chapter the student should be able to:

1. Explain seven requisite or possible criteria for news.
2. Explain the greater advantages of radio news during emergencies.
3. Name and describe the two American wire services and the workings of their two primary types of radio service.
4. Describe the advantages to a station of carrying local news.
5. List and explain four ways in which time signals may be given to talent in radio or television, and describe the hand signals for 30 seconds, 15 seconds, and "wrap it up."
6. Explain two terms that may be applied to radio news packages and discuss the preferred types of quoted content for short packages.
7. List three video news sources (other than the wire services and networks) that supplement a local news-gathering staff.
8. Describe three positions within a package in which a reporter may use a "stand-up."
9. Explain three functions of a news consultant.
10. Describe five common on-air studio presentation problems of beginning television news anchors or reporters.
11. Explain the difference between "freedom of the press" for the print media and for the electronic media, and why press freedom is important in a democracy.
12. Explain the importance of avoiding libel, and practices usually followed to avoid lawsuits.
13. Briefly explain copyright and fair use as they apply to broadcast journalism.
14. List four types of actions described in the chapter that might be deemed unethical.

The Gulf War in 90 seconds.

A murder in a nearby town gets half a minute.

The story of a fatal bus accident in Canada is bumped in favor of a lion cub's birth at the zoo.

TV news is selective. Its time is limited. And what it does best is capture moments. The elation of the elected. The downcast of the defeated. The joy of a mother's face when her child is found. The blank stare of a stoned teenager.

Stories with pictures.

Summaries of what matters most.

That's TV news on a daily basis.[1]

DELIVERING THE NEWS

Americans get more of their news from television than from any other source,[2] in spite of its brevity and selectivity. Most Americans seem to prefer their news "with pictures," pre-selected, served up in a convenient capsule of less than 30 minutes. The most reliable, immediate source of news locally, though, in time of emergencies is often radio. Whether it is radio or television, however, the electronic media provide Americans with a constant supply of news.

NEWS DEFINED

What is news? *Hard news* is information that is timely, unusual, factual, and of interest to a large number of people. The reporter or editor might also ask these questions: Did it happen nearby? Is the person involved well known? Can audience members empathize with the event? Is there conflict? Is there competition involved? Often forgotten is the question: Do our listeners need to know this to make wise decisions as voters in a democracy? Hard news concerns events that change life for people near and far away.

Soft news is perhaps less timely and usually less momentous. Yet most of the other news criteria can be expected to apply.

To be news the story needs to be out of the ordinary. The unusual makes news: a scheduled airliner landing safely at the airport probably is not news. A plane crashing at the airport, or even having a treacherous landing—this is unusual. This probably is news.

If it happens every day in about the same way, it is not hard news (though it could conceivably be a feature of some sort if there is an angle that can be exploited).

Of course news is expected to be true. If you've been on the scene where news was being made, then have seen the event on television or heard about it on the radio, you may have had the feeling, "But that's not the way it was." News

---

[1] Knight-Ridder, "Is TV News Shallow?" advertisement in *Channels,* November 1987, p. 19.

[2] "Cable Comes On Strong in Last T10 Roper Poll," *Broadcasting,* April 3, 1989, p. 27.

that is "as factual as possible" might be a better way to describe the product. News is what happened through the eyes of a camera or a reporter, probably both. Value judgments have to be made by reporters based on what they think is important—what they think is news, or what they think their editor wants.

Timeliness, of course, is a critical element of news. The very word "news" suggests that the information is of recent origin. One of the advantages of radio or television news is its immediacy. Most newspaper stories are at least 12 hours old. Radio and television can be on the scene, showing and describing the event as it unfolds.

Is it of interest to a great number of people? This is one place where a decision has to be made, and it helps to know the demographics of your station. Who the listeners are can pretty well determine the approach you should take to a story and whether, in fact, the story belongs in your station's newscast.

One element that relates directly to the interest of the people in your listening area is that of *proximity*. Is the event something that happened nearby? Does it concern people and places with which the audience is familiar? A murder in your city is news in your city, but a murder in another city a few hundred miles away (or less) may not make any difference to the listeners of your station unless it seems to be a serial killing, or it concerns a local person, or a celebrity many people recognize.

The prominence of the person or persons in the story often determines the story's newsworthiness. One study showed that of the hundreds of members of Congress and other politicians, only about 50 are in the news regularly.[3] Well-known names such as those of the Kennedy clan tend to make news, sometimes almost as much as the president or presidential candidates. Everything the president does is news. The same things happening to unknown people just are not news to the average listener. An exception is the human interest story.

The human interest story is usually considered "soft" news. It may very well be of interest to listeners if the listeners can empathize with the individuals involved. Sometimes the angle that receives the most attention in national or international stories is an emotional appeal that the listener can identify with.

SELECTING STORIES

Defining what news is and knowing your station's target audience help news selection, but there are other elements that also need to be considered.

When there is conflict or a competition—between countries, companies, or almost anything else, including politicians—this is usually news. The election story often is not "Who is in favor of what issues?" Rather, it is "Who is ahead in the polls?" The race itself is often the story, in spite of what the critics may think best serves the public interest.[4]

---

[3] Herbert J. Gans, *Deciding What's News: A Study of CBS Evening News, NBC Nightly News, Newsweek & Time* (New York: Pantheon Books, 1979), pp. 8–31.

[4] Doris Graber, *Mass Media and American Politics,* 3rd ed. (Washington, D.C.: CQ Press, 1989), pp. 80–105.

Determining the importance of a news story can be based on whether the story is timely, unusual, factual, of wide interest, or meets any of the other criteria that define news. The newspersons must carefully weigh stories to be sure that these stories are important to their audiences.

ON-THE-SPOT NEWS

"If you hear it, it's news. If you read it, it's history." This was a slogan radio stations used in the 1970s. Certainly radio has had the capability of getting on the scene first and delivering the news first, because of the very portability of the remote equipment and the ease of communicating from field locations using the telephone or remote transmitters that can relay a signal back to the radio station. The advent of the cellular telephone has made some on-the-scene reporting for radio much easier.

While radio equipment has gained some in portability in recent years, television has been able to catch up in many ways with successively smaller portable equipment and access to satellite and microwave links, which make it almost as easy for TV to be on the scene as it is for radio.

Figure 4–1 The satellite truck makes SNG possible

Electronic news gathering (ENG) refers to electronically capturing the story with a video camera and videotaping the event and relaying or taking the story back to the studio for editing and airing. Or, the story may be reported "live" from the scene without being recorded first. The signal sent to the station is often transmitted via microwave from the station's mobile unit. When the mobile unit is equipped with a satellite uplink, the news may be relayed via satellite. ENG then becomes SNG (satellite news gathering).

Probably only in natural emergencies (hurricanes, earthquakes, and floods), where people must depend on portable receiving equipment, does radio remain the most important immediate source of crisis information in a local area. When a power blackout hit New York City some years back, radio stations with supplementary emergency power supplies provided news and reassurance to people on their battery-operated portable radios. Even though TV stations usually also have some source of backup power, the public's access to emergency power supplies for television sets is limited. The public does have portable radios, however, backed up by those in their automobiles.

Wire Services

The backbone of most radio and television newscasts at both the local and the network levels has been the news collected by the Associated Press (AP) and the United Press International (UPI).

The Associated Press is a cooperative owned by its member stations and newspapers. Originally founded in the nineteenth century by newspapers to provide news of events outside a paper's normal news-gathering area, the press association grew in tandem with the telegraph. As telegraph systems expanded their coverage, so too did the news wire services grow to become key sources in the news-gathering process. Since the AP was a cooperative organization, much of the coverage was originally provided by the newspaper members, who shared their coverage with papers in other areas. Even today, local AP papers and stations are expected to contribute information on stories breaking in their local areas that otherwise might not get covered.

The primary method of transmission of news stories (originally sent by the dots and dashes of Morse code) became the teletype machine, which printed stories on typewriter-like machines over a wide geographical area via leased telephone lines. The original bulky teletype printers have given way to compact rapid printers and computer data banks, while the leased wire transmissions are now sent primarily via satellite. However, the name "wire service" remains.

The same electronic impulses that feed teletype machines can also be directed into a computer database. The days of the hard copy teletype may be numbered as more stations adopt computerized news systems.

Wire services provide not only teletype news, but voice actualities as well (though not all stations subscribe to the voice service). Actualities are "the voices of the people that make the news." These comments and answers to interview questions as recorded by wire service reporters are sent via satellite and leased wire at preset times to stations subscribing to that additional service. In addition, on-the-scene reports of late-breaking events are covered by wire service reporters and are made available to subscribers to the audio service. The audio networks also make available regular five-minute hourly newscasts. "Billboards" are listings of forthcoming actualities printed out on the teletype to alert station personnel as to when the audio reports will be sent and what topics and persons will be covered. The stations, in turn, record the materials they can use. Even without a major full-service network, a local radio station can put together a complete, interesting, and sophisticated newscast.

United Press International is a private organization that has served newspapers and broadcasters in much the same ways as the AP. It has functioned at a distinct disadvantage, however, since it has been expected to make a profit without the type of member cooperation that the AP organization elicits. In recent years UPI has tried to differentiate itself from the AP by focusing primarily "on 15 states near four regional hubs in Chicago, Los Angeles, New York and Atlanta.[5] It has intensified its reporting of "business and finance, economics and trade, government, crime, and other quality of life features," particularly on a regional basis.[6] By using stringers (part-time reporters paid on a per-story basis) UPI has managed to cut much of its overhead and remain a viable, competing source of important news stories to many newspapers and broadcasters.

Local News

News programming based primarily on the information delivered by a wire service can be relatively inexpensive. Local news gleaned from the city's newspapers and rewritten also entails little expense, and it can be reasonably easy to do once the techniques of broadcast news style are mastered.

Rewriting of newspaper material means doing away with the newspapers' traditional "inverted pyramid," where "who, what, where, when, why, and how" are expected in the first sentence. Broadcast news style involves shorter sentences, conversational style, and usually writing in present tense. Radio and television news-writing tradition as it has developed with the media is considerably more than this, of course, and can be the basis for another intensive college course.

Local actualities recorded from telephone interviews provide authenticity without a reporter on the scene. It is possible for a radio station to do a passable news job without spending much in the way of resources. If your station caters to an audience relatively unconcerned with breaking world and local events, these methods probably will suffice.

On the other hand, an all-news format is probably the most costly of the radio formats. Factors contributing to this are the cost of facilities and staff for (1) the possible dispatching of mobile units to a news scene for live reports, and

---

[5] Patrick J. Sheridan, "UPI Pins Its Survival Hopes on Differentiation," *Broadcasting*, October 22, 1990, p. 80.
[6] Ibid.

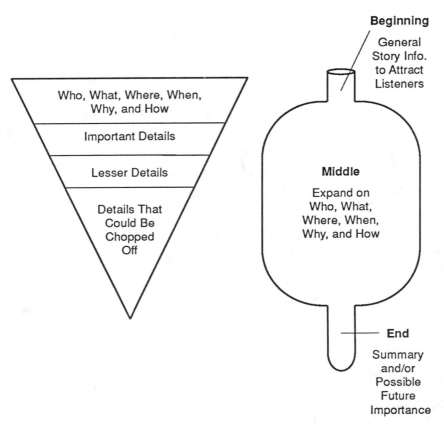

Figure 4–2   The structure of a news report in the print media versus the
                 broadcast media

(2) the getting of actualities at news conferences. Also of importance are (3) staff
for frequent rewrites and updating to keep the news fresh, and (4) multiple on-air
newscasters required by the intensity of the format. Any of several radio networks
can provide national and international news. It is the local coverage that is expensive.

Benefits of Local News

One of the criteria for news is proximity. The closer to home the news
transpires, the more it affects the local audience and the more this audience can
relate to it. Local news—almost by definition—is an important part of broadcast
programming in fulfillment of the FCC policy of stations serving their local areas.
Because news attracts a large, concerned audience with an above-average income,
news programming likewise attracts advertisers who want to sell their goods to
thinking citizens who have money to spend. Local news is frequently a station's

major profit-making center, especially in television. Local news programming is also a focal point around which other programming can be positioned because of its strong audience attraction. While most stations with an important news image carry network news and commentary, they feature and promote their local news because of its profit importance.

News programming is often the primary image producer for a radio station as well as for a television broadcast organization. Good local news coverage is often seen as the vital element in creation of a desirable station image. When important news happens, most concerned citizens turn to the television or radio station they think does the best job of covering the news—the one with the best news image.

Part of the news-generated image is the result of news credibility, created by a station that is on the site (or gets there quickly) when news happens and reports live from the scene. Local stories with pictures from the scene and sound bytes also receive more credibility from the audience than word-only stories. Most news directors want to be first with a story or to have it "exclusively"; therefore they monitor police band radio, check repeatedly with police and ambulance services, and listen to their competition. Thus, a competing medium's scoops are short-lived, as are a station's own exclusive stories (when the competition is on the job).

Investigative reporting also does much to enhance a station's image. It was in vogue for awhile shortly after Watergate, but most stations have found it much too expensive to pursue on a regular basis and have opted for syndicated human interest materials or consultant-prescribed local features.

A station's news personnel also represent an important source of credibility. People want trusted local anchors and reporters. Trust and credibilty, of course, come from reliable news coverage and presentation style that helps give stories authenticity. Part of the credibility of a TV weatherperson comes from the electronic devices the station has to tell the weather story.

help station's image.

WEATHER

Weather is an important element in broadcast news. The existence of cable's Weather Channel tends to reinforce the concept of weather as a basic field separate from news information. Weather's importance is additionally emphasized in the Midwest. There, weather often is the leading segment of a newscast, partly because of the severe extremes in the weather possible, and partly because knowledge of the weather is so important in making farming decisions. Almost all radio and television stations in the United States have some form of weather report. The wire services provide the National Weather Bureau reports for a number of zones in most states. Announcers can determine which zone they are in and read the appropriate forecast. In addition, some stations subscribe to the National Oceanic and Atmospheric Administration's weather wire, which carries weather information exclusively.

Radio stations may subscribe to a weather service such as Accu-Weather, which supplies not only forecasts but meteorologists as well, who identify themselves as bringing the current local weather and national weather "exclusively" for that particular station. Even with this service, however, most radio board operators will find themselves presenting the weather at some point.

Accu-Weather, ColorGraphics, and similar organizations syndicate maps and other services for television station weathercasters, providing graphics via telephone lines or satellite transmission. Of course some stations still create their own maps of the ever-changing weather, and have the electronic technology and personnel to do the job. One of the primary weather graphics may be the station's own radar or the radar of a nearby U.S. Weather Bureau station.

Training

Television stations that have their own meteorologists usually hire weatherpersons with a bachelor's or master's degree in meteorology. Some colleges offer courses in meteorology that can be taken by broadcasting students. The American Meteorological Society sets standards for its members and allows its seal to be used by approved television weathercasters. Large TV stations have meteorologists (often more than one) who are "personalities" and become household names. They appear on the local nightly news and try to explain why the weather is the way it is and what to expect for the ensuing period.

Most of these weathercasters have degrees in meteorology, but at some stations one of the general announcers may be assigned as weatherperson backup or weekend weather reporter. In some instances a regular weathercaster may not have been formally trained as a meteorologist, but learns on-the-job, so to speak. Knowledge of meteorology and skill as a weathercaster can be an important plus for the beginning TV announcer. If you want a career as a meteorologist, however, at least a four-year degree in meteorology is recommended.

Chroma-Key

Though chroma-key has been replaced as a means of supplementing video on most news stories, it is still the preferred method of projecting the changing maps of a good TV weathercast. The chroma-key technology replaces one color (usually blue or green) with the image from another source. In this case data have probably been stored on a computer disk to be seen by the viewing audience, though not by the weatherperson, except as it appears on monitors adjacent to the news set. So, though the announcer may appear to look at the map, he or she is really looking at a nearby TV monitor.

Perhaps it can be said of weather reporting as it has been of politics: all weather is local. People want to know what the rainfall or snowfall or temperature is, has been, or is going to be where they are, have been, or are going to be. Extensive floods in Texas and drought in California are most relevant to Texans or Californians, unless audience members know people there or the conditions are

Figure 4–3 The weathercaster looks at a monitor to see where he is pointing

reflected in some way locally as in the economy, perhaps in the cost of grapefruit or lettuce. Whatever the effect, weather can be expected to be an important television programming element for the foreseeable future.

TELEVISION NEWS

Just as television entertainment programming evolved from radio and film, so too television news was the outgrowth of radio news and movie newsreels. Most early television stations and networks were owned and operated by radio stations and networks, and early television reporters and operational formats were like those used in radio.

The newspaper-radio wire services likewise became television's important news sources. While early television picture-transmitting gear was extremely cumbersome compared with radio's sound-sending technology, the story coverage methods otherwise remained much the same. The news-writing style developed for radio obviously fit the new television medium better than the more literary writing style of newspaper reporting, with its "who, what, when, where, and how" first sentence (lead). Each story on radio or television tends to be a mini-drama

---

WEATHER TERMS

air mass—a large body of air with similar conditions throughout; may be dry or humid, warm or cool

barometric pressure—the weight of the air pressing down on the earth as measured by a barometer

dew point—the temperature at which dew will form

freezing—32 degrees Fahrenheit, 0 degrees Centigrade; temperature at which water solidifies; precipitation may be snow or hail

front—narrow band of changing weather between two air masses

high—an area of high pressure; winds blow clockwise around a high in the northern hemisphere, counterclockwise in the southern hemisphere

humidity—the amount of water vapor or moisture in the air

hurricane—a severe cyclonic tropical storm with wind speeds in excess of 73 mph

isobars—lines on a map connecting points with the same air pressure

isotherms—lines on a map connecting points with the same temperature

low—an area of low pressure; winds blow counterclockwise around a low in the northern hemisphere, clockwise in the southern hemisphere

precipitation—any form of moisture condensation, such as rain, snow, sleet, etc.

tornado—localized, violently destructive cyclonic winds formed over land; winds often over 300 mph

trough—an elongated area of low pressure, often related to hurricanes

weather warning—issued by the Weather Bureau to indicate that a storm is in the immediate vicinity

weather watch—issued by the Weather Bureau to warn of a possible impending storm

wind direction—based on the direction from which the wind comes; e.g., a north wind

---

with a beginning, a middle, and an end. Of course, live on-the-scene reports on radio and television can deliver the news in a much more timely manner than the print media, though involved, detailed explanations are still primarily a newspaper function. Events staged for the media, such as news conferences, are particularly important since coverage can be planned ahead by media personnel.

Syndicated Sources

Besides generating network news programming, the networks supply their affiliated stations with pictures and commentary that the networks have gathered, but that may not make the networks' scheduled half-hour news shows. In addition, stations' traditional network sources are often supplemented by independent video news-gathering organizations such as the Cable News Network and Conus. These agencies have become international in their distribution as well as their news gathering.

Local Packages

An *actuality* is a recording for radio of an event in progress with voices and sounds of the event, or it may be an interview with the voice of the interviewee. A *voicer* is a story recorded by a radio reporter for later airing. It may or may not contain actualities.

When getting the voice of the newsmaker or a bystander, it is usually preferable to ask the interviewee to make comments or state opinions to be used in the story, while the reporter furnishes the facts (the who, what, where, etc.) to be neatly packaged at the beginning and the end of the story.

As with radio, where actualities and voicers are prepared for subsequent newscasts, television reporters create "packages" using recorded video for hard news events and features. The reporter may do a *stand-up* (a reporter presentation in front of the camera) to introduce the piece, as a transition in the piece, or (most usually) to conclude an on-the-scene news report. While news anchors may narrate stories that have no video (except perhaps a generic still-store image beside them on the screen), the number of relevant local video packages that a newscast contains is often an indication of the competitiveness and the vitality of a station's news organization.

News Consultants

Media consultants have been around for a long time. Those who have done something often, or sometimes even for the first time, become "experts." Those who conduct and study the polls and surveys may also become experts. Those in a position to see the overall broad scene nationwide—who can see what has succeeded in other markets—are also experts and have information valuable to local stations. In the mid-1970s Frank N. Magid and Associates and McHugh-Hoffman set themselves up as experts and showed amazing ratings increases for the stations with whom they worked. Their restructuring of local television newscasts on stations in some major U.S. markets made the rest of the industry sit up and take notice.

News consultants look at what is drawing ratings in other markets around the country and try to modify them for the station being advised. This may result in special local features, such as a local medical update, or a regular feature on homeless children.

Consultants may offer advice on the presentation style: the set, the dress and makeup, and interaction between news personnel. Consultants may evaluate package editing and content. At times local survey research may be done by consultant organizations to determine such things as the station's image and audience wants and needs.

"Happy talk" news and "action" news were two of the formulas developed by consultants that seemed to work. Happy talk involved getting the formerly stiff presenters of the news to become more "relaxed," making informal patter and friendly comments to each other as well as to the audience. Feel-good type happy news was also an important element, leaving the audience with an upbeat feeling. The action news concept included featuring events where something was happening, such as at a fire, a picket line, or a demonstration. Visual action had priority. Critics have complained that emphasizing the visual tends to leave out other important events or informational needs of the public. Yet, since broadcasting is primarily a profit-motivated endeavor, ratings are critical to a station's success, and news consultants (or "news doctors," as they have been called) have flourished. Initially there tended to be resentment among news directors when top management brought in consultants to "help" them in the ratings game. However, as the 1980s ran their course, news directors generally seemed to accept and even seek the advice of consultants.[7]

TELEVISION PERFORMANCE

As with radio performance, experience is an important factor in making a television presentation that appears relaxed and credible. As with radio, being able to read TV news in a conversational manner, *telling* about what happened in a believable, authoritative way, is essentially all that is required.

Some of the common problems that students may have in trying to adapt to the medium of television are:

- slouching in their chairs. Being relaxed does not mean being so relaxed that the newscaster appears not to be alert or not to care.
- sitting so erect and stiff that one appears mechanical. Reporters should appear alive and concerned, certainly not like a robot.
- leaving the script flat on the desk when reading so that it is difficult to look at the camera, especially when not using an electronic prompter. Anchors who are not using an electronic prompter should hold the script at about a 45-degree angle, low enough to be out of the picture on a close-up, high enough that they can glance down without bowing their heads.
- losing their places in the stories being read. Students are advised to keep a finger on the line where they are reading so that they can grasp a sentence or a phrase, look at the camera, and return to their script, knowing where they are in the copy.
- wearing a low-hanging hairstyle (such as bangs) that shades a person's eyes. Remember that most lighting comes from an angle above the newscaster. The audience needs to see the reporter's eyes for good communication.
- acknowledging time cues. This can be done with a very slight nod or blink of the eyes that the audience does not see, but that the floor director catches.
- having nervous habits, such as turning in a swivel chair or tapping a pencil or fingers on the desk, that are readily picked up by the camera or microphone.
- making sudden movements that may catch a camera person off guard. "Telegraph" movements before you make them. Lean into a major movement such

---

[7] Roger David Maier, *News Consultants: Their Use by and Effect upon Local Television News in Louisiana,* unpublished master's thesis, University of Southwestern Louisiana, Lafayette, Louisiana, 1986.

Figure 4–4 The script appears over the camera lens so the newscaster can read and look right at the audience at the same time

as moving from a sitting to a standing position. Make major head movements slowly.

- stretching the microphone cord by moving too far from the point where it is plugged in. This may happen when on camera (very awkward) or when finished and moving off the set (could damage equipment).

All of the mistakes that a radio announcer can make can also be expected to show up before the TV camera. As with announcing for radio, a key element that cannot be overemphasized is the importance of preparation. Reading over your copy out loud, so that you know what it's going to sound like, can help you immeasurably in being able to project a meaningful understanding of the news.

Electronic Prompters and Prompt Cards

Since an important objective of newscasting is to give the impression that the announcer is talking directly to each member of the audience, it is important for the newscaster to look directly into the camera lens much of the time while

Figure 4–5 Students may keep their finger on the script where they are
reading

reading the news script. This can be done with an electronic prompting device
(described more fully later in this chapter). Also required of the newscaster,
however, is the ability to read effectively from a script, because any prompting
device may fail or get out of synchronization.

Some newscasters may even prefer to use a paper-printed script in certain
situations. David Brinkley, for example, prefers a script of hard copy just below
the camera's point of view on ABC's *This Week* program on Sunday mornings.
Though much of the program is ad lib, Brinkley is able to maintain an informal
manner as he introduces, narrates, and comments during various segments of the
show from a script. If you look quickly during cover shots in discussion segments
of the show, you may see his script on the coffee table.

Cue cards are probably the original verbal prompting device. These may
still be used in a studio where the more expensive electronic prompting devices
are not available, such as in a college TV studio. While it would be extremely
difficult to try to do an entire 30-minute newscast with cue cards, they can be
appropriately used for a 30-second spot, or for interview questions. Of course, as
mentioned elsewhere, cue cards serve well for time cues, often being more visible
than other cueing methods to newscasters with bright lights in their eyes.

The studio prompter has two configurations. The newest is all-electronic, with news scripts typed into a computer, where they are edited and projected line by line onto a reflective surface in front of the camera lens where the newscasters can read the prompter as they look directly into the camera. The computer also provides a hard copy of the script for the newscasters and production personnel.

With an older system, scripts are typed on multiple paper copies in large letters. One copy is taped together to be fed onto a crawl, which slowly rolls the script past a small black-and-white television camera. A television monitor above the camera lens then displays the words on a reflective surface over the television camera lens, which the newscaster can read while appearing to look directly into the camera. It is usually recommended that the announcer try to read at about the middle line on the prompter script, to provide a cushion in reading ahead and to avoid being rushed because the words are about to slip out of viewing range. Keeping a finger on the correct line in the printed script, and glancing down occasionally at that, not only insure that the announcer is prepared for a prompter breakdown, but that the viewer does not feel the reporter is trying to stare him down.

While it is, of course, desirable to be able to practice on an electronic prompting device, it is a skill that most announcers grasp without any problem. Effective reading from a script, however, is a skill that may take some practice. The student announcer can gain confidence and poise by practicing for as many situations as possible. This may mean rehearsal under bright studio lights in a necktie or other restrictive clothing.

APPEARANCE

Be sure clothing fits correctly: neither so loose that it appears you need to grow into it, nor so tight that it restricts breathing or movement. While the style of dress may vary slightly with the formality of your station or your newscast, it is generally accepted that men should wear ties and sports jackets or suits, while women should wear conservative business dress. Sweaters, blouses, and dresses are acceptable, though sparkling jewelry of any kind or dangling earrings can detract from the total newscast, and are to be avoided. Overly frilly, shiny, or provocative dress may also be seen as undesirable.

An expanse of white (as in a shirt or blouse) should not be in immediate juxtaposition with a area of black or near black (as in a suit or dress or even very dark skin). Most cameras cannot properly process this much contrast. The black may appear to have bleeding streaks of white shooting into it, or all detail will be lost as the camera automatically stops down to compensate for the brightness of the white. Pastel shirts and blouses do much to solve the problem.

Persons appearing on camera should always be careful not to wear narrow stripes or checks. They can cause the camera to produce a moiré effect, in which the design on the piece of clothing confuses the camera to such an extent that the figures in the design appear to "dance" on the screen. Both the black and white bleeding and the moiré effect can be annoying to viewers and distract from the content of the newscast.

Where most stations now use chroma-key only for the weather maps behind the weatherperson, this too can affect the talent's apparel selection. In the chroma-key process all of one color (usually blue or green), is, in effect, removed from the screen to let the background image from a different source "show through." The brightly lit wall behind the meteorologist is all of this particular color, so the weather maps appear to the viewing public to be on that wall. The problem may come if the weathercaster is wearing the same shade of blue or green as the background wall. In this case the map or other projected image may appear in place of the same colored article of clothing. When chroma-keying is used for still-store inserts or background weather effects, the weatherperson must be careful not to wear colors that may chroma-key out. Blue or green are selected because they are not usual skin tones. When the shade of the color used becomes transparent to the camera, some strange effects can occur—when the background visual appears through a weatherman's necktie, for example. Chroma-key was once used for most television news graphics. It was said that Walter Cronkite was always chroma-keyed in green because his eyes were blue and because he had so many blue suits in his wardrobe.

The newer method of inserting graphics for stories for which there are no other visuals is down stream keying, where the image appears to be on a plane in front of the anchor (instead of behind, as with chroma-key). When down stream keying is the system used, the anchors must be careful not to move extensively or rapidly when the camera is on them on close-up shots, or they may become hidden by the visuals. These graphics may partially cover newscasters until the camera operator is able to follow their movements.

Bright lights may fade the complexions of newspersons. With women, their regular street makeup usually looks fine. Men, on the other hand, may need powder or pancake makeup to avoid a washed-out look or to cut excessive shine on their skin. This may be particularly true with bald heads. In extreme cases, with early color equipment shiny bald pates could result in green halos over the person on camera.

When you open your mouth, it is distracting to see uneven, protruding, or otherwise imperfect teeth. If you plan to be on camera and your teeth are not straight and white, you probably will need to see a dentist for corrective dentistry. Similarly, if your eyesight is less that perfect, you may wish to consider contact lenses.

Furthermore, the camera adds ten pounds to your weight! People who are overweight usually learn to turn their bodies away from the camera at a 45 degree angle while keeping their heads looking straight. This tends to deemphasize their weight. Better yet, if you are overweight, lose a few pounds before applying for an on-camera job.

In general, if your clothing or makeup causes comment, it should not be worn. It is detracting from the newscast. Though newscasters sometimes are promoted as "stars," it is important for them to remember that what they say can affect the lives of many thousands of people. And while appearance may increase credibility, a beautiful smile and attractive attire can never overcome obvious lack of understanding and insight into the news.

Hand Signals

Since segments of the news must be carefully timed to begin and end as scheduled, several methods are used to advise talent of time remaining. One of the most universal is hand signals. These apply whether in the studio or on remote. Hand signals evolved in radio at different stations and have continued to be used in television. Since signals often were invented as needed, they may vary from station to station. There are, however, certain signals that are almost universal and well worth knowing. If you are doing an audition, of course, you'll want to check with the person who will be doing any signaling to be sure you are in agreement as to meanings.

In the studio a sweep second hand clock or timer may be set so that the performer can see the elapsed time without additional signaling. Other studios will have a digital timing device that the announcer can see, showing elapsed time or time left in the segment or the show. One of the most common methods is the

Figure 4–6 Floor person signals must be clear to the talent

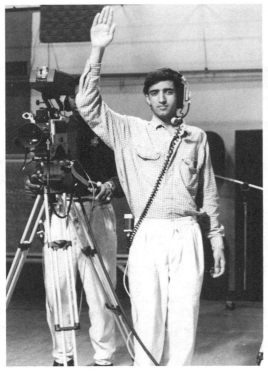

Figure 4–7(A) ''Stand by . . .''

Figure 4–7(B) ''You're on . . .''

Figure 4–7(C) ''Three minutes to go . . .''

Figure 4–7(D) ''Stretch it out . . .''

Figure 4–7(E) ''One minute to go . . .''

Figure 4–7(F) ''Thirty seconds . . .''

Figure 4–7(G) ''15 seconds . . .''

Figure 4–7(H) ''Cut . . .''

use of time cards that show the talent the time remaining. On a remote such sophistications may not be available, and at times in the studio hand signals for timing may be desirable or necessary. The thoughtful director or floor director will indicate before your performance just when time signals will be given, so that you know when to look for them.

Hand signals in television should be given directly under the lens of the camera that is on the air, except for the change-of-camera pointing motion, where the floor director broadly indicates on-the-air camera as the director calls for that camera and the camera becomes "live." This change-of-camera motion needs to be extremely broad and sweeping so that the announcer can see it with peripheral vision. A red light on the camera usually indicates which camera is on the air. If a newscaster finds that he or she is looking at the wrong camera, the reporter should glance briefly down at the script, casually coming back to the proper camera to avoid highlighting the error.

Standard time signals may be for the program as a whole or for a segment of the show. A newscast that has separate segments between commercials will often be timed in segments. A hand held beneath the camera lens with five fingers extended indicates five minutes to go; four fingers indicates four minutes, etc. Thirty seconds is indicated by fingers or arms crossed to simulate the one-half fraction. A clenched fist often indicates 15 seconds remaining. A hand-over-hand rolling motion is often used for "wind it up." Students need to practice reading in a timed situation to get a feel for how much material is needed to fill a minute, 30 seconds, or 15 seconds.

The writing of news, the reading of news, and the electronic technology for presenting news are important for broadcasting students to understand. Though we have freedom of speech and freedom of the press, there are limits to each of these rights. Some of these are covered by laws, others are primarily ethical considerations.

LAW AND ETHICS

Broadcasting is not a right. It is a *privilege*. For this reason, those who broadcast are often held to higher standards of performance than others. As used here, *ethics* refers to the good or bad conduct of individuals based on moral precepts. *Law,* on the other hand, refers to conduct expected and enforced by governmental agencies such as the police, the courts, and the Federal Communications Commission.

The Law and Broadcasting

Freedom of the press is guaranteed by the Constitution of the United States. Citizens are free to publish newspapers or handbills as they please (as long as they adhere to certain rules that have been established by the Supreme Court regarding libel and the public good). Freedom of the press is a *right* deemed essential for the function of a free society in which people govern themselves by way of the ballot box.

Broadcasting has been held to be different from newspapers in that the broadcast spectrum is finite. "Anyone can start a newspaper," the argument goes, "but you have to have an assigned frequency to start a radio or TV station." There are only a limited number of channels on which broadcasting can be done. In most metropolitan areas all of the allotted channels have been assigned.

Broadcasting freedom resulted in airwave bedlam when broadcasters first started taking to the air in the early 1920s. The Radio Act of 1927 set up the Federal Radio Commission to establish rules and issue licenses that restricted frequency use, power, and hours of operation. The Federal Radio Commission later became the Federal Communications Commission (FCC), whose primary duty has become to set engineering and performance standards and to regulate the use of the broadcasting frequencies "in the public interest, convenience, and necessity."[8]

Licensing, then, limits the number of people who can operate radio or TV stations, and it is a privilege to own and operate a radio or TV station. The Supreme Court has held that the airwaves "belong to the people," that licensees hold this resource in trust for the citizens of the country. It was the scarcity of frequencies and concept of responsibility that resulted in the Fairness Doctrine.

The concept of the Fairness Doctrine, which says that broadcasters must give equal time to all sides of controversial issues, does not have the force it once had, yet conscientious broadcasters recognize their responsibilities and try to provide a hearing for all sides of issues in newscasts. In order for the democratic system of government to function properly, people must be informed. Voters cannot make wise decisions without knowledge of the issues and the candidates. Section 315 of the Communication Act does require equal time opportunities for candidates for federal public office.

The first amendment to the Constitution of the United States guarantees free speech. Yet this does not mean that individuals can say anything they want to. Moreover, it does not mean that the media may ruin a person's reputation or that copyrighted materials belonging to others may be used indiscriminately.

Libel as defined by the law is the making of false statements or reporting information that might defame an individual or group. For this reason news reports are filled with such terms as "alleged" and "purported," which imply that the reported information is only hearsay and may not be true. The primary reason for this is to avoid costly lawsuits. Even though "truth" is an acceptable defense against libel in court, "truth" is often hard to determine or to prove, and the cost of defense in such litigation can often run into millions of dollars.

Attribution of a statement to an authority on the subject can also relieve the reporter from full responsibility. The quoted statement must, of course, be completely correct, and is best if recorded on tape.

---

[8] Communications Act of 1934.

Since one of the primary functions of free speech is to provide information to the citizens for self-government, statements made on the floor of the legislature or in open court are what is called *privileged speech* and are exempt from libel suits. In addition, persons such as politicians and performers, who have chosen to be "public figures," are more exposed to public view. It is important to note here, however, that court decisions tend to change as to the degree of privacy that may be accorded public figures (if not politicians).

Invasion of privacy is the reporting of information about a person's past so intimate as to be considered private and not something the public has a "right to know." Again, civil lawsuits may result in payment of extensive damage claims. Excessive intrusion on a person's personal, physical solitude and holding someone before the public in a false light have also been held to be illegal.

When reporting at the scene, it is particularly important that story items be reported as objectively as possible. Exaggeration may seem to make a better story, but ethically the reporter is expected to report "just the facts."

Though the news itself or facts of an event cannot be copyrighted, particular treatments of those facts can be and often are. It is in all probability a violation of the copyright law to read extensively directly from a copyrighted story in a newspaper or magazine on the air without permission from the publisher. *Plagiarism* (directly copying another's work and claiming credit for oneself) may not always be prosecuted under the law, but certainly it is always unethical. *Fair use* of copyrighted work does allow short quotations (usually up to 250 words) from copyrighted works with proper credit for the purpose of reviewing the work. Statements by newsmakers need to receive attribution even when paraphrased (as they usually are).

Gaining a proper understanding of the laws governing broadcasting is a lifetime career in itself. Broadcasting law is an ever-changing milieu of subtle differences of intent and meaning, and it is important that a station's news director and editors have a broad knowledge of what is proper under the laws of the country, and that newscasters be sure that they are following station policy on the points raised here or other issues whose legality is unclear. If in doubt, ask your news director or station attorney before airing material that may be questionable.

Applied Ethics

As pointed out repeatedly, the Bill of Rights of the U.S. Constitution guarantees freedom of speech and freedom of the press. All U.S. citizens can practice all of the freedoms of the first 10 amendments to the Constitution except one: freedom of the press is a right that can be practiced only by print and electronic journalists. Ethically this right also includes the assumption of responsibilities beyond strict adherence to the law. Society expects *ethical behavior* (actions that are morally correct) even though the law may not specifically spell out what the exact procedure should be.

With the priviledge of holding a broadcast license or a cable franchise comes the responsibility of personnel and the licensee or franchise holder to be good citizens, adhering to the truth, fairness, and free from the influence of those with economic and political power. Although such groups as the National Association of Broadcasters (NAB) and the Radio and Television News Directors Association (RTNDA) have laid out codes of ethics, there is little that enforces these codes except the desire to be responsible citizens. These codes of ethics include such things as the right to privacy, news objectivity, and not accepting objects of value that might influence news or programming.

As part of a person's (and his or her family's) right to privacy, many news media feel that it is improper to reveal a victim's name in cases of rape or suicide.

If a person's actions are reported as part of an episode that could ruin his or her reputation, at the least that person should be given the right to make a statement explaining his or her side of the situation.

A station's sponsors may *expect* to receive favored treatment in cases of scandal or product problems or to have certain incidents overlooked. Failure to report or glossing over facts is distortion of the news and, of course, is unethical.

News people need to know where their station stands on various ethical questions. Here are some that are important:

SOME ETHICAL QUESTIONS OF STATION POLICY

Should names of minors be used (with the possibility of marking them for life)?

Should the names of possible sexual assault victims be withheld?

Is it acceptable to have principals reenact an event for the cameras?

Is it necessary to label file footage in all cases?

Should news staff not be permitted to partake in outside activities where there might be the appearance of a conflict of interest?

Can reporters accept free lunches or other favors?

Should station advertisers receive special consideration?

Is the public perception of impropriety by station personnel to be avoided?

If a report may disturb listeners or advertisers, should it be downplayed or not used?

Are commentary and editorializing carefully identified?

News people need to carefully consider their ethical standards when they report a story. Here are some questions they might ask themselves:

REPORTER-ANNOUNCER ETHICAL QUESTIONS

Do I need more information to be sure before reporting this?

Do I need more points of view?

If roles were reversed what would I want the reporter to do?

Should I slant the story a little because it's a good cause?

Does reporting the story this way conflict with personal ethics or station guidelines?

What are my alternatives?

Will I be able to justify my decision and actions to others? to myself?

Will a nonguilty party suffer unnecessarily?

Is the well-being of the nation at risk?

> Based on Caesar Andrews, "Ethics: A daily story at newspapers," *Gannetteer*, March-April 1991, pp. 11–13.

The public may see ethical problems in a different light than either the station or the reporter. The viewer may be inclined to ask questions such as the following:

PUBLIC'S ETHICAL QUESTIONS

Who selected you (the news announcer) to determine what my neighbors and I need to know?

Why is my grief or that of my neighbor anybody else's business?

Whatever happened to our right to privacy?

Why don't you spend more time on the topics in which I'm most interested?

Why does your news coverage tend to miss the real issues?

Why is your coverage so narrow and encapsulated?

It is up to the news media to report only the truth, and to report the *whole* truth. Objectivity and accuracy should be paramount to the news reporter. If possible, all sides of a question should be revealed. There is a question that arises, however: is it possible to be completely objective? The answer is probably "no." Every time a story is reported, every time a camera is pointed, the medium is saying, "This is important; this is what matters." Information that a reporter reports is filtered through this person's previous experiences, prejudices, and beliefs, and so again, cannot help but be at least slightly biased because of the reporter's perception of "truth."

Reporters are expected to refrain from building personal relationships with government officials, since this is apt to distort the reporter's view of that official or his or her department.

A big flap in the 1950s erupted when it was revealed that record companies were dishing out thousands of dollars in payola to disc jockeys to play specific records. Accepting any kind of gifts or favors by dee-jays or news reporters is still seen as improper influence since this can distort public perception or public opinion, resulting in windfall profits or reputation enhancement for the giver of the gratuities.

Other unethical deception by programmers occurred during the 1950s when the big money quiz shows, such as *The $64,000 Question,* found that it built ratings (and therefore profits for the network and the sponsors) to rig the results. Contestants were rehearsed and given the answers in advance, and they performed in a prearranged manner. This led Congress to amend the Communications Act to prohibit such practices.

Electronic and print journalism are the primary means by which citizens can acquire the knowledge required to function effectively in a democracy. It is obvious that the images of reality as projected by the media must be protected and held in high esteem if the system is to work properly. See also Undesirable Commercials, Chapter 6.

INFLUENCE

Radio and television have become an integral part of the information system of a democracy. Not only is television America's primary news source, as noted earlier, it is also the one most trusted by the populace.[9] For the people of a nation to govern themselves, they must be informed. The voters need to have a grasp of the issues in order to make intelligent decisions. Keeping the population informed is a grave media responsibility. It is often said that the news is not covered in sufficient detail for people to completely grasp the issues, yet with the cable news networks (including C-SPAN) and the public broadcasting system's news programs, national news is available to those who want to be informed even without the print media.

EXERCISES

1. Mark the copy provided at the end of this chapter as recommended with underlining, overlining, slashes, parentheses, quotation marks, and any additional markings that might be useful in helping you read your copy better.

[9] "Roper Poll," *Broadcasting,* April 3, 1989, p. 27.

2. Follow the instructions for studying this chapter's word lists as suggested for previous chapters. Be prepared to pronounce the words correctly, write the correct phonetic transcriptions when tested, and define the words when used in a sentence.

3. Read your marked copy for Chapter 4 onto your cassette tape to be handed in. You may also reread paragraphs from previous word lists to review. Your tape will be handed in for evaluation. Marked copy for the current word lists should be handed in with your cassette.

4. Read this chapter's copy until you have done the best you possibly can, or until you have read for a full hour. When you feel that you have done your best, proceed to reading the news copy at the end of this chapter on the balance of your hour tape. Again, repeat until "perfect."

5. Bring your marked copy to class. Pick your best 60 seconds to be read "live" for the other members of the class.

6. Be sure that the assigned material (the best you can do) is at the end of your tape since your instructor will pay particular attention to this to evaluate your improvement.

7. Prepare a two- or three-minute newscast (as assigned by your instructor) to present for the TV camera in class. You may use the news copy found in the text or other appropriate news sources. It is recommended that only one camera be used with a member of the class acting as floor director giving "you're on," two-minute, one-minute, 30-seconds, 15-seconds, and wrap-up cues; this gives you a feel for timing as well as reading well.

8. Prepare a second (different) two- or three-minute newscast (time as assigned). This time two cameras should be used, with the added objective of being able to change cameras on direction of the floor director at appropriate times. The newscasters need to be able to indicate a story's ending by slowing in pace, dropping in pitch, and pausing.

9. Prepare a five-minute newscast with another member of the class. Put together a script in which story segments and different stories are assigned to each newscaster. Prepare up to 30 seconds of "ad-lib happy talk." Duplicate copies of the script for each announcer and the director.

VOCABULARY WORD LIST   Unit 4-A

1. tertiary (adj)—quality of being third, as in order, rank, or formation

   _____   *tur' shee er ee*

2. meteorologist (n)—a person who studies something beyond in the air or studies mete-

   orology, which deals with the phenomena of the atmosphere

   _____   *mee tee or ol' u jist*

3. bivouac (n)—temporary military encampment

       (v)—to make camp

   _____   *biv' oo ak* or *biv' wak*

4. rendezvous (v)—to present oneself at a place of meeting

       (n)—a meeting place

   _____   *ron' day vew*

5. laser (n)—acronym: light amplification by stimulated emissions of radiation; concentrated beam of light used in surgery and fiber optics

_____   *lay' zur*

6. altimeter (n)—an instrument that measures height or altitude

_____   *al tim' u tur*

7. perigee (n)—the point in the orbit of a heavenly body or satellite at which it is nearest to the earth

_____   *per' u jee*

8. peripheral (adj)—pertains to the external boundaries

_____   *per if' ur ul*

9. wonder (v)—to feel doubt or curiosity

   (n)—that which arouses awe or admiration

_____   *won' dur*

10. aeronautical (adj)—relates to the art of flight, especially the design and construction of aircraft or aircraft navigation

_____   *air u naw' ti kul*

11. Nazi (n)—right-wing German political movement

_____   *not' see*

12. wander (v)—to proceed or go aimlessly about without a plan or fixed destination

_____   *waun' dur*

13. apogee (n)—the point in orbit of a heavenly body or satellite at which it is furthest from the earth

_____   *a' pu jee*

14. impinge (v)—to encroach or collide (or, used with upon, or against)

_____   *im pinj'*

15. astronomical (adj)—pertaining to or connected with astronomy; extremely large, enormous

_____   *as troh nom' i kul*

16. astronautical (adj)—pertaining to astronautics or astronauts

_____   *as troh nau' ti kul*

17. protocol (n)—the customary or recommended procedure

————————————————   *proh' tu kaul*

18. protegé (n)—one whose career is advanced by a person of influence

————————————————   *proh' tu zhay*

19. irreparable (adj)—not capable of being repaired

————————————————   *i rep' ur u bul*

20. itinerant (n)—one who travels from place to place

————————————————   *igh tin' ur unt*

21. communiqué (n)—an official announcement issued by a government

————————————————   *ku myew' ni kay* or *ku myew ni kay'*

VOCABULARY WORD LIST   Unit 4-B

1. anarchist (n)—a person who believes in no government and therefore chaos and disorder; one opposed to government

————————————————   *an' ur kist*

2. legislator (n)—lawmaker, member of a lawmaking body

————————————————   *lej' is lay tor*

3. legislature (n)—body of lawmakers, a lawmaking assembly

————————————————   *lej' is lay chur*

4. Bethesda (n)—a city and naval hospital in Maryland; a Biblical healing pool

————————————————   *bi thez' du*

5. constituency (n)—persons represented by an elected official

————————————————   *kun stit' yew un see*

6. viscount (n)—a nobleman above a baron and below an earl; title denoting nobility

————————————————   *vigh' kount*

7. titular (adj)—holding a title; existing in title only

————————————————   *tich' u lur*

8. inaugural (adj)—having to do with a formal ceremony of induction into office

_____   *in aug' gyew rul*

9. gubernatorial (adj)—relating to or of a governor or his or her office

_____   *gew bur nu tor' ee ul*

10. solon (n)—wise legislator

_____   *soh' lun*

11. envoy (n)—a representative of state; an official who may or may not be attached to an embassy; a diplomatic courier

_____   *on' voi*

12. counsel (n)—advice given by a lawyer; one who represents and offers advice

_____   *kown' sul*

13. consul (n)—an appointee sent to protect the interests of his or her countrymen in a foreign land; head of foreign consulate

_____   *kon' sul*

14. attaché (n)—the official attached to a diplomatic mission

_____   *at' a shay*

15. laissez-faire (n-adj)—the doctrine of economic freedom or theory permitting people to do as they please in economic matters with little or no governmental interference

_____   *les ay fair'*

16. emirate (n)—the realm of an Arab chieftain or prince

_____   *em' ur it*

17. infamous (adj)—having an extremely bad reputation

_____   *in' fu mus*

18. ingenious (adj)—extremely clever

_____   *in jeen' yus*

19. ingenuous (adj)—innocent, free of reserve, naive

_____   *in jen' yew us*

20. ingenue (n)—innocent female character in a drama

_____   *on' zhu new*

ANNOUNCING PARAGRAPH   Unit 4-A

In the secluded rendezvous the meteorologist finds his initially tertiary objective has become primary. The laser will not solve his problem, nor can the altimeter. Interest will wane if the satellite should wander and fail to meet its predetermined apogee and perigee. Troops on bivouac closely follow the satellite's course; and a galaxy of top scientists, whose reputations are at stake, no longer need wonder as to their own fates. Only the meteorologist has yet to prove his ability. In the meantime, the protegé of the meteorologist has found that the prescribed protocol impinges on his freedom, doing irreparable damage to his psyche, and he has become an itinerant in search of security.

VOCABULARY WORD LIST   Unit 4-B

Although the legislator had a visa, he could not convince the attaché that the viscount knew about the intended agenda. The legislature was to sponsor an inaugural ball for the governor, yet the gubernatorial candidate saw that his laissez-faire attitude toward the Iranian consul could lead to trouble. Not only was the party's titular head expecting a rout, but several of the solons had given counsel that the legislator was in fact an incognito anarchist from a Middle Eastern emirate. He was said to be infamous for his ingenious schemes, constantly preying on the ingenuous and trusting, much as a villian in an old-time melodrama might try chicanery to seduce the comely ingenue.

v2859int--

r a AP-LISTTRIAL (DETAILS)   04-12   0294
/\AP-LIST TRIAL (DETAILS)

/\

(ELIZABETH, NEW JERSEY) -- PROSECUTOR ELEANOR CLARK SAYS THAT IN THE CASE OF JOHN LIST, JUSTICE DELAYED IS NOT JUSTICE DENIED.

A JURY IN ELIZABETH, NEW JERSEY, FOUND THE 64-YEAR-OLD FORMER ACCOUNTANT AND SUNDAY SCHOOL TEACHER GUILTY OF THE PREMEDITATED MURDERS OF HIS WIFE, HIS MOTHER AND THREE CHILDREN IN 1971.

A GAUNT, WHITE-HAIRED LIST SHOWED NO EMOTION AT THE VERDICT, WHICH FOLLOWED NINE HOURS OF DELIBERATIONS OVER TWO DAYS. HE FACES A LIFE TERM WITH PAROLE POSSIBLE AFTER 15 YEARS. LIST'S SENTENCING IS SCHEDULED FOR MAY FIRST.

LIST HAD BEEN ACCUSED OF SHOOTING FAMILY MEMBERS AT THEIR WESTFIELD, NEW JERSEY, HOME IN 1971. HIS ATTORNEY ACKNOWLEDGED THAT IT HAPPENED ON NOVEMBER NINTH. POLICE DISCOVERED THE BODIES ON DECEMBER SEVENTH. DIRGELIKE RELIGIOUS MUSIC WAS PLAYING OVER AN INTERCOM SYSTEM AND LIST HAD LEFT A SERIES OF MATTER-OF-FACT NOTES EXPLAINING HIS ACTIONS AND APOLOGIZING. LIST HAD DISAPPEARED.

HE WAS FINALLY ARRESTED IN VIRGINIA LAST JUNE. AUTHORITIES WERE TIPPED TO HIS WHEREABOUTS AFTER HIS CASE WAS HIGHLIGHTED ON T-V'S "AMERICA'S MOST WANTED."

WITNESSES IN THE TRIAL DESCRIBED LIST AS A MILD-MANNERED MAN WHO WAS DEEPLY RELIGIOUS. AND DEFENSE PSYCHIATRIC EXPERTS TESTIFIED THAT LIST HAD AN "OBSESSIVE-COMPULSIVE" PERSONALITY DISORDER. AND THAT, COMBINED WITH A TWISTED SENSE OF RELIGION AND A SERIES OF PRESSURES ON HIS LIFE, MADE HIM AN UNTHINKING KILLER.

THE DEFENSE CONTENDED THAT LIST FEARED FOR HIS FAMILY. HIS WIFE WAS DYING OF LATE-STAGE SYPHILIS CAUGHT FROM HER FIRST HUSBAND IN 1943. HE WAS ASHAMED. HE ALSO FELT UNABLE TO SUPPORT HIS FAMILY AND DREADED THE PROSPECT OF WELFARE. AND HE FEARED HIS FAMILY WAS FALLING AWAY FROM THEIR RELIGION AND FACING DAMNATION. THE AIM WAS TO WIN A CONVICTION ON A LESSER SECOND DEGREE MURDER CHARGE.

BUT A PROSECUTION PSYCHIATRIST DESCRIBED LIST AS A MAN
WHO SUFFERED FROM LITTLE MORE THAN A MIDLIFE CRISIS. AND
PROSECUTORS POINTED TO HIS OBVIOUS EFFORTS TO ELUDE CAPTURE
AS PROOF THAT LIST ACTED WITH PREMEDITATION.

/\

AP-NP-04-12-90 1345CDT<+

v286llntg-

r d AP-15THNEWSWATCH (THREETA   04-12   0256
/\AP-15TH NEWSWATCH (THREE TAKES) <

by Ira Dreyfuss

/\

HERE IS THE LATEST FROM THE ASSOCIATED PRESS:

/\

FROM THE CRIMES OF THE NAZIS TO THE FUTURE OF THE NATION,
THE NEW GOVERNMENT OF EAST GERMANY IS MAKING BIG
CHANGES—EVEN SETTING THE STAGE FOR ITS OWN DEMISE.

/\

THE NATION'S FIRST FREELY ELECTED LEGISLATURE CONVENED
TODAY, TO CHOOSE CONSERVATIVE LEADER LOTHAR DE MAZIERE (LOH'-
TAR DUH MAY-ZEE-AIR') AS PRIME MINISTER AND BACK A SWEEPING
AGENDA FOR REFORM. HIS COALITION LOOKS TOWARD RAPID
UNIFICATION WITH WEST GERMANY—MAKING ITS PRIME GOAL TO BE
ITS REPLACEMENT BY A SINGLE GERMAN GOVERNMENT. BUT
LAWMAKERS ALSO CALLED FOR KEEPING SOME SOCIAL BENEFITS, SUCH
AS JOB GUARANTEES, DATING FROM THE OLD DAYS OF COMMUNIST
GOVERNMENT.

/\

THE PARLIAMENT ALSO MADE A STRING OF CONCILIATORY
GESTURES TO THOSE WHO SUFFERED UNDER THE LAST UNIFIED

GOVERNMENT OF GERMANY—THE NAZI GOVERNMENT. IT RECOGNIZED
THE LEGITIMACY OF THE CURRENT BORDERS OF POLAND, WHICH
INCLUDE LAND GERMANY LOST AFTER WORLD WAR TWO. IT ALSO
APOLOGIZED TO JEWS FOR THE NAZI HOLOCAUST AND PROMISED
REPARATIONS.

/\

JEWS IN ISRAEL AND AMERICA WELCOMED THE EAST GERMAN
STATEMENT. ISRAELI OFFICIALS SAY IT COULD MAKE IT EASIER TO
ESTABLISH TIES BETWEEN THE TWO NATIONS. BUT THE SPEAKER OF
ISRAEL'S PARLIAMENT—A DEATH-CAMP SURVIVOR—SAYS HE'LL
NEVER GRANT FORGIVENESS FOR THE HOLOCAUST.

/\

PRIVATE ENTERPRISE IN THE SOVIET UNION? POSSIBLE, SAYS ONE
TOP LAWMAKER—PAVEL BUINCH (PAU'-VEL BYEW'-NITCH) SAYS A
MOVE TO PUT UP TO 70 PERCENT OF THE ECONOMY INTO PRIVATE HANDS
COULD START NEXT YEAR. HE SAYS HE'S NOT SURE IF THE GOVERNMENT
WILL PRESS HARD ENOUGH TO BRING OFF REFORMS SO GREAT—BUT,
HE SAYS, SMALL STEPS WILL LEAD NOWHERE BUT "GENERAL COLLAPSE."

/\

AP-NP-04-12-90   1347CDT(+

v3142int--

r d AP-20THNEWSWATCH   04-12 0406
/\AP-20TH NEWSWATCH<

by David Shapiro

/\

HERE IS THE LATEST FROM THE ASSOCIATED PRESS:

/\

IT'S ACKNOWLEDGED THAT IT HAS CHEMICAL WEAPONS, IT'S
WIDELY BELIEVED TO BE BUILDING A NUCLEAR BOMB, AND NOW THERE

ARE NEW ALLEGATIONS AGAINST IRAQ. BRITISH CUSTOMS OFFICERS
HAVE SEIZED A HUGE STEEL TUBE ORDERED BY IRAQ. IT'S 131 FEET
LONG, AND ARMS EXPERTS SAY THE TUBE IS BIG ENOUGH TO OUTFIT A
GUN TO FIRE NUCLEAR OR CHEMICAL WARHEADS HUNDREDS OF
MILES—INTO IRAN AND ISRAEL.

/\

AN IRAQ OFFICIAL IS CALLING THE CHARGE BASELESS. AS FOR THE
BUSH ADMINISTRATION, IT SAYS IT'S ASKING THE BRITISH
GOVERNMENT FOR INFORMATION ON THE IMPOUNDING ACTION AND
WILL NOT ISSUE ANY COMMENT FOR NOW.

/\   *A Federal study as shown*

NEARLY EIGHT PERCENT OF THE 465 WOMEN IN A FEDERAL STUDY
HAD USED COCAINE, OPIATES OR OTHER ILLEGAL DRUGS TWO DAYS
BEFORE GIVING BIRTH. THE REPORT BY THE U-S CENTERS FOR DISEASE
CONTROL LOOKS ONLY AT WOMEN IN RHODE ISLAND, AN URBAN STATE
THAT RESEARCHERS SPECULATE IS LIKELY MORE PRONE THAN RURAL
STATES TO DRUG USE. STILL, THE REPORT SAYS THE FIGURES PROBABLY
UNDERESTIMATE THE SCOPE OF ILLICIT DRUG USE AMONG WOMEN
GIVING BIRTH.

/\

HE'S NOT SUFFERING FROM IMPAIRED VISION, BUT DOCTORS HAVE
FOUND THAT GLAUCOMA HAS STARTED TO DEVELOP IN THE LEFT EYE
OF PRESIDENT BUSH. THE WHITE HOUSE SAYS BUSH HAS BEEN GIVEN
AN EYEDROP PRESCRIPTION TO CONTROL THE PROBLEM. BUSH
UNDERWENT A PHYSICAL AT BETHESDA NAVAL HOSPITAL TODAY, AND,
EXCEPT FOR THE GLAUCOMA, HIS DOCTOR SAYS THE PRESIDENT WAS
FOUND TO BE "IN EXCELLENT HEALTH."

/\

THE PULITZER PRIZES HAVE BEEN HANDED OUT, INCLUDING THE
61ST ONE FOR "THE NEW YORK TIMES." THAT AWARD GOES TO NICHOLAS

KRISTOF AND SHERYL WUDUNN, A HUSBAND AND WIFE TEAM WHO
COVERED LAST YEAR'S DEMOCRACY PROTEST IN CHINA. AN OFFICIAL OF
THE NEWSPAPER CALLS THE PRIZE "A GREAT VICTORY FOR THE
INSTITUTION OF MARRIAGE."

/\

AP-NP-04-12-90 1853CDT(+

v3450lal--

r h AP-8THNEWSMINUTE   04-12   0166
/\AP-8th NEWSMINUTE

/\

    HERE IS THE LATEST FROM THE ASSOCIATED PRESS:

/\

    "NASA'S" STILL WATCHING THE WEATHER AS IT COUNTS TOWARD
THE SPACE SHUTTLE LAUNCH AT 8:47 A-M, EASTERN TIME. CONDITIONS
AT KENNEDY SPACE CENTER ARE NOW 80 PERCENT FAVORABLE FOR
LAUNCH. BUT POOR WEATHER HAS SHUT DOWN TWO EMERGENCY
LANDING SITES—AND IS QUESTIONABLE AT A THIRD.

/\

    THREE EUROPEANS ARE FREE IN BEIRUT, LEBANON, TODAY, AFTER
LONG MONTHS AS HOSTAGES. PALESTINIAN GUNMEN DELIVERED A
FRENCH WOMAN, HER BELGIAN BOYFRIEND AND THEIR DAUGHTER
BORN IN CAPTIVITY TO THE FRENCH EMBASSY IN WEST BEIRUT.

/\

    TODAY'S HOSTAGE RELEASE MAY HAVE LITTLE TO DO WITH THE
FATE OF 18 WESTERN HOSTAGES HELD IN LEBANON. THE THREE PEOPLE
FREED TODAY WERE BELIEVED HELD IN LIBYA, AND NOT CONSIDERED
PART OF THE LEBANON HOSTAGE SITUATION.

∧

PRESIDENT BUSH HEADS TO CANADA TODAY FOR HIGH LEVEL TALKS AND A LITTLE BASEBALL. BUSH WILL MEET WITH CANADA'S PRIME MINISTER TO DISCUSS NEXT MONTH'S U-S - SOVIET SUMMIT. THEN, THE TWO MEN WILL TAKE IN A TORONTO BLUE JAYS GAME.

AP-NP-04-10-90 0704CDT(+

5

Off the Cuff

OBJECTIVES

Upon completion of this chapter the student should be able to:

1. List three elements of successful ad libbing.
2. List six possible types of information sources for an upcoming remote.
3. List five representative periodical indexes that would probably be the most useful for most remote broadcast research.
4. Explain the use of written materials on radio and on television talk shows.
5. List and explain three possible ad lib formats.
6. Describe a fourth step that might be added to all interview formats.
7. List and give examples of the seven types of sensory imagery.
8. Demonstrate the use of five grammatical techniques for creating imagery.
9. Explain the author's attitude about "How do you feel [after your traumatic experience]?" questions.
10. Suggest three ways a dee-jay might prepare for his or her air shift ad libs.

AD LIBBING

The security of having a script or a television prompter may not always be there to lean on. Yes, you need to be able to read well and with expression, but you also need to be able to express ideas without a script, either from notes or strictly impromptu. The successful announcer must know how to *ad lib*.

SUCCESS STORIES

Walter Cronkite won the admiration of his colleagues and the respect of CBS management when he was able to fill in and expound almost endlessly with relevant insightful statements at a Democratic National Convention some years ago. This was a key factor in his elevation to the position of nightly anchor on the CBS Evening News.

Dan Rather first came to the attention of the nation as a capable newsperson when he reported live during a hurricane in Galveston when he worked for a Houston television station.

The ability to ad lib effectively can *make* a career. But good ad libbing doesn't just happen. It entails preparation, organization, and an ability to put your knowledge and observations into words.

PREPARATION

Preparation consists to a large extent of various kinds of research. (See also Chapter 8.) In addition, preparation includes practicing the ad libbing skill and should also include careful thought as to logical organization of the information to be discussed.

Topic Research

Let's look at a hypothetical situation: a radio reporter is going to be doing a remote at an upcoming event. Perhaps the governor is coming to town. How does a good reporter research the topic? If the station has access to a computer database of the news services and other news publications, it may be easy to access this information by typing in a key word (perhaps the name of the governor). Suddenly there is a wealth of information at the reporter's fingertips, probably more than can be used. As you have probably found in researching for term papers or speeches, it is important to narrow the topic. Perhaps the type of event at which the governor will be appearing will help the researcher select a more specific aspect of the topic. *Narrow the Topic*

If the event is the opening of a new highway link, the reporter will need to know the governor's position on road construction and his or her part in the building of this particular road. The reaction of local legislators is also relevant. How is the roadway being financed? What economic benefits are to be expected? All of these things may be included in the computerized database, but the local angles may well not be included. If the local newspapers are not included in the database, the reporter will need to find some of this information in the station's files (if they exist), or more probably at the local library.

There are advantages to working for a member of a chain of news organizations. Gannett newspaper and broadcast properties, for example, maintain a large centralized library. Should there be Gannett employee questions anywhere in the country, the USA TODAY/Gannett library is primed to find the answers. The Gannett library has over 5,000 reference books, several million photos, and on-line databases such as NEXIS, DataTimes, Vu/TEXT, and DIALOG.[1]

While many stations may not have computer database access, the local library probably has access to computer databases that might give a reporter some of the needed information. There may be a small charge, but (depending on the reporter's skill at choosing proper descriptors for the search) rapid finding of the information should be well worth the expense involved. A reporter's time is worth money.

In locations where computer database access to the particular topic a reporter needs to research is not available, or where the information provided is obviously inadequate, the traditional research tools of the library are important.

Before computer databases were widely available, the rule of thumb was, "look first in a general research source," such as an encyclopedia. This is still a good rule, and it may be the one to follow if the topic has not been covered recently by the popular media. An encyclopedia should be able to provide a reporter with important dates and names as well as a bibliography for further investigation.

One of the problems encountered here is what to look up in the encyclopedia. If the governor is coming to open a new highway, the reporter may want to look under the name of the relevant state. He or she may want to look under "roads and highways," which can give information on road construction, funding, mileage by states, history of road building, and, in the case of one encyclopedia at least, nearly 50 related articles within that one reference work.[2]

Names from the bibliography may well appear in the card catalog, where one can also find information by topic or publication name.

The *Reader's Guide to Periodical Literature* should be one of the first indexes to which one refers. But it often does not include more specialized publications that can help make a reporter an authority. The list of periodical indexes that follows should be of particular value for reporters who wish to really understand the topic they are investigating.

Data bases used in Research.

[1] Laura Dalton, "Library Goal: Leave No Fact Unfound," *Gannetteer,* September 1991, p. 8.
[2] "Roads and Highways," *The World Book Encyclopedia (1975),* 16, pp. 334–41.

SELECTED LIST OF REPRESENTATIVE INDEXES[3]

Columns on this chart containing an "X" refer to the index on the right.

The column labels are as follows:

A—the index includes *abstracts*
B—the index catalogs *books*
P—the index lists *periodicals and professional journals*
G—an important source of *government documents*
M—material is often found on *microforms*

A	B	P	G	M	
		X			Applied Science & Technology Index
	X	X			Art Index
	X	X			Bibliographic Index
		X			Biological and Agricultural Index
X		X			Biological Abstracts
X		X			Book Review Digest
		X			Business Periodical Index
X		X			Chemical Abstracts
X			X		CIS (Congressional Information Service)
X				X	Dissertation Abstracts
		X			Education Index
		X	X		ERIC* Current Index to Journals in Education
X			X	X	ERIC* Research in Education
		X			Essay and General Literature Index
	X				Granger's Index to Poetry
		X			Index to Economic Journals
	X				Index to Plays
	X		X	X	Monthly Catalog to U.S. Government Publications
		X			Music Index
X		X		X	New York Times Index
X	X	X	X		PAIS (Public Affairs Information Service)
		X			Poole's Index to Periodical Literature (1802–1906)
X		X			Psychological Abstracts
		X			Reader's Guide to Periodical Literature
	X				Short Story Index
		X			Social Sciences Index
	X				Speech Index
		X			Subject Index to Children's Magazines
		X			Topicator

* Educational Resources Information Centers

One resource researchers often fail to highlight, but that they need to acknowledge, is the librarian. Asking questions of a librarian may be very rewarding, especially for locating sources in a particular library.

[3] William L. Hagerman, *The College Library* (Lincoln, NE, Nebraska Educational Television Council for Higher Education, 1973), Unit V, p. 16.

The reporter is not limited to the library or a database for doing research. Personal interviews may well serve as a source of information available nowhere else. Earlier library investigation can help frame the proper questions to ask. Who are the local authorities? Perhaps their aides are more available and could give the same information. At local colleges, there usually is a professor willing to impart some of his or her understanding. Being able to quote a credible source in relation to a topic may give reporters and their audiences unexpected insights.

Many university libraries also house a government documents section, which is in effect almost a separate library since much of it is indexed separately using a different system of material organization. If government is an important part of the remote to be covered (and maybe even if it is not), the reporter may want to ask the government documents librarian to help find information because of the unusual arrangement of this section. Since the U.S. government is the world's largest publisher, government documents can yield a wealth of information. Above all, the researcher should remember the importance of getting information as the remote or ad lib broadcast is planned.

Practice

Johnny Carson is reported to have said to his producers that it was time to practice the ad libs. Indeed, good ad libs sound as if they are spur-of-the-moment comments. Sometimes they are. More probably, however, the good ones have been thought out and quite probably practiced. To be sure, according to the dictionary ad lib means "to act, speak, etc., without preparation,"[4] but the person capable of consistent, exemplary ad libs is *prepared* with at least a knowledge of the topic from research. For the person trying to develop the ad libbing skill, it is important not only to be prepared with necessary information but also to practice answers to anticipated questions or situations.

The practice session should not be an attempt to practice repeatedly exactly what is to be said in a given situation. Rather, the practice should be of the expression of ideas. Certain phrases will tend to recur, but the reporter should not try to memorize a pat answer that will be automatically triggered by a comment or situation. Practice of rehearsed answers may make a presentation sound "canned," as the would-be ad libber concentrates on trying to recall specific words rather than listening to what is being said and being able to respond conversationally.

Using an Outline and Notes

On radio, written notes can be ideas announcers have organized as a result of their research. To keep their ad libs organized, concise, complete, and factually correct, it is recommended that announcers keep their notes at hand. Good notes are intended to be used, and the announcer should continue to add to them even

[4] *The Random House Dictionary, Unabridged* (1967), p. 19.

as an event being covered continues. All of the statistics about an <u>athlete or sporting event can hardly be expected always to be carried in the announcer's head,</u> though many sportscasters live and breathe sports to such an extent that much of the important data will be on the tips of their tongues.

Talk show hosts who discuss current events keep up with the news with ardor, but it certainly is expected that they should have a card file or other source of specific information to supplement their expertise, especially on radio, where the notes are not obvious to the listener. How often have you been amazed by the seemingly endless information on a topic that a good talk show host displayed? He or she probably had notes.

Notes on cue cards held under the camera lens or on an electronic prompter, as mentioned in Chapter 4, are methods used by television hosts to remind them of certain data or key ideas they want to be sure to cover. Where quotations or specific numbers are part of what is to be said, written notes in the performer's hand or on the talk show host's desk may even lend credibility to the overall presentation. The prepared "ad libs" of some would-be stars reading cue cards while describing the Pasadena Rose Bowl Parade or Macy's Christmas parade or other such event have sometimes been so obviously <u>scripted that the term ad libbing should not be abused for this type of performance.</u>

ORGANIZATION

With ad libbing, as with any other kind of presentation—be it written, acted, or narrated—the proper juxtapositioning of ideas and images gives a more coherent meaning than a random as-you-think-of-it scramble of thoughts, even though many of the same points are expressed. Announcers can take a cue for organizing from the academicians who have helped students organize their speech making. The presentation on radio or television is, after all, a form of speech making. Organizational methods that seem to lend themselves well to radio and television are (1) space and proximity, (2) the chronological sequence, and (3) question and answer.

Space and Proximity

The *space-proximity* organization provides a framework in which announcers can describe the scene that they see before them. Though the initial input may suggest general conditions, the second step includes description of the scene from left to right and from distant to close-up. Then the announcer will describe a primary object of attention in some detail. Essentially, then, this is a three step formula:

- Step one: General conditions—temperature or weather, time of day, and the occasion for the remote.
- Step two: A more detailed description of the environment from left to right, or distant to close-up. This is arbitrary and may depend on the scene to be described.

Resue Team is working to pull people out of their SNOWED up house TRAP PAST 3 DAYS.

Old People in Their seventy's

The announcer should try to create suspense or build to the more important elements to be described. So if it may be more logical, the spatial progression may be right to left, top to bottom, close to distant, or outside to inside, etc.

- Step three: A detailed description of the element that is the intended focus of the broadcast. The announcer should try to *find action* to describe.

Compare this to the standard sequence of shots used in most situations when shooting film or video. The normal sequence is wide shot, medium shot, close-up.

The space-proximity formula may be used particularly when the announcer has time to fill or is trying to set the scene for an upcoming event such as a ball game or a parade. It might also work effectively for a break in a parade or a half-time game description.

Chronological

Chronological, of course, means that elements are described in the order in which they have happened. After a general description of the occasion, it is the announcer's task to describe what has happened previously. If the event is a fire, the reporter may have described the scene using the space-proximity formula. He or she should proceed to describe what is known about the chronology of the event as it has unfolded. The final step is a description of the scene as it now exists and what is happening on the scene.

- Step one: A general description of the present scene and why it is deemed important enough to be the subject of a remote broadcast.
- Step two: The event as it has happened up to now. It may be the history of the event. If it is an annual event, the reporter may describe why or how the first event happened; how and when the event has been continued, with previous year highlights; then what has happened so far this year in relation to the event. Another element that may be worth investigating is the cause of the action taking place.
- Step three: The final step in this formula is the explanation or description of what is currently happening, giving a blow-by-blow account, so to speak. This may be seen as the effect of the previous information and actions.

Question-and-Answer Sequence

The *question-and-answer* method of arranging ideas is based on the idea of answering the questions you think are most likely in the minds of the listeners.

- Step one: Again it is important that the announcer advise the audience of the location of the remote broadcast and why it is important to the listener.
- Step two: Prepare a list of questions the announcer thinks the audience is most apt to want to have answered. How does this event relate directly to audience members and to their lives? If there is a chance before going out on the remote, the announcer may ask a representative group of people just how this event may be important to them. The announcer might ask what things they might be

interested in knowing about the event. A logical way to arrange these questions and answers is to create basic categories so that you can lump similar ideas together. These ideas then can be grouped in a logical manner such as "cause and effect," "problem-solution," or "familiar to unfamiliar."

- Step three: As usual, the final step includes a description of the action that is currently taking place on the scene.

4th step

An additional step that should be added to all of the formulas listed here is a summary and future projection. As the announcer describes the scene that's unfolding, he or she may even want to keep notes (as with a sporting event) so that the closing summary will be complete. What is going to happen as time passes? What will the scene be like 10 minutes, one hour, or 24 hours from now?

These suggested formulas can be combined where appropriate. Knowledge of the event and its background are important for an interesting and audience-holding performance.

CREATING IMAGERY

Word pictures are your reason for being on the scene when doing a radio remote, but there are also imagery elements that can be inserted when doing television on-the-spot broadcasts as well. With radio you need to create visual images. These are mostly supplied by the medium with television. But taste and smell sensations, tactile, and emotional feelings often need words to bring them to life.

Ehninger, Gronbeck, and Monroe suggest seven types of imagery. They are:

1. Visual (sight)
2. Auditory (hearing)
3. Gustatory (taste)
4. Olfactory (smell)
5. Tactual (touch)
   a. Texture and shape
   b. Pressure
   c. Heat and cold
6. Kinesthetic (muscle strain)
7. Organic (internal sensations)[5]

Visual Imagery

Here is where radio's "theatre of the mind" comes into being. The announcer creates it. The announcer suggests to the audience the sizes, shapes, colors, and movements of objects in the environment and of the event being covered.

[5] Douglas Ehninger, Bruce E. Gronbeck, and Alan H. Monroe, *Principles of Speech Communication,* 8th brief ed. (Glenview, Ill.: Scott, Foresman, and Co., 1980), pp. 163–69.

The most vivid visual images for radio are created with the use of descriptive words and action verbs. Descriptive words include nouns with built-in adjectives, such as "limousine" used in place of the more generic term "car." For instance,

> The presidential candidate is briskly emerging from his long, black limousine.

creates a much better word picture than,

> Now he's getting out of the car.

"Limousine" has built-in modifiers: large, luxurious, tinted glass, chauffeur-driven, and whatever one's experience and imagination can conjure up. The built-in modifiers of "car" (if any are suggested) are much more mundane: motor-driven, four-wheeled, rubber-tired, etc. Note also the use of the specific adjectives used with "limousine": *long* and *black,* and use of the adverb *briskly.* The verb "emerge" also has more interesting built-in modifiers than does "getting out," though both do show action. Saying "he was in his car and now he's out" implies action perhaps, but there is no specific action stated. Try to avoid using forms of the verb "to be" as the only verbs when describing a scene. The "to be" verbs show *state of being* rather than action. (The "to be" verbs are *be, am, is, are, was, were, been.*)

Instead of saying,

> There are trees along the street.

say something with more action, such as:

> The wind is gently swaying the stately palm trees that line the boulevard.

Example of a prepositional phrase that describes might be:

> The president's wife with her hair *of silver-gray* . . .

Obviously, the announcer is not going to use all of the techniques suggested here at the same time. The announcer does, however, need to be aware of the kinds of words that can be used to create imagery. If there are notes to be used or phrases to be remembered, they should probably include these methods.

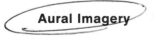 Aural Imagery

As the visual imagery is provided by the television picture, so too the sound of radio and television tend to provide much of the auditory imagery. There are times, of course, when sounds are discussed that have happened previously, that are expected to happen, or that are happening off camera and out of mike range. ABC reporter Beth Nissen was in Panama when Noriega had surrendered to the United States and described the reaction of the Panamanians:

> They banged pots and pans with spoons.[6]

Note too the use of *onomatopoeia* (a word that sounds like the sound it denotes), in this case the word "banged." What better way to indicate a sound?

Gustatory and Olfactory Imagery

The announcer may not often have a need for projection of a taste, but when that time does arrive, hopefully the planning professional will be able to use something other than the trite "nice," "good," "wonderful," or "delicious." The announcer should be specific in telling listeners about the scene. A reportable action associated with the taste may make it more real.

> GOOD: The Cajun food is hot and spicy.
> BETTER: The hot and spicy Cajun food is bringing tears to her eyes.
> GOOD: The crackers are crisp and salty.
> BETTER: You can hear the crispness of the lightly salted crackers as the diners bite into them.
> GOOD: The wine is said to be robust and fruity.
> BETTER: The guests are making a toast with the robust and fruity wine.

Taste and smell tend to overlap. Technically taste includes only those elements that can be distinguished on the tongue: sweet, sour, salt, and bitter, or combinations of these. "Fruity" then probably is an aroma rather than a taste. When it comes time to describe an odor, the use of an analogy is perhaps the simplest and the best way. A wine aroma has been described as

> fruity, floral, spicy, yeasty, yellow plums, peaches.[7]

The descriptive prepositional phrase obviously also works well.

> Your nose can pick up the aroma of freshly fried onions and bell peppers.

> The carnival midway combines the odors of cotton candy and diesel fumes.

The use of familiar odors with which the audience can relate helps listeners create the olfactory image the announcer is encountering.

[6] Beth Nissen, *ABC Special Report*, January 3, 1989.
[7] Eleanor and Ray Heald, "Sur Lie: Aging White Wine on the Lees," *Practical Winery and Vineyard*, X, no. 6 (March/April 1990), p. 13.

Kinesthetic and Organic Imagery

Kinesthetic refers to the use of muscles, often the stress or strain sensations that accompany the ultimate athletic effort. Similarly, organic imagery calls forth bodily experience.

> The expression on the face of the runner plainly shows the wrenching pain of his muscle cramps.

> The young man's drunkenness was confirmed by his obvious dizziness, wrenching nausea, and uneasy steps.

Though the announcer may not often be called on to project kinesthetic or organic imagery, it is the kind of thing that can really bring home to the audience a feeling of being on the scene. The on-the-scene reporter needs to be aware and ready to invoke kinesthetic and organic imagery when the proper moment arrives.

Emotional Imagery

The ability to transmit the feelings of the people involved in the action and being able to describe this is one of the important aspects of on-the-scene reporting. ABC Sports for years used the slogan "the joy of victory and the agony of defeat" to describe the emotion its cameras caught and its reporters described. One of the clichés of too many beginning or unimaginative reporters is the question, "How does it feel to . . . (whatever the experience has been)?" In most cases the reporter probably should try to avoid this. Surely an announcer can describe feelings of agony or elation without asking the principals of the action how they "feel." Better to discuss their winning strategy or the strong competition they overcame.

"How does it feel to see your brother run over by a truck?" shows poor taste on the part of the reporter and of the station that runs such a story. The announcer on the scene should have the good taste to allow the victims of a tragedy to have their privacy unless they really want to express themselves.

The techniques of language use that have been discussed for visual or aural imagery work equally well for other imagery. Be sure to think in terms of analogy (especially simile and metaphor) in all of the imagery types. Adjectives, adverbs, active verbs, and words with built-in modifiers need to be practiced so that the announcer is alert and ready to use these resources.

AD LIBS ON THE AIR

Perhaps the remote broadcast of a news or sports event is the ultimate ad lib situation, but certainly the ability to think on one's feet is also apparent in many of the other types of programming announcers are expected to perform.

The talk show program, in which a guest is interviewed or telephone calls are taken, is much like an ordinary conversation but is one to which an audience is privy. (See interview techniques, Chapter 8.)

The dee-jay's ad libs are best planned in advance, especially for the beginning announcer. A comment that has become a cliché among dee-jays is, "I'll be with you until . . . ." Who cares? Probably only the dee-jays themselves care when they get off. Like preparing for the typical college class, the conscientious dee-jay spends two hours in preparation for every hour on the air. For the tyro, additional time may be necessary to do a professional quality job.

How does the dee-jay prepare? Obviously, it depends on the station and the format, but the student should consider how these steps might work on many stations.

1. All announcers should check the news wire and know what's going on locally and around the world. This is important even if the announcer is not doing news programming. Dee-jays should especially look for news items that relate to artists that might be featured on their shows.
2. Announcers should check the music to be played and get as much background as they can on the music and the artists. They should listen to the music: they need to know how to get in and out of the music and in and out of the show gracefully. (See Chapter 11.)
3. Conscientious announcers use the library or their own resources to find quotations, jokes, news features, and other material to inform and entertain. There are many collections of anecdotes and stories about famous people as well as other types of collections of humor. Audiences like to laugh or snicker. If announcers can create original humor, that is great. But if they can't, they can quote others (giving them credit, of course). And how about checking out a topic that can be used as a theme for the show?

On the television news set, happy talk appears to be ad libbed. Again there is a certain amount of planning that goes into this. Certainly, being up on current events in each of the major news areas is essential to be able to respond appropriately to one's news peers. When leading into or promoting an upcoming segment or feature, newscasters should not quote the other reporter's first line or give away the story's punch line. Rather, it is up to the reporter to suggest a general view of the topic.

Describing sports takes a particular kind of person, one who eats and sleeps sports. The good sportscaster is often one who seems to believe that sports are the most important events of the day. This is discussed in Chapter 9.

Ad libbing is something that is developed to an art form by many of those who practice its intricacies. It is a skill well worth having, probably essential in various degrees for all who expect to appear before the camera or before the microphone on a professional basis.

EXERCISES

1. Mark the copy provided at the end of this chapter as recommended with underlining, overlining, slashes, parentheses, quotation marks, and any additional markings that might be useful in helping you read your copy better.

2. Follow the instructions for studying word lists as suggested in the previous chapter, this time doing word lists 5A and 5B. Be prepared to pronounce the words correctly, write the correct phonetic transcriptions when tested, and define the words when used in a sentence.

3. Read your marked copy for Chapter 5 word lists onto your cassette tape to be handed in. You may also reread paragraphs from previous word lists to review. Your tape will be handed in for evaluation. Marked copy for the current word lists should be handed in with your cassette.

4. Record the ad lib assignments onto your tape, doing the best you possibly can, or until you have read and ad libbed for a full hour.

5. Bring your marked copy to class. Pick your best 60 seconds to be read "live" for the other members of the class.

6. Be sure that the assigned material (the best you can do) is at the end of your tape since your instructor will pay particular attention to this to evaluate your improvement.

7. Write out a 60-second "ad lib" using three of the seven types of imagery discussed in the chapter and following one or more of the chapter-recommended organizational methods. Describe:
   a. The noon-time activity in your student union.
   or
   b. The scene at half-time at the last football or basketball game you attended.
   or
   c. A man-on-the-street reporter's visit to the student cafeteria or a local fast-food restaurant. (DO NOT DO AN INTERVIEW for this assignment.)
   or
   d. A campus event taking place this week where a crowd of people is expected.

8. Take your cassette recorder and describe one of the scenes in exercise 7 above "live." If there is another remote scene you could fit better into your schedule that you would like to describe, be sure to clear it first with the instructor.

9. Looking out of a window, take two minutes to describe what you see using the three-step space-proximity method of description.

10. Ad lib scenario #1
    It has been raining hard for several hours. You have been assigned to do a remote using the chronological approach. Here is some basic information:

    Streets are flooding around campus. Sidewalks cannot carry off the water fast enough. Students are taking off their shoes and rolling up their jeans to get where they're going. The ground is saturated, so walking around flooded sidewalks is no solution.
    The grounds director, Mike Bridges, says that flooding has been a problem as long as the university has been here. The difficulty, he says, is caused primarily by leaves backing up in the drainage pipes. The crews try to clean out the pipes before the rains come, but they can only do so much with the limited size of their crew. Students and faculty are urged to call the trouble line (231-6440) when they see trouble developing so that it can be headed off. It is the responsibility of the city to take care of the streets. The city has said that it would like to hire another 13 persons to work on drainage, but again finances are limited. As the city has grown over the past 10 years, many roadways have been added to the city street crews' responsibili-

ties. Yet these crews have been reduced, according to Pat Logan, director of capital improvements for the city. Logan says that the city is aware of the problems around the campus and does its best to keep drains clear of leaves and debris. He pointed out that the city has appropriated $800,000 for drainage improvement for the new buildings scheduled for erection on the east campus.

This is an ad lib assignment. You are to speak extemporaneously. Do not read this information verbatim in your simulated broadcast. You may make notes and use them. You may not "make up" things. You may, however, use experiences or memories you have relating to similar flooding problems. This report should run two minutes.

11. Ad lib scenario #2

AD-LIB NEWS remote   (60 seconds)

SITUATION: school board meeting still in progress, but this is to be a one-minute report on what's happened tonight.

LOCATION: school board office

OCCASION: selection of final candidates for superintendent

Finalist candidates announced:

Walter Lee   Caddo Parish Superintendent
Max Skidmore   Fairfax County, Va., Supervisor
Lois Chapman   Superintendent, Edinburg, Texas
Thomas Tocco   former Superintendent, Cobb County, Ga.

SALARY: Jay Floyd Hall has been retained to negotiate the contract with the new superintendent (Hall to be paid $1,000).

BACKGROUND: Screening process has been going on for six weeks; originally 47 applicants for the job. Board members have done personal interviewing and visited local school districts where they work.

Meeting started at 8 o'clock.

Final choice to be announced Saturday.

12. For the next three ad lib scenarios, research is required. Using the techniques suggested in this chapter, find out additional information relating to one of these events that you can use to expand your ad libbing to three minutes. Use an organizational plan from the chapter and at least three different types of imagery. Prepare by recording your ad lib onto this week's cassette tape. Be ready to present your ad lib description of events and background material in class.

Scenario #3   The governor is coming to town to officially open a new stretch of interstate highway, which includes important interchanges near the heart of the city.

You have been assigned to cover the event live on the air. While the segment is not long, you are expected to ad lib with useful information for two minutes prior to the ribbon cutting. Prepare with information from the library by using some of the sources recommended in the chapter as well as the local newspaper(s) if appropriate. You may use notes, but you should not read the material as if you have a prepared script. This needs to sound like the ad libs of a competent reporter on the scene. After your two-minute description using one or more of the frameworks as suggested in the chapter, you may describe the actual ribbon cutting as you might envision it to take place. (Take about 15 seconds for this.) Then conclude with a summary that runs about 30 seconds.

Scenario #4   A new city entrance way–park is opening. At the center of the park is the tourist information center. Research tourist information and tourist income generally for the state and the area. Describe the park as you envision it. Look at the history of the park (if one exists in your area, research it). Tell about the visitor points of interest in the surrounding area that this tourist information center can highlight. As in Scenario #3, spend about two minutes giving the above background. Then take about 15 seconds to describe the actual ribbon-cutting ceremony, and 30 seconds to summarize your on-the-scene report.

You may use notes as in the preceding scenarios. Try to sound informal but proficient and professional.

Scenario #5   Research an upcoming event for which a distinguished guest is expected in town and a ceremony is planned. Do a three-minute description of the ceremony or speak for three minutes describing the person's arrival in town without calling on others for comments or descriptions. Be sure to use organization and imagery.

VOCABULARY WORD LIST   Unit 5-A

1. subpoena (n)—a legal writ for summoning of witnesses before a court

   _____   *su pee' nu*

2. indict (v)—to charge with an offense or crime; to accuse of wrongdoing.

   _____   *in dight'*

3. allegation (n)—an assertion made without substantial proof

   _____   *al u gay' shun*

4. litigation (n)—a lawsuit

   _____   *lit i gay' shun*

5. subject (v)—to bring under influence, control, or domination

   _____   *sub jekt'*

6. liaison (n)—the contact made between units of any organization

   _____   *lee ay' zon*

7. amortization (n)—the act of liquidating a mortgage or other debt by periodic payments

   to the creditor

   _____   *am ur tu zay' shun*

8. in absentia (adj)—while not present (in a court of law)

   _____   *in ab sen' chee u*

9. amnesty (n)—a general pardon for offenses committed against a government

   _____   *am' nus tee*

10. subservient (adj)—serving or acting in a subordinate capacity

_____   *sub sur' vee unt*

11. arraign (v)—to call or bring before a court; to answer to an indictment

_____   *u rain'*

12. indemnity (n)—protection against damage or loss; compensation for damage or loss

_____   *in dem' ni tee*

13. impugn (v)—to challenge as false or to call into question

_____   *im pyewn'*

14. alleged (adj)—doubtful, suspecting, or supposed

_____   *u lejd'*

15. allegation (n)—an assertion made without proof

_____   *al u gay' shun*

16. nomenclature (n)—a set of names or terms used in a particular art or science

_____   *noh' men klay chur*

17. reciprocity (n)—an exchange on a mutual basis

_____   *re si pros' i tee*

18. recognizance (n)—an obligation often assumed in lieu of bond

_____   *ri kog' ni zens*

19. recalcitrant (adj)—resisting control or authority

_____   *ri kal' su trunt*

20. renege (v)—to not keep a promise; go back on one's word

_____   *ri nig'*

VOCABULARY WORD LIST   Unit 5-B

NOTE: On French terms, there may be an option of several different syllables that can be accented correctly, though only one preferred pronunciation is listed here.

1. carte blanche (n)—unconditional authority; full discretionary power (literally, "white card")

_____   *kart blaunsh'*

2. potpourri (n)—any mixture, especially of unrelated objects or subjects

———————————————   *poh pu ree'*

3. rout (n) or (v)—a defeat attended with disorderly flight

———————————————   *rowt'*

4. suave (adj)—person who is smoothly agreeable or polite; agreeably or blandly sophisticated

———————————————   *swawv'*

5. soirée (n)—evening party or social gathering

———————————————   *swor ay'*

6. blasé (adj)—being unimpressed, filled with boredom from an excess of worldly pleasures

———————————————   *blaw zay'*

7. ricochet (n) or (v)—rebound or skip made by an object or projectile after it hits a
   glancing blow against a surface

———————————————   *rik' oh shay*

8. faux pas (n)—a blunder in manner or conduct

———————————————   *foh paw'*

9. et cetera (Latin)—and others; and so forth and so on

———————————————   *et set' u ru*

10. esprit de corps (n)—a sense of union and of common interests and responsibilities

———————————————   *es pree' du kor*

11. chamois (n)—a soft pliable leather dressed with oil

———————————————   *sham' ee*

12. forte (n)—a strong point; that in which one excels

———————————————   *fort'* also *for tay'*

13. fete (n)—a festival, celebration, or entertainment; a holiday

———————————————   *fayt'* or Cajun French: *fet'*

14. gendarme (n)—a policeman in any of several European countries, especially France

———————————————   *zhon' darm*

15. facade (n)—the front of a building; a false appearance

———————————————   *fu saud'*

16. apropos (adj)—to the purpose; with respect to

_____   *ap pru poh'*

17. fiasco (n)—complete and ignominious failure; usually refers to an event

_____   *fee as' koh*

18. pique (n)—a feeling of irritation; displeasure as from a wound to the pride

_____   *peek'*

19. piquant (n)—agreeably pungent or sharp in taste or flavor; provocative or lively

_____   *pee' kaunt*

20. piqué (n)—a tightly woven, ribbed cotton fabric

_____   *pee kay'*

WORD LIST COPY   Unit 5-A

Once the subpoena was issued for the witness to appear before the grand jury, it was evident that they would indict the prisoner. The allegation of the liaison with the drug cartel led to litigation. Though the recalcitrant witness appeared in absentia, the prosecutor found it easy to arraign the alleged drug dealer. Try as they might, the defense could not impugn the witness. Indemnity was assessed. Yet the suspect was released on his own recognizance. The court did subject the suspect to subservient community service. The allegation of further wrongdoing through amortization of a previous debt suggested nomenclature not usually used on radio or television. The defendant pleaded for amnesty, saying that he did not renege on his promise, and swearing that any obligations were the result of agreed-upon reciprocity.

WORD LIST COPY   Unit 5-B

The winning basketball team may be given carte blanche on campus, a potpourri of favors and privileges. A soirée may even be given in the team's honor, or a fete to celebrate victory. A frilly carpet of piqué may be laid before the conquering heroes. But, let the suave athletes suffer a rout, or even a narrow defeat due to the ricochet of the ball, and the blasé facade seems to crumble. The faux pas that brings the fiasco may also destroy the esprit de corps, et cetera. A chamois is no longer apropos, for there is no trophy to polish. A gendarme no longer protects the former heroes, for their forte is no longer victory. They have suffered a pique. The piquant flavor of victory has given way to the bitter pill of defeat.

6

The Commercial and Narration

OBJECTIVES

Upon completion of this chapter the student should be able to:

1. Explain the circumstances surrounding the first radio commercial.
2. Explain the usually intended functions of broadcast commercials. Note the expected positive effects on the economy and possible negative effects on society.
3. Explain three ways in which narration or voice audio for television may be produced in relation to production of the video portion of a spot.
4. Describe a basic first step in doing a good job of voicing a commercial.
5. List and explain five elements of a commercial spot that the announcer should look for to emphasize or differentiate when delivering that spot.
6. Explain 10 possible objectives of commercials.
7. Describe four techniques that might be used to lengthen the audio of a commercial, and four techniques to shorten one.
8. Differentiate between the three kinds of sponsorship and three kinds of production for broadcasting spots.
9. Describe the requirements and restrictions of straight copy.
10. List four production elements for radio spots and four television production elements that might be used for production spots.
11. Explain the structure of a radio doughnut and its television counterpart.
12. Describe the difference between hard sell and soft sell in attitudes, copy style, and style of delivery.
13. List and describe the elements of form as recommended by Aristotle.
14. List and explain the three elements of persuasion suggested by Aristotle and how they can be related to broadcast commercials.

ANNOUNCING THE COMMERCIAL

The selling power of television and radio is sometimes almost beyond comprehension for the uninitiated. It is difficult for most of us to comprehend how a million-dollar-a-minute television spot can be worth that much. (This was the going rate for spots on the Super Bowl from the 1980s into the 1990s.)[1] Yet your voice on the airwaves may someday create millions of dollars in sales, thousands of jobs in industry, and a better way of life for hundreds of thousands of consumers.

With the advent of mass production it became necessary to stimulate sales of merchandise by showing people the marvels of the new age. Mass production created a surplus of production capability in relation to consumer demand, so it became necessary to create demand for goods. Things unknown only a few years ago are now considered necessities of modern life, largely because of advertising. The industrial revolution, in effect, created the need for advertising.

EARLY RADIO

Many of radio's pioneers were repulsed by the idea that the miracle of radio might be used to sell goods, though actually the first radio stations went on the air in order to sell radio "music boxes." The makers of radios (RCA, Westinghouse, General Electric, Crosley, and others) operated early radio stations so that the radios they had for sale would have programming to be listened to. In the early days the function of radio was unclear. It had been pioneered as a point-to-point communication medium like the telegraph or telephone, and as a common carrier.

A *common carrier* makes its service available to all, but the buyer provides the entity to be processed. For example, the post office and the telephone system are common carriers of messages provided by the buyer of the service, while the railroads or airlines transport more tangible things (people and cargo), again provided by the purchasers of the service.

Commercials Are Born

American Telephone and Telegraph continued to think of wireless as a type of telephone or common carrier well into the 1920s. Their radio service was under the supervision of the long lines (long-distance) division of the corporation. AT&T's philosophy was that radio time (as with other telephone common carrier uses) should be leased, much as people leased telephone lines when they made long-distance phone calls, and as with phone calls the lessee provided the message being transmitted.

What is generally accepted to be the first commercial was a 10-minute leased air-time explanation of the joys of suburban living in a Long Island real estate development named for Nathaniel Hawthorne. It was presented on August

---

[1] "Price Hinders Bowl Sales," *Advertising Age* 55, (Oct 1, 1984), p. 1.

28, 1922, at 5:00 p.m. on WEAF New York and cost $50. Rules adhered to later prohibited direct selling or price mention, though this one presentation was certainly meant to sell real estate. The program opened with this:

> This afternoon the radio audience is to be addressed by Mr. Blackwell of the Queensboro Corporation, who through arrangements made by the Griffin Radio Service, Inc., will say a few words concerning Nathaniel Hawthorne and the desirability of fostering the helpful community spirit and healthful, unconfined home life that were Hawthorne ideals. Ladies and gentlemen: Mr. Blackwell.[2]

The commercial itself followed:

> It is fifty-eight years since Nathaniel Hawthorne, the greatest of American fiction-ists, passed away. To honor his memory the Queensboro Corporation, creator and operator of the tenant-owned system of apartment homes at Jackson Heights, New York City, has named its latest group of high-grade dwellings "Hawthorne Court."
> I wish to thank those within sound of my voice for the broadcasting opportunity afforded me to urge this vast radio audience to seek the recreation and the daily comfort of the home removed from the congested part of the city, right at the boundaries of God's great outdoors, and within a few minutes by subway from the business section of Manhattan. . . ."[3]

Most early commericials were more like the public radio grant announce-ments of today. Singing groups and orchestras bore the names of their sponsors to get air mention without appearing to plug a product. As it became clear that the AT&T philosophy wouldn't work, and that philanthropic organizations would not fund the new medium to the extent necessary (as some had hoped), commercials became an important element in financing broadcast programming. However, the deciding factor was, of course, that radio proved to be an effective advertising medium. William Paley's father's La Palina Cigar Company got feedback for the first time from the public about its advertising when the elder Paley cancelled radio advertising authorized by his son. Paley's father is reported to have said:

> Hundreds of thousands of dollars we've been spending on newspapers and maga-zines and no one has ever said anything to me about those ads, but now people are asking me, "What happened to the *La Palina Hour* [radio show]?"[4]

William Paley, seeing a great potential for the medium, convinced his father to invest in a struggling new radio network. Paley became president of CBS at age 26. Not only did the new network sell cigars and other products, but Paley's leadership broke new ground for programming and network-station relationships as well.

---

[2] *A Tower in Babel: A History of Broadcasting in the United States* (New York: Oxford University Press, 1966), p. 111.

[3] Ibid.

[4] William S. Paley, *As It Happened* (New York: Doubleday & Co., 1979), pp. 32–33.

Commercials Around the World

Marketers throughout the world continue to develop products that make life better and that contribute to a constantly expanding economy.

Even in countries where the government controls major industry, advertising has been seen as necessary to stimulate consumption of surplus production items where they may exist. Indeed, in many of these countries the media are controlled by the government. Though Americans may consider the message of the mass media in totalitarian states and third world countries to be propaganda, propaganda must be considered a form of advertising if we define *advertising* as a method of changing people's attitudes via the mass media. The connotation of propaganda tends to be negative. So too advertising can be negative, if it promotes products or habits that may be unhealthy or antisocial.

Undesirable Commercials

Even in a land of free speech, the U.S. Congress has seen fit to outlaw the advertising of tobacco products on the electronic media. The policies of most major networks and stations prohibit the advertising of distilled spirits (whiskey, gin, vodka, etc.). Many well-known performers have turned down lucrative advertising contracts because they opposed the use of a product or service. Animal rights proponents have declined to be seen in spots or dramas that promote the wearing of fur coats. Announcers sometimes have the option of saying ''no'' if they find that the material they are asked to perform does not meet with their approval.

There has long been objection to some of the materials designed for children that are shown on television. Since young children are more gullible than the average consumer, media advertisers have at times exploited young viewers. Michael Jacobson, advertising industry critic, complains:

> Advertising, even if scrupulously honest, . . . promotes materialism, envy, insecurity, greed, selfishness . . . values that pervade the way people think and the way our society works.[5]

Conscientious announcers consider the ethics of their actions as well as the recompense to them that may result.

Right of Refusal

In some situations more than others, it is easier to refuse to do a spot. If you are working at a small station where you have a four-hour board shift, are expected to produce spots for two hours, and maybe even serve as salesman for another two hours of your eight-hour day, it may mean that you do assigned

---

[5] ''Jacobson: Battling 'Excess of Marketing,' '' *Advertising Age*, 62, no. 24 (June 10, 1991), p. 12.

material, or you lose your job. In this situation it depends to a large degree on your station management's policies as to acceptable advertising and its acceptance of any moral obligation. Every situation is different. Your success in turning down certain assignments may depend on your ability to convince people to accept the validity of your point of view, or, indeed, that you be "allowed" to have a point of view.

On the other hand, if you are working for a large or prosperous station, you may be paid extra to do certain production commercials. Announcers may also free-lance, doing production work for advertising agencies or production houses. This applies to both radio and television. In these situations, you have much more freedom to select the spots to which you lend your talent (see also Ethics in Chapter Four).

Television Audio

Where television once did commercials live (before the days of video tape), chances are pretty good now that any announcing you do for television commercials will be recorded, so the timing is precise and the errors are eliminated. Announcers, as you have probably noticed, may not be visible on major television commercials, though celebrity announcers quite often are. In addition to simultaneous production of audio and video there are essentially three ways the announcer works with television spots:

Audio First, Add Video:

1. The voice-over (copy read in conjunction with pictures on the screen) may be done first, then prerecorded music and the video are edited to match as is often done with news stories. This is probably the most efficient manner to correlate the video and audio if there is sufficient video available and the video is sufficiently flexible.

Video First, Add Audio:

2. Sometimes the video is done first; the announcer is expected to insert the audio at the proper moment to match the pictures as they are projected on the screen. In this case you need to have the script well in mind because you must watch the television monitor much of the time.

Audio and Video Separately:

3. A third alternative is recording the video and the audio separately and editing the audio or video to match the other and conform to time limitations. This is best achieved if both are carefully timed to start with.

If you free-lance (offer your services independently), or if you are paid extra for the commercials you do, you probably are able to select the commercials you provide talent for, though the techniques of production will be up to the producer or director. See also "Narrator" later in this chapter.

SELL YOURSELF

Doing a good job means more opportunities to perform in the future. How does one best use one's talents to do a selling job on radio or television? As suggested above, it is important that you sell yourself on the product or service. If you do not believe in the product or service of the advertising, probably you should refuse the commission. When you are delivering a commercial on radio or television, you are a salesperson every bit as much as the "Fuller Brush man" or the "Avon lady" is. You are "knocking on the potential customer's door" and being invited in to tell about your product or service. You probably will not be an order taker, as is the door-to-door sales representative. On the other hand, you may. Consider direct marketing via the home shopping networks and infomercials on cable and nonprime-time television or other direct marketing ads, especially for CDs and tapes. With all of these, the listener is asked to call in and order the product.

"Knocking on the door" is the manner in which the door-to-door salesperson gets the attention of the would-be buyer, much as the announcer must get the attention of the listener before the advertiser's pitch can be made. Just about all advertising has an attention-getting device of some kind. (If you don't get the listener's attention, the rest of the sales message is wasted.) On radio it may be an unusual sound; on television, an unusual picture. Often it is up to the announcer to get and hold the audience's attention. Most listeners or viewers are really not paying close attention, especially when it is commercial time. The announcer is being paid to get the audience's attention.

The copywriter is usually responsible for the method used to get attention. It may be a question, a startling statement, reference to a common problem, or some other technique. But it probably is the announcer's responsibility to see that the method used truly does attract the attention of the listener. Different announcers have different ways of getting attention; different products or producers may change your approach. Perhaps the most important thing to consider is the audience demographics of the station or the programming. What will appeal to the person who likes this type of programming? Obviously, it takes a good deal of investigation, insight, and plain old common sense to know the right approach. If the announcer is producing the spot, this research and understanding is his or her responsibility. Announcers performing for an advertising agency producer may find that the producer has the research in hand and knows what he or she wants, so you do what you are directed to do.

After getting the listener's attention (knocking on the door), the announcer needs to be "invited in" to the listener's consciousness. Is the manner of presentation such that the audience will want to continue to pay attention while the announcer extols the benefits of the product or service? Even more importantly, can the announcer be intriguing enough and have enough credibility that the listener will want to buy the product? This is an awesome responsiblity for the effective use of a company's resources. A company's future and people's jobs (possibly the announcer's own job) may be resting on the proper execution of the intended message.

The objective of a spot often is assumed to be an immediate sale and rapidly increased market share, but this is not always the case. Perhaps the spot is intended to create familiarity for a name so that when the listeners are ready to buy, this is the first name that pops into their heads. Most of the soft drink ads, for example, do not urge you to stock up now (though some of them do). The makers of Coke and Pepsi want the names of their products to be strong enough in the consumer's consciousness that a call for a cola product when the occasion arises will almost automatically be for their particular brand. In addition, the message reiterates that their cola product will be appropriate at almost any time. At the other end of the purchase spectrum, the real estate broker, who sells a once-in-a-lifetime purchase such as a home, may not be expecting an immediate sale to result from his or her advertising either. Here is another advertiser who may feel that the results expected are name recognition and trust.

Although advertising probably first came into being (1) to sell the large quantity of merchandise created by mass production, (2) to inform the public as to what was available for purchase, and (3) to introduce new products or services, Madison Avenue has found many more functions.

Other objectives of a commercial may be (4) to gain package or logo recognition; (5) to stress product benefits; (6) to provide information about the advertiser, the product, or the service; (7) to create good will for the advertiser, the product, or the organization; (8) to point out a product or service's unique qualities (how this one differs from the competition); (9) to create a positive image for the product or service in the mind of the consumer; (10) to show availability of the product or service (where or how it may be obtained); (11) to create a need for what is being advertised; (12) to implant a slogan or mnemonic in the minds of the public for easy recall; or (13) to instill loyalty.

Announcing the commercial combines the communication techniques previously discussed as well as several others.

TIMING

Timing is critical in broadcasting. Time, after all, is what a radio or television station has to sell. The audio of most 30-second television spots is expected to run 28 seconds. Radio spots must not run even a fraction of a second long. Yet you want to be sure that advertisers get their money's worth. The practice of reading to get the feel of the length of 10 seconds, 30 seconds, or a minute is important to the beginning announcer.

Sometimes at the request of an anxious advertiser, the copywriter is expected to put more copy into a commercial than can effectively be read in the allotted time. An agency producer or writer may correct the problem during the production session. If, however, the announcer is producing the spot, it becomes important for him or her to be able to cut material to the time ordered without destroying the feel and the message of the copy. What can be done? First, the objective of the spot must be determined so that the spot's purpose is not defeated. Then, carefully, the announcer/producer can:

- look for and cut redundancies. (A good commercial is usually expected to state the key concept of the spot three times in different ways.)
- cut wordiness. (Instead of "the reason is that," usually just "because" will give the same meaning. There are many extra words in most conversations that can be cut.)
- look for unnecesary articles. (Sometimes "a," "an," or "the" can be eliminated without changing the meaning.)
- change descriptive prepositional phrases to adjectives. (Instead of the "eyes of blue", say the "blue eyes.")

These last two techniques do not cut much, but hopefully much cutting may not be required. If the spot is still too long:

- use common sense in cutting or rephrasing as you find necessary.

Often local retailers' commercials have a tendency to run long because the advertiser has more to say than will fit into the allotted time. Occasionally, however, spots may run short. Obviously, you want the advertisers to get all that they are paying for. In this case you may need to pad. This is usually extremely easy:

- Repeat the last lines of the commercial, particularly if they sum up the sales message.
- Repeat the slogan or summarize the key idea of the spot. Remember, you are selling differences and benefits.
- Especially punch the name of the advertiser, the product, or service.
- Repeat where or how the product or service may be obtained.

KINDS OF SPOT SPONSORSHIP

We often use the terms spot and commercial interchangeably. And it is true that commercials are spots. However, all spots are not commercials. *Spots* may be commercials or public service announcements or promos. This categorizes spots according to function.

Commercials

Commercials are spot announcements paid for by an advertiser that usually explain benefits that may accrue to the listeners if they utilize the product or service that the advertiser has to offer.

A *sponsor* is an advertiser (and sometimes producer) financially responsible for a segment of time on radio or television. Television time is so expensive that very few programs have a single sponsor, as once was the case. (One exception for many years has been the *Hallmark Hall of Fame*, which has been always fully sponsored by Hallmark greeting cards.) At one time most network programs on radio and television were sponsored by a single national or local advertiser. Today, local radio may have one sponsor for a traffic update or a weather report, but even short local newscasts are rarely sponsored by one advertiser. Joint sponsorships, however, are fairly common. With a joint sponsorship the advertiser probably gets a "sponsored-in-part-by" announcement at the beginning and end of the program (such as a sportscast) along with a number of spots within the body of the show.

Public Service Announcements

Public service announcements (PSAs) are spots that promote the public good, are aired without cost, and are normally written or produced by a government agency or other nonprofit organization. PSAs were once required of all commercial radio and television stations as part of their operation "in the public interest, convenience, and necessity." While the public interest part of the law has not been repealed, deregulation in the 1980s brought different interpretations of the law by the Federal Communications Commission. The license renewal obligation of broadcast stations no longer requires these announcements, but most stations still see them as one way of showing their commitment to public service. Some stations have adopted a method whereby many public service announcements do not receive a detailed explanation; rather, the interested listener is asked to call for further details. If the telephone number given is the station's, the caller then receives the phone number of the sponsoring organization to call for further details. This may be a practical way of functioning, since few people are sitting with paper and pencil waiting to write down a phone number in case something of interest might come on.

The means of delivery and construction of the public service announcement tends to be quite parallel to commercial spots.

Promos

Promos are spots that are intended to promote the station's or the network's image or programming. Sometimes promos will promote the programming or image of another station or network if there is a joint ownership. For example, you may see the programming on the Headline News Network promoted on the Cable News Network or on Turner Network Television. Announcer-only promos on television often are inserted over closing credits to alert the audience to an upcoming program. Local promos may come in conjunction with a station break (the pause between programs when stations identify themselves by giving their call letters orally or visually or both). Promos often follow the same form as commercial spots but are usually shorter.

KINDS OF SPOT PRODUCTION

Spots can also be categorized according to production method. Production methods separate spots into straight copy, production spots, and doughnuts.

Straight Copy

Straight copy spots are made up strictly of material to be read by an announcer. There are no sound effects, no music, and only a single voice. Straight copy is often the greatest challenge to announcers because there are none of the crutches that may help an otherwise poorly written or delivered spot to be effective. Straight copy spots may be delivered live on radio and they are usually to be found in a continuity book, which the announcers follow as they proceed through their board shifts. The continuity book may also contain such things as PSAs, promos, and show openings or closings that may be done live and outlines for ad lib commercials, as noted in Chapter 5.

Production Spots

Obviously, those spots that entail production, and are therefore tape re-corded, are *production spots*. These include just about all television spots, including the earlier mentioned credit roll voice-overs, which, of course, are audio only. For radio production, techniques may include:

- music beds (recorded selections over which copy is read),
- multiple voices (either for contrast or for a dramatic sequence),
- sound effects (to attract attention or fill in a mini-drama), or
- sound distortion or enhancement (usually done with a wide array of digital electronic wizardry).

The audio effects are available for television, of course, as are visual elements. Visual elements may include:

- persons on the screen (actors, announcers, musicians, and sponsors, to name a few of the possibilities),
- printed words that sometimes scroll or crawl across the screen,
- digital effects and keying, which also lend themselves well to interesting effects on television, with images squeezed, twirled, inverted, duplicated, distorted, enhanced, or superimposed to the limit of one's imagination,
- dramatic situations, which can offer the chance for audience members to project themselves into the mini-drama, or
- product demonstrations, which may be particularly attractive to the advertiser, especially if the product's effectiveness can be shown in a convincing or unusual manner.

Doughnuts and Co-ops

Another type of spot is a co-op campaign commercial. In this instance the advertising agency that represents the advertiser prepares or produces copy that is aired and paid for jointly by the manufacturer and the retailer. The produced spot may be tagged with the name of the retailer, usually at the end of the spot, or it may be in the form of a *doughnut,* where the beginning and end are produced by the manufacturer's agency. The local announcer or merchant then fills in the hole in the middle. (The hole in the middle makes it a doughnut.) It is the announcer's task to insert the copy at the end or in the middle, in the spirit of the spot and within the allotted time.

Though they may not be called doughnuts, television promos often use a similar format, except that the announcer copy may be at the beginning and the end with an excerpt from the upcoming program being plugged in in the middle.

HARD SELL VS. SOFT SELL

The intention of the advertiser, the agency, or the copywriter should give the announcer a hint as to how the commercial is expected to be read. The reasoned, low-pressure approach to soft sell of some national companies can be contrasted with the harsh, demanding approach of many local merchants. The following chart should give you some insights into the differences in the two approaches.

	HARD SELL	*SOFT SELL*
ATTITUDE	demanding threatening superior coercive	rational calm feeling of equality reasonable
COPY STYLE	superlatives sells price stresses bargains imperative mood	logical explanation sells quality stresses value active voice
DELIVERY STYLE	evangelistic flamboyant shouting commanding	conversational informed cool and collected explanatory

Most commercials use several of these appeals to attempt to influence the potential customer. It is up to the announcer to be sure he or she understands the importance of finding and emphasizing each of these elements.

As an announcer, you are expected to be able to adapt to what the advertiser wants, to what the audience expects, and to what will do the best selling job. Hopefully all three are the same.

NARRATION

Many radio and television spots depend on narration to carry the primary message. Another type of selling job for the announcer is the "voice over" (VO) narration for documentary-type productions. As in advertising, the narrator is essentially selling an idea. Narration can be said to combine the credibility and authoritativeness of news with the persuasion and conviction of advertising.

CBS's top-rated "60 Minutes," and other series featuring mini-documentaries, have gained an increasing importance in network programming because the cost is less that for most dramatic productions requiring many highly paid actors, writers, and production personnel.

Even more of a selling job for the narrator may be present in corporate (industrial) television, educational, and public relations television. Corporate television, of course, includes both instructional and public relations production. Among other things, it may also include videos intended to recruit personnel or raise funds for important projects. (By producing a video, the organization is, in effect, saying, "This is important.")

Public relations television has become an important way for many organizations to get their messages across. Most people still think of television as entertainment and are often willing to watch a television program on a topic about which they might not bother to read.

The skills required for effective narration are the skills required of any experienced announcer, with the use of variety of pitch and pace, as well as voice placement and energy, being important factors. Announcers who are effective narrators and who can project a positive image for an organization, are increasingly in demand.

Documentaries are not limited to the format below. In fact, most documentaries are a combination of several formats. This listing suggests that narrators

---

DOCUMENTARY NARRATION MESSAGES

The announcer is asking the audience to
PAY ATTENTION

NEWS: Here is a problem that you may or may not be able to do something about.

HISTORICAL: Here are some factors responsible for the way things are today.

INSTRUCTIONAL: Here is what you need to know in order to do this particular task correctly.

PUBLIC RELATIONS: You should have this positive image about this particular institution.

TRAVEL: Enjoy this vicarious trip to somewhere.

NATURAL SCIENCE: This universe is a strange and wonderful place.

LABORATORY SCIENCE: Man's inventions and discoveries are fascinating.

MESSAGES OF COMMERCIALS

The announcer should be looking for these elements which say
THIS IS IMPORTANT

IMAGE: Here is a positive, lasting impression of the product or company.

FEATURES: These things enhance the product or service.

BENEFITS: The customer receives this type of satisfaction from using the product or service.

DIFFERENCES: This is how this product, corporation, or service is better than the competition.

CREDIBILITY: This presenter has a positive image for believability.

EMOTIONAL APPEAL: This combination of words and images influences the feelings of the audience.

LOGIC: Here are facts the audience can use to justify their belief in the message.

---

must approach their documentary narrative knowing the general impression to be made on the listener.

IF ARISTOTLE HAD DONE COMMERCIALS
AND DOCUMENTARIES . . .

Some theories have lived through the ages. Among these are many of the teachings of the ancient Greek philosopher Aristotle. To the best of our knowledge, Aristotle was the first to analyze how best to change attitudes and how best to conceive drama. Aristotle observed and studied the most successful rhetoricians and dramatists of his time and developed criteria that have lived to this day.

Beginning, Middle, and End

Every well-written commercial or documentary is like a drama or a speech. It has a beginning, a middle, and an end. In making speeches you have been taught that your speech should have an introduction, a body, and a close. Aristotle's rules live on.

An announcer should be able to look at a piece of copy and break it into its component parts so that he or she can clearly explain to the audience the message to be delivered. As discussed earlier, getting the audience's attention is critical to a successful commercial or documentary. Without the audience's attention, the commercial may as well not be presented. In most cases the "undivided" attention is to be desired, but it has been shown that only partial attention may be all that is needed for advertising in some instances. People purchase brands they are familiar with from broadcast commercials, even if they do not get the full intended impact of the commercial, and often even if they have found the commercial to be irritating.

The middle of a commercial or documentary is essentially the important message that describes, demonstrates, or informs.

Many advertising theorists tell you that people do not buy a product or a product's features; consumers buy the benefits that the product will presumably deliver to them: Sweeter breath (feature); ergo, friends and lovers (a benefit). As an announcer doing commercials, it is important to note the difference between features and benefits and to focus on the benefits.

Another selling strength is "differences." How does this product differ from the competition? The announcer needs to be aware and make the audience aware of the differences that make this product superior.

In a documentary the central and principal section focuses on describing what the documentary is about, often highlighting opposing views.

The conclusion of a commercial or documentary should leave the intended audience with a feeling of completeness. It should not just quit; rather, it should have an aesthetically pleasing ending. The advertising spot ending often includes reaffirmation of the product name, its slogan, its logo (or trademark), or where the product is available. A documentary may summarize the intended points of the production or point out the future expectations for the topic. One of the duties of the announcer is to give the production a feeling of completeness.

Ethos

Through the years the meanings of words often change. *Ethos* refers to an ethical approach to attitude change and selling: trustworthiness of the speaker. But it really refers to much more. We have previously referred to it as "source credibility." Everything that makes an announcer or salesperson a believable, reliable, trusted source of information is included in ethos. Often publicly respected authorities are asked to do commercials: the athlete who endorses Wheaties, for example. The assembly-line workers at Ford or the president of Chrysler should know their product and are considered experts. Sometimes unknown "experts" (the common man or woman like you or me) endorse a product or an idea sometimes with use of a "hidden" camera for "unbiased" testimony. Still other endorsers may be movie stars who really know little more about the product or a topic than the audience members do. People may buy the product in this instance not because they consider the stars to be experts, but because they respect these "beautiful people," or because they are stricken with a star to such an extent that they feel the star can do no wrong. This is probably less a case of the star's expertise (ethos) than it is of star-related pathos.

Pathos

Pathos refers to the emotional element of persuasion. Most of us are largely ruled by our emotions when it comes to making purchasing decisions. We want to be loved, to be admired, or to feel in command. Often we want our neighbors to envy us. We want to feel good about ourselves. The word "pathos" may suggest empathy for the person in the commercial or documentary. When used in reference to attitude change or enhancement, pathos refers to all kinds of emotion, including joy, happiness, and anger, as well as the resulting physical manifestations from laughter to fist clenching. Announcers must be able to effectively pluck the heartstrings, tickle the funny bone, and excite the palate.

Logos

Most people like to think that they use *logos* (rational, logical reasoning) in making decisions. At times they probably do. In most cases, however, they probably do *not* use reasoning when making purchases. Emotions usually seem to win out.

> Psychologists unhesitatingly state that the main appeal which advertising uses and the one on which we place our main reliance is the emotional. . . . [6]

However, since buyers need to rationalize the logic of their choices to themselves, rational reasoning is provided in most advertising and certainly must be the basis of most documentaries. People want to be able to give you many logical reasons why they believe in something. It is therefore of great importance that announcers can effectively point out the reasons for attitudes their listeners should adopt, as well as making attractive, emotional appeals while maintaining source credibility.

Ethos, pathos, and logos—Aristotle's three methods of attitude change—constantly influence the lives of all of us. Commercials in the mass media are responsible for much of the success of capitalistic society, and documentaries which promote a point of view increasingly suggest solutions to viewers' or society's problems.

EXERCISES

1. Mark the copy provided at the end of this chapter as recommended previously.
2. Follow the instructions for studying word lists as suggested in the previous chapters, this time doing word lists 6A and 6B. Be prepared to pronounce the words correctly, write the correct phonetic transcriptions when tested, and define the words when used in a sentence.
3. Read your marked copy for the word lists for Chapter 6 onto your cassette tape to be handed in. You may also reread paragraphs from previous word lists to review. Read with your best and most convincing manner the spot announcements at the end of the chapter.
4. Select two of the spots at the end of this chapter to be read as "Hard Sell" spots and then as "Soft Sell" spots. What are the specific differences? Practice these on your audio tape. Be prepared to show in class how you differentiate between "Hard Sell" and "Soft Sell."

[6] Pierre Marineau, *Motivation in Advertising* (New York: McGraw-Hill, 1957), p. 15.

5. Bring your marked ad copy to class. Pick your best 60 seconds to be read ''live'' for the other members of the class.

6. Select three to five minutes of documentary copy to read. Allow time for the visuals as noted in the video column of the script. Be prepared to present this in class.

7. Be sure that the assigned material (the best you can do) is at the end of your tape since your instructor will pay particular attention to this to check your timing and evaluate your advertising style.

WORD LIST: MORE COURT TERMS (AND MORE)

BROADCAST VOCABULARY WORD LIST   Unit 6-A

1. venireman (n)—a juror

   _____   *ven igh' ri man*

2. venue (n)—the place from which the jury is drawn and in which a trial is held; location

   _____   *ven' yew*

3. advent (n)—the period beginning four Sundays before Christmas and continuing until

   Christmas Eve; arrival of, coming into being

   _____   *ad' vent*

4. advocate (v)—to defend by argument

   _____   *ad' vu kayt*

5. advocate (n)—a defender, one that pleads the cause for another

   _____   *ad' vu kit*

6. vociferous (adj)—boisterous, making insistent outcries

   _____   *voh sif' ur us*

7. compensatory (adj)—serving to repay

   _____   *kum pen' su tor ee*

8. recompense (n)—compensation; a return for something done, suffered, or given

   _____   *re' kum pens*

9. comparable (adj)—worthy or capable of being compared

   _____   *kom' pur u bul*

10. incommunicado (adj) or (adv)—to be deprived of communication

    _____   *in ku myew ni kaw' doh*

11. adjudicate (v)—to make a judgment after hearing evidence.

　　_____   *a jew' di kayt*

12. compromise (n) or (v)—to reach agreement through mutual consent

　　_____   *kom' pru mighz*

13. conflagration (n)—a large fire; a raging war

　　_____   *kon flu gray' shun*

14. prejudicial (adj)—having prejudice or being prejudiced

　　_____   *pre ju dish' ul*

15. reggae (n)—a particular style of Caribbean music

　　_____   *re' gay*

16. escargot (n)—an edible snail

　　_____   *es kar goh'*

17. conspicuous (adj)—obviously intended to be seen

　　_____   *kun spik' yew us*

18. judiciary (n)—judges or the courts

　　　　(adj)—having to do with judges or courts

　　_____   *jew dish' ee air ee*

BROADCAST VOCABULARY WORD LIST   Unit 6-B

1. anesthesia (n)—a loss of sensation with or without loss of consciousness

　　_____   *an us thee' zhe u*

2. anesthesiologist (n)—a physician who specializes in anesthesia and anesthetics

　　_____   *an us thee zee ol' u jist*

3. anesthetist (n)—one who administers anesthetic

　　_____   *u nes' thu tist*

4. appendectomy (n)—the surgical removal of the appendix

　　_____   *a pen dek' tu mee*

5. chiropractic (n)—a therapeutic system utilizing adjustment of the spinal column

_____   *kigh   roh   prak'   tik*

6. glaucoma (n)—a disease of the eye causing progressive loss of vision

_____   *glaw   koh'   mu*

7. inhalator (n)—an apparatus providing pure air to breathe

_____   *in'   hu   lay   tur*

8. malady (n)—a disease or disorder of the body

_____   *mal'   u   dee*

9. malignant (adj)—disposed to cause harm or suffering

_____   *mu   lig'   nunt*

10. maniacal (adj)—pertaining to a maniac

_____   *mu   nigh'   u   kul*

11. medicinal (adj)—pertaining to or having the qualities of a medicine

_____   *mu   dis'   u   nul*

12. pharmaceutical (adj)—of or pertaining to pharmacy or pharmacists

_____   *farm   u   sew'   ti   kul*

13. resilience (n)—the power or ability to return to the original form or position

_____   *ree   zil'   yunts*

14. benign (adj)—not malignant; mild and gentle

_____   *bi   nighn'*

15. resuscitate (v)—to revive from apparent death or from unconsciousness

_____   *ree   sus'   i   tayt*

16. carcinogen (n)—a cancer-causing agent

_____   *kar   sin'   u   jen*

17. amniocentesis (n)—a prenatal test for malformation or disease

_____   *am   nee   oh   sen   tee'   sus*

18. herpes (n)—a viral disease causing skin eruptions

_____   *her'   peez*

19. Kaposi's sarcoma (n)—a skin disease; often an AIDS symptom

_____   *ka poh' zeez sar koh' mu*

20. dyslexia (n)—a reading disorder in which figures or letters appear to be inverted or reordered

_____   *dis leks' see u*

21. anorexia nervosa (n)—a disease of compulsive noneating

_____   *an or eks' see u ner voh' su*

22. cryogenics (n)—the "science" of freezing bodies to be brought back to life at some undetermined future date

_____   *krigh oh jen' iks*

WORD LIST PARAGRAPH   Unit 6-A

The change of venue could not occur after the veniremen had been selected by the court. Then on the objections of the Rastafarian, it became evident that the advent of this vociferous advocate was not comparable to the accompanist who issued the communiqué. He advocated compensatory recompense for those with anorexia nervosa. They could not be held incommunicado, nor sent a subpoena, nor forced to perform cyrogenics experiments, or eat escargot. The judiciary would only exacerbate the problem. Yet someone had to adjudicate the fate of those who continued to deplore reggae.

WORD LIST COPY   Unit 6-B

Under certain conditions two operations might be performed one after the other. While the anesthetist prepared the anesthetic, the anesthesiologist stood by with an inhalator in case it was necessary to resuscitate the patient. The anesthesia came swiftly, and the appendectomy was soon over. Then doctor number two performed an operation in an attempt to arrest the patient's glaucoma and restore the resilience of the eyeball. This malady had been attributed to a spinal condition and chiropractic was advised by a maniacal friend. Obviously medicinal help was not the answer. Only an operation could produce a positive result. This would then be followed by pharmaceutical ministration. The condition was not curable. Nor was it malignant, though exposure to a carcinogen had been suspected. It was almost certain that the operation would grant respite from pain.

Amniocentesis is being used more and more to test for inherited diseases. It cannot test for such things as AIDS, where Kaposi's sarcoma may result, or herpes, which is also sexually transmitted. It cannot determine minor brain disorders such as dyslexia. Modern medicine works many near miracles, but it still has a long way to go.

COLLEGE PROMO
60 SECONDS

Preparation for a successful future need not be costly. A degree from [INSERT NAME OF SCHOOL] means not only career skills, but also a background in the humanities and the arts. A career that is rewarding . . . leisure-time pursuits that are intellectually stimulating . . . these are the educational goals at [INSERT SCHOOL ABBREVIATION]. Prepare for your future on the friendly, progressive campus at the [SCHOOL NAME] in [SCHOOL LOCATION] for less cost than at many other schools. The future belongs to those who prepare for it. The future can belong to you when you prepare at [NAME OF SCHOOL].

Note: This promo runs short. Using the techniques discussed in the chapter, extend this spot to run 60 seconds.

H-2-0 P-S-A
30 SECONDS

What do you do when you're thirsty? Many Americans have a soda, a beer, coffee or tea. Some have spirits that quench their thirst with a potent high. However, what about a drink of water when you're thirsty? Is water enough, or does your taste demand sweeter juices? Have the purveyors of conspicuous consumption reached you with their clever gimmicks? You may still have a mind of your own if you recognize that simple, clear water has no equal . . . that highly advertised drinks really only satisfy a need that has been created by the advertising. Enjoy one of life's essential pleasures . . . . Water—life's simple thirst quencher.

Note: This spot probably will run long. Try to apply the rules for cutting copy discussed earlier so that you can deliver this spot in 30 seconds.

ANDRUS INSURANCE
30 SECONDS

Now you can find lower insurance rates. Keep listening to learn how your auto and homeowner's insurance can be taken care of quickly with reliable companies and Dwight W. Andrus' friendly, informed representatives. Confer with an efficient Dwight W. Andrus representative at an agency computer terminal while he or she rapidly checks for the lowest rates from many fine, reliable companies. You can save money and get friendly, reliable service at the Dwight W. Andrus Insurance Agency. Check for the Dwight W. Andrus Agency in the yellow pages of your phone book under insurance.

GENERIC UNIVERSITY
PSA COPY
30 SECONDS

Lots of people do it twice a year. Others do it three times. You can do it too. Enroll at the ——————————————— for the spring, summer, or fall
                                    (NAME OF SCHOOL)
semester.

————————————————— continues to excel. ———————————————
(SCHOOL INITIALS)   (SCHOOL NAME)
offers specialized studies in an area that can lead to a successful career for you. Join the successful people who enroll at ——————————————— in the fall,
                                                          (NAME OF SCHOOL)
in the spring, and sometimes in the summer. Start or advance in your career.

Stop by the campus or call today. ———————————————————

—————————————————————————————————.
(NAME OF SCHOOL AND SCHOOL SLOGAN)

PERDIDO (PUR DEE' DOH) WINE CO.
30 SECONDS

ANNCR: I have something here that will really excite your taste buds. It's cool, refreshing, and fruity. It comes in white, red, and rosé.

Have you guessed it yet? Well, it's made in Perdido, Alabama, right in the heart of the South.

Here, let's sample it.

SFX: SOUND OF LIQUID BEING POURED AND TASTED

ANNCR: Ahhhhh . . . pure pleasure.

You've guessed it right. It's Perdido wine. Perdido wine made with Alabama's fine muscadine (MUS' KU DIGHN) grapes, native to the South. Perdido wine has a distinctive taste, cool, refreshing, and exciting.

Perdido wine, Alabama's contribution to grape-ious (GRAYP' SHUS) living.

DOUCET (DEW SAY') ACE HARDWARE
AD LIB COMMERCIAL
30 OR 60 SECONDS

SPONSOR:	Doucet Ace Hardware 4509 Altamont Hometown
HOURS:	8 to 5:30 Monday–Saturday
FEATURE:	one-stop personalized service; locally owned and operated
PRODUCTS:	hardware, tools, plumbing and heating supplies, electrical supplies, lawn and garden supplies, hand and power tools.
SERVICES:	saws sharpened; propane bottles filled
SPECIAL FOR APRIL:	round or square-end shovel; reg $9.95, now $6.95 Armor-All protectant: 32 oz. refill size: $5.95 value for $3.95
SLOGAN:	"Ace is the place with the helpful hardware man" (or folks?)

AIDS TESTING P-S-A
ADLIB COPY MATERIAL
30 SECONDS

Should you get tested for HIV? (HIV–human immunodeficiency virus)

infection with HIV can lead to AIDS

transmitted in body fluids, especially blood and sperm

becoming more and more a disease that can infect anyone

HIV infection possible from: used drug needles

blood transfusions

unprotected sex with HIV-infected person

Each time you have sexual relations with someone new, you are in effect sleeping

with all of that person's previous sex partners.

HIV testing is testing for the antibodies the body builds up.

often six months before antibodies show up in the test . . .

a false negative can result if exposure in previous six months

New drug treatments (AZT and several other similar drugs)

can help prevent symptoms

hoping for treatment as for diabetes

treatment with vaccine a possibility

Testing by the local AIDS task force at University Medical Center

each Monday from 6 to 7 p.m.

includes pre-test and post-test counseling

Testing is anonymous! Testing is free!

For more information: Call 233-AIDS.

Outside the metro area: 1-233-AIDS (toll free)

TELEVISION
DIRECTION
(EXERPT)

Note: This script is intended to be done "live" in a television studio. The narrator should
be able to see the screen and pace him or herself according to what is on the screen. For
abbreviations used here see the glossary.

WS TV STUDIO SHOWING 2 CAM-
ERAS WITH OPERATORS POSI-
TIONED TO TAKE NARRATOR

NAR: The preparation for directing a
live studio television production needs to
include an understanding of three directing
essentials.

LIST ON THE CG WITH NARRATION:

1. continuity
2. transitions
3. camera blocking

These are . . .

continuity . . .

transitions . . .

and camera blocking

MS OF NARRATOR
CG: "CONTINUITY"

By continuity is meant keeping a constant
flow of interrelated concepts and pictures.
Images and ideas must merge with each
other logically and naturally. Video and
explanations need to logically interrelate.

VTR: CONTROL ROOM SCENE
SHOWING DIRECTOR AT
WORK

Commands by the director must be followed precisely by the crew and the talent.
One of responsibilities of the director is to
keep the viewer constantly in mind. Pio-
neer television teacher, Rudy Bretz first
expressed it . . .

KEY: "Show the viewers what they
want to see when they want to
see it."

Show the viewers what they want to see,
when they want to see it. This axiom is
aimed at providing viewer comfort.

VTR: COLLAGE OF UNRELATED
OBJECTS

It can be jarring to the viewer to be supplied with visuals in a random or haphaz-
ard manner.

MS OF NARRATOR

People raised on television expect there to be logic in the sequence of scenes on the screen, and most viewers will try to create

STILL STORE: PUZZLED VIEWER

one, even if none exists. This tends to be harder work than most viewers wish to

STILL STORE: EXHAUSTED VIEWER

expend, and they will change channels unless they are a captive audience as in a classroom. Here, attention will wander.

KEY CG: CONTINUITY

To retain viewers and get the desired message across, the director must interrelate pictures and ideas in the manner the viewer expects.

KEY CG: "Show viewers what they want to see when they want to see it.

In other words, show viewers what they want to see when they want to see it in the ways in which visual literacy traditions dictate.

**EXERPT: DOCUMENTARY
OPELOUSAS JUNIOR HIGH**

by Stephen Foster

Note: This script would probably be narrated on video tape with video added to match the narration both in pictures and allotted time. It is important that the narration be energetic and enthusiastic.

FADE IN

WS of front of OJH

WORK . . . LEARN . . . PROGRESS . . . Opelousas Junior High School has a tradition of almost 30 years of providing quality education to the community.

MONTAGE OF TREES/BUILDINGS

The twelve acre campus of Opelousas Junior High is one of the most beautiful in the area . . . providing a comfortable, serene environment conducive to learning and growing.

TWO OR THREE SHOTS OF TEACHERS IN CLASS OR WITH STUDENTS

The faculty and staff are energetic and dedicated to student development. Over half of the faculty members have advanced degrees.

MS OF COMPUTERS, VIDEO EQUIPMENT

Well-equipped, modern classrooms help the teachers to interest and guide the students and facilitate development of learning skills.

GUIDANCE COUNSELOR/PRINCIPAL/TEACHERS IN CONFERENCE SETTING

Students are scheduled in classes where they can be taught at their own level of achievement. Students' performance determines to which group they are assigned. Parents can request that a student be moved to another group. Schedule changes are made through the guidance office with the approval of the principal.

TEAMS/INTERVIEWS

For the more dedicated athlete, organized team sports include basketball, football, and track. There are two teams in each sport. One team consists of seventh and eighth graders while the second team is

MS OF TROPHY CASE	made up of ninth graders. Girls also have two teams and compete in basketball. A look at the trophy case reveals the success of the teams.
CLUB MEETINGS/STUDENTS HAVING FUN WHILE LEARNING/BAND PRACTICE	Eighteen different organizations, including the junior optimist club and the national junior honor society, are active at Opelousas Junior High. Special interest clubs like 4H, the Math Club, and the Science Club are also popular with students. Some organizations, like the Pep Squad and cheerleaders, are just for fun. The band and choir practices involve many students.
FACULTY/STUDENTS/ COMPUTERS/VIDEO	• A well-rounded faculty • Advanced placement • Specialized classes • Individual attention • Excellent facilities • The latest in educational technology and resources
SCHOOL EMBLEM	Quality education is a tradition at Opelousas Junior High.
FADE OUT	

7

The Theatre and Broadcasting

OBJECTIVES

Upon completion of this chapter the student should be able to:

1. Describe three roles you might play as a radio announcer.
2. Explain what "art" is and what "art" is *not.*
3. Describe three elements of oral style that announcers should strive to attain.
4. Define "style clone" and explain how to avoid possible related hazards.
5. Explain the importance of mimicry and sensitivity as broadcaster qualities.
6. Explain two timing techniques valuable to announcers.
7. Describe Duerr's five common failings of performers in the broadcast media, and describe recommendations to overcome these failings.
8. Compare the discipline of the actor and the announcer in three important aspects.
9. Explain microphone placement for three different mike types or situations.
10. Describe microphone perspective and the physical actions an announcer may use to create this perspective.
11. Describe a technique for recalling an accent you can successfully execute.
12. Describe three methods that can help the communication of ideas and feelings in radio drama.
13. Indicate three oral techniques used to portray an elderly person.
14. Explain five other techniques that can be used to create caricatures.
15. Give examples of expressions a copywriter may add to help create characterization.

INFLUENCES OF THE THEATRE

We impose the form of the old on the content of the new.

—*Marshall McLuhan*[1]

All the world's a stage,
And all the men and women merely players:
They have their exits and their entrances;
And one man in his time plays many parts. . .

—*William Shakespeare*[2]

ROLE PLAYING IN LIFE

We all play many roles. You probably now play the roles of student, son or daughter, brother or sister, grocery clerk or student aide. You play the role of driver when you are behind the wheel of a car. You play the role of concerned citizen when you vote. You play the role of audience when you watch a stage play, a movie, or television. So, playing the role of an announcer on radio or television is not particularly different in many ways from what you have been doing in everyday life.

ROLE PLAYING IN THE ELECTRONIC MEDIA

Role playing in broadcasting may mean that you play only one role—a dee-jay, a newsperson, or a talk show host. Chances are, however, that you will be expected to play more than one media role when you are starting your career, and perhaps during much of it.

You are a board announcer. Then you are a newscaster. Later, you may be a sportscaster, a call-in talk show host, or a voice on a commercial. When you shift roles in everyday life, you probably don't consciously make a change (though, in fact, you do change hats subconsciously). As a driver, you pay careful attention to what is happening immediately in front of you on the road, though many of the physical responses of shifting gears or even steering take little conscious effort. As a voter, you carefully study the materials put out by the candidates or their supporters to make an educated choice.

When you change roles within a small radio station, you may not make as much of a change as you might if you were to change stations. For example, consider the change from a beautiful music station to one playing contemporary hits. CHR (contemporary hit radio) tends to take a more rapid, hyped presentation,

---

[1] Marshall McLuhan and Quentin Fiore, *The Medium Is the Message* (New York: Bantam Books, 1967), p. 82.

[2] William Shakespeare, *As You Like It*, Act II, Scene vii.

whether it is announcing a piece of music, doing a commercial, or reading the news. Whether there should be differences in the style of announcing for different types of broadcast content at a particular station may be up to the station's program manager. The announcers on most stations tend to sound pretty much alike, regardless of whether they are doing weather or sports or introducing the next song. Part of this similarity may be due to hiring practices. The program manager or other management personnel who make hiring decisions tend to want people with a certain sound. On the other hand, it is also true that there is a tendency to pick up the pitch and the rhythm of people that you associate with, particularly in a professional environment. If you feel you must conform to the style of a station, be sure you have control of your actions. If you allow yourself to become a *style clone,* you should continue to practice other styles of announcing as well, so that you can turn off or turn on any style you want to adopt. Flexibility and diversity are important for development in most announcing careers. Announcers need to be aware of their performance styles as they become more like other announcers on the same station.

Playing a Role

Take advantage of those characteristics that make you a unique individual. Use your voice effectively, make it pleasant to listen to, but let it be you. One of the advantages youth should be able to offer is unbridled enthusiasm. Excitement is a mark of distinction that is much sought after by both program directors and advertisers. As a dee-jay, you may have unique information on a particular type of music or a particular group of artists. If you are not an expert, become one. Study and learn about a particular entertainment facet. The study techniques you've learned in school can be put to use as you research and study in relation to your broadcasting career. This can make you more valuable to your employer and will become part of your extended personality—part of who you are.

Assuming a Character

Some rather meek-mannered and retiring people become dynamic personalities when they assume the role of disk jockey or of newsperson. A laid-back dee-jay can also change roles, becoming an excited and enthusiastic sportscaster when he is assigned to do play-by-play football. Rather ordinary, matter-of-fact newscasters can radiate excitement and relevance when they are on the scene of an important news event. The role you play depends in part on the situation in which you find yourself, and partially on the image that you see for yourself and want to project.

The Art of Theatre

You may be considered an artist in what you do. Is there an "art" of announcing? Perhaps. Certainly many of the skills of the theatre arts can be applied to radio and television announcing. It has been said that one man's art is another man's garbage. What is art? Is it the ability to mimic another's efforts in painting, music, acting, or announcing? Probably not.

Defining Art

Art is not life, is not a carbon copy of something in reality, is not the mere duplication of an actual event or experience, is not limited to a mere recording or reproduction of the objective world. Art is infinitely more than that; it is the revelation of *a state of mind and spirit* resulting from experiences in the world. . . .
— The artist . . . does whatever is necessary and whatever he can to the object or the event he has experienced . . . for the purpose of communicating to others, in the way or medium he has chosen, the quality of his own peculiar experience.
— In art a uniqe experience is somehow so intensified and clarified that one man's emotion . . . is transmitted to an audience.[3]

Leo Tolstoy said:

Art is the transmission of feeling.[4]

Skills of a Radio-Television Artist

Training as an actor can do much to enhance the broadcasting skills of the announcer. The study of announcing can use some of the theories and techniques that produce actors of excellence to create announcers of distinction.

The Actor's Voice

Good stage actors have mastered voice control, as discussed in Chapter 1. They breathe from the diaphragm for what appears to be effortless projection of their utterances to the last row of the proverbial third balcony.

Projecting to the last row of the balcony is not a trait required or even necessarily desirable in radio or TV, though voice control, of course, is.

Good actors do not always project to the balcony. In a small and intimate theatre, they know how to modulate and control their voices for the most desirable level. As an announcer, this is a skill well worth attaining. Though a well-modulated, theatrically full voice is desirable, the emphasis of modern radio also is on naturalness and conversationality. This may sound contradictory in a sense. Yet the announcer, who makes a well-modulated voice sound natural and distinctive, certainly has achieved a desirable voice quality.

[3] Edwin Duerr, *Radio and Television Acting: Criticism, Theory and Practice* (New York: Rinehart & Company, 1950), pp. 2–3.

[4] Leo Tolstoy. *What Is Art and Essays on Art,* translated by Aylmer Maude (London: Oxford University Press, 1962), p. vi.

When we consider microphone techniques, it is obvious that sounds that are too loud can create a problem of overmodulation with the VU indicator in the red and periodically "pinning the needle." Another part of microphone technique, however, is knowing the proper distance from the microphone. And part of voice technique is being able to adapt to the particular situation in which speakers find themselves.

Mimicry

Though art is not mimicry, mimicry is a quality that has value for announcers, especially announcers who also serve as characters in commercials produced by their station or by others who have found that their versatility makes them desirable as talent. Being able to re-create character voices can be a lucrative sideline for the talented announcer.

Sensitivity

As with actors and other artists, you as an announcer can best demonstrate an affinity to interact with the audience if you are fully informed as to what is currently occurring in your audience's world. You must be sensitive to what's happening to the listeners economically, sociologically, and politically. Important in projecting a knowledgeable authority are having a broad educational background and being well informed.

Timing

One characteristic often attributed to good actors is what is called a "sense of timing." Timing is knowing when to pause, when to increase or decrease delivery speed, and when to continue at a rate that is consistent with the message being communicated. There are two dramatic timing techniques so important in and of themselves that they deserve special attention. They are the "dramatic pause" and "picking up cues."

The Dramatic Pause   One of those notable to the older generation for use of the dramatic pause was Edward R. Murrow. Unlike most of radio's other newspeople, Edward R. Murrow studied speech rather than journalism in college in preparing for his career. At the suggestion of his Washington State College speech teacher, Murrow began his wartime presentations from London with "This [PAUSE] is London." It became his trademark, later becoming, "This [PAUSE] is the news." In later years the announcer who closed Murrow's news show also used a punctuating pause: "Listen to Murrow [PAUSE] tomorrow." Murrow had a fine sense of timing and combined this with a conversational style and an authority that made him one of the important news voices of broadcasting for all time.

Paul Harvey has used the dramatic pause by building to a climax and pausing, or repeating his last phrases and pausing, before revealing the climactic element of particularly dramatic stories. Gabriel Heater, H. V. Kaltenborn, and many of the famous news commentators of World War II used similar techniques.

Cue Pickup   Another particularly important element of timing is what theatre people call "picking up your cues." This means that you begin talking before the person who speaks before you quits. "Stepping on the other person's lines" (starting too soon) is not considered good form. But, starting to speak before the other person finishes—timed correctly—can mean that speeches are immediately back-to-back with no break between them. For a dee-jay this means running a tight board—a good, fast pace, with no pauses. As an announcer in a spot or a mini-drama, a rapid pickup of cues keeps up a lively pace, which holds the interest of listeners, and may mean the difference between finishing within the allotted 30 or 60 seconds or being long.

Imagination

A critical factor that can make announcers into artists is that important element of acting, *imagination*. Imagine that you are talking to one individual about half-way across the room as you speak. Envision the situation or scene you are describing to lend greater meaning to your words. Taste the food you are describing. Smell the flowers or perfume you are selling. Become part of the commercial or part of the news or sporting event as you tell your listener about it. Imagination used creatively, combined with experience, knowledge, and understanding, can enhance one's performance both as an announcer and as talent in a commercial.

COMMON FAILINGS

Duerr points out that there are five common failings of actors in the electronic media. See if these apply to announcers you've heard. The problems are reading copy (1) in an artificial manner, (2) in a monotonous tone, (3) with a mechanical sameness, (4) with a superficial facade, or (5) in a careless or inaccurate manner.

Artificial Manner

When announcers pay more attention to how they sound than to what they are saying, the manner cannot be other than artificial. The golden tones and perfect articulation are wasted if the announcer has not carefully examined the copy for meaning. Announcers must fully understand and have a feeling for their copy and understand their audience. Think about what you are saying and to whom you are saying it. Be concerned with how what you are saying can influence the lives of your listeners. Be enthusiastic about the good things. Be restrained about those that are negative. Contrast ideas that are different. Show parallels in your phrasing of complementary concepts. Talk to your listeners with understanding.

Monotonous Delivery

The monotone announcer has a sameness of tone and pitch that almost completely lacks variety. Announcers often fail to let their voices rise and fall in pitch to create variety within each sentence or paragraph. This situation may provoke the criticism of the beginning announcer to be more conversational.

One method that helps overcome monotony is this:

1. Read a sentence, getting the idea in mind.
2. Then, without looking at the copy, tell someone what you have just read.
3. Look for meaning in your copy. Think about what you are saying. Present ideas, rather than words. In short, be conversational. These techniques also help overcome mechanical sameness.

Mechanical Sameness

Mechanical sameness may be the result of a voice pattern that includes the repetition of a rising pitch at the beginning and a falling pitch at the end of each sentence, phrase, or paragraph. This mechanical sameness also often exhibits a lack of variety in pace. Students must recognize that emphasis for a word or phrase can be gained by slowing down that phrase or word sequence. Conversely, a more rapid reading can relegate a section of a sentence to relatively less importance or confirm its redundancy. While just not being able to read aloud with confidence is probably the most common beginning announcer problem, voice pattern tendencies are probably next. Mechanical sameness is certainly one of the greatest offenses of beginning announcers.

Mechanical sameness may also be the result of reading as you were taught to do when reading aloud in elementary school—reading each syllable carefully and with equal emphasis, paying special attention even to each article ("a," "an," or "the") so that it could be clearly determined that you were reading correctly. Reading "correctly" is a secondary objective. The primary objective is to transmit thoughts, ideas, and concepts; to transmit *meaning*. When you think about what you are saying (or reading), you de-emphasize the unimportant words such as helper verbs, prepositions, and articles. If you are not de-emphasizing some words, the problem should be obvious when you listen to tapes of yourself as you read. Marking copy as suggested earlier is a key to overcoming these problems. By keeping yourself conscious of your bad habits, you can overcome them.

Pinpoint your problems. Mark your copy to prompt yourself to change pitch and pace, to emphasize key ideas, to phrase ideas together, and to pause appropriately. Get rid of mechanical sameness.

The Superficial Facade

When a piece is read in a pleasing manner with what appears to be great style, using clear diction as well as variation in pitch and pace, one might think that the announcer is communicating effectively. Perhaps this is the case. But even with all of these desirable attributes, the piece may be being presented in a manner that is routine, shallow, and uninspired. The announcer not familiar with the ideas he or she is describing is reciting words rather than communicating ideas.

Actors might call this not understanding the "subtext." For announcers it is the result of not fully comprehending the material they are reading. If it is a commercial, does the announcer really know what the competition has to offer, why the product in this particular commercial has certain advantages? Do announcers reading the news know the world ramifications of the material being read and the effects at the local level? The *subtext* refers to the deeper meaning and motivations, which can be projected only with a full understanding of the copy.

Carelessness

Lack of preparation is the usual culprit for misreading material. Beginning announcers who think they can read copy cold often discover that their reading is almost gibberish. Words are skipped; other words are inserted. The meaning is (at best) almost completely lost. One persistent cause of this problem is trying to read at too rapid a rate. When you are admonished to slow down, there is a reason. Often the reason is inaccurate reading of words or groups of words that have almost no meaning to the listener when delivered at a machine-gun pace. The careful announcer has read through the material, understands and can pronounce all the words, and reads ideas and phrases rather than a string of words.

THEATRICAL DISCIPLINE

Persons who wish to break into the theatre have to be dedicated to their cause. Before rehearsals start, extensive research often is done, preparing a role and studying the historical or sociological environments of the action before rehearsals start. Rehearsals proceed for weeks before a word is uttered in public. Many hours are spent in memorizing lines. Careful direction makes sure that each actor is standing or moving in the right place on stage at the right moment.

Contrast this with announcing duties. Research may be more extensive for announcers doing a conscientious job because new material is constantly being covered. Newscaster research should be a regular, ongoing part of normal duties. Since stage actors may only do two or three different shows a year, research for them may not be an ongoing activity. Newscasters need to search out and grasp new information rapidly, keep ideas clearly in mind, and be capable of ad libbing effectively. (See Chapter 5.) (Memorizing, too, can be a useful skill for the broadcaster.) The radio broadcaster usually has a script to use. Television announcers usually rely on an electronic prompter, except perhaps on remotes. While announcers have comparatively little rehearsal time and may have little or no memorizing, actors do much of their rehearsal with a director and usually have weeks of preparation time. On the other hand, announcers must pretty much depend on their own resources: practicing, marking copy, and evaluating on their own.

Radio announcers generally read from scripts or computer screens. Modern technology can create problems for those who religiously mark traditional paper copy. The computer newsroom may be paperless, projecting the newscast on a computer screen from which the announcer is expected to read. So, as an announcer it is recommended that you perfect your style before you take a job at a station with a computerized newsroom.

Students often think that announcing is an easy, fun-filled job. If that is their belief, they are in for a rude awakening. Exciting, challenging, and fun-filled the career may be, but easy it is not when well done. Good announcing takes fully as much dedication for the announcer on the air as does drama for the thespian on the stage.

While the stage actor may spend weeks preparing for a single scene, announcers must continually be preparing, alert to the events they may need to interpret. Announcers also need careful planning, and beginners often need extended practice to sound professional.

COMMERCIALS TALENT

Announcers often may be called upon to act in commercials, especially when ''dramatic'' commercials are done at the local level. Though most announcers may not think of themselves as actors, many of the techniques used by actors are valuable, especially when announcers are expected to be believable in commercials.

Using the Microphone

In most cases as an announcer, you have one position in relation to the microphone: the position that is right for you with the level of projection that you normally use. True, on a remote, with an omni-directional mike, you may need to adjust to compensate for the ambient noise level that you wish to use to enhance your presentation, and that must not be allowed to overwhelm you. Of course, if you use a headset microphone (often the case with remotes) your microphone placement is pretty much predetermined. (See also Chapter 9.)

One reason to use a floor stand microphone when doing commercials is to be sure that your breathing is unimpaired. Deep breathing using the diaphragm can be difficult when you are cramped in a sitting position. Especially when doing a commercial with implied action, it is important to use a floor stand microphone so that you may change your position relative to the mike easily and quickly. For dramatic types of commercials, the speaker's relation to the microphone can vary considerably. If the scene calls for you to shout, it is imperative that you not be too near the microphone to avoid blasting. To sound as if you are shouting—to get the effect without the volume—it is necessary that you step back from the microphone. Excessive volume may distort your voice, or the station's limiter could put you off the air. So that loudness will not distort, the shouter may use a thin voice quality, calling slowly as if trying to overcome distortion of the echo that nearby mountains or buildings might create.

> The use of perspective is essential to creating the radio picture. When a production is in stereo, the relationship of characters can be suggested by positioning the mikes for each channel: when a speaker or effect is away from the center of focus, the speaker or sound effect can be heard more distinctly on one stereo speaker or the other to indicate relative position. Even in monaural production, the location of a person can be suggested by positioning the character away from the mike (OFF MIKE), to create the illusion of a person across the room or at a distance from the point of perception.[5]

Sound effects, too, may seem to move to or from the point of perception on radio by varying the sound's intensity. Often, however, sound is established to suggest location, then faded into the background to maintain the feel of the environment. It may appear in a script something like this:

SFX: ESTAB CAR & FADE TO B.G.

> SFX is short for *sound effects*.
> ESTAB CAR means *establish* the sound of a car at a level that leaves no doubt in the listener's mind as to where the scene is taking place. This is usually done by rapidly fading in the sound.
> FADE TO B.G. means to fade the sound to *background* level (loud enough to be heard, but low enough not to overwhelm the speaker).

To create microphone perspective for a person, the speaker must at times be OFF-MIKE or FADE-ON or FADE-OFF mike. Your being able to move in relationship to the microphone helps the audience visualize the performance in the "theatre of the mind." Your director will help you achieve the correct balance and the effect desired. Speaking at the point of perception (the microphone location) places the individual closer to the mike than someone shouting from a distance away, for example.

Fading-in or fading-out may be done by backing away from or approaching the microphone as you speak. "Fading-out," proceeding from being on-mike (in the primary pickup pattern) to being off-mike (out of the primary pickup pattern), can also be executed by turning the head away from or into the pickup pattern of the microphone as you speak.

Intimacy is achieved by speaking at low volume close to the mike. On a cardiod mike this close proximity may result in an apparent lower pitch of the speaker's voice (the proximity effect). Some microphones have a bass roll-off

[5] William L. Hagerman, *Broadcast Advertising Copywriting* (Boston: Focal Press, 1990), p. 111.

switch, which allows this effect to be de-emphasized if the added bass emphasis is not desired.

Normal conversation is usually best achieved by speaking at full volume at from 10 to 12 inches from the mike. Place your 8½-by-11-inch script between you and the mike to measure 11 inches. This should be about right if you project properly.

Assuming a Character

Often in a commercial you will be expected to be a particular type of person, a specific person, or perhaps a character you create. As with the subtext knowledge necessary for narrating a commercial, or the background required to do a good job with the news, you need to know about the character you are portraying. Doing a one-minute spot is a long way from doing a two-hour drama, yet you are, in a sense, doing a drama—a mini-drama. If it is a historical character that appears in the spot, such as Benjamin Franklin or George Washington, you will need to conform to the common expectation of what these gentlemen would be like. Are they young or old at the time depicted in the spot?

On spots where the characters have been invented to fit the situation, it may be up to you to portray the character envisioned by the copywriter or the sponsor. Chances are that you will create a *caricature* rather than a character. The person creating a caricature exaggerates peculiarities or defects. Since time is extremely limited in a commercial, character traits may be overdone to get the intended idea across or to give the spot the extra punch necessary to stand out from the competition. On radio, about the only thing that you have to work with is the character's voice.

Some accents are easy for some people. For most Americans, a Southern twang, a Brooklyn accent, or a Texas drawl may be easier to mimic than a foreign accent, since they have heard these American accents for much of their lives. Persons who were exposed to a foreign language or ghetto talk early in life may be able to do an accent of that particular type without practice.

Part of the distinctiveness of an accent is the rhythm of the speech involved. A simple phrase that includes the accent's sound and rhythm may be used sometimes to get into that particular speech pattern. If you're doing an Irish accent, the phrase may be as simple as "Sure, an' b'gorra." Authentic accents can add much to a commercial. Poorly performed accents are best left out.

Mini-drama Communication

To make any dramatic piece believable, there must be communication between the characters. You will probably find this much easier if microphones are set up so that characters who have scenes together can make eye contact with each other. The old two-sided ribbon mikes were ideal for this.

Movement on stage and facial expressions on television often communicate feelings visually. The audience can tell from the manner of the movement or the telling look in the eyes (on TV) what is meant as a character delivers a line. On radio, some of this type of expression must be transmitted by repetition, grouping words together, or pausing between ideas to emphasize and enhance meaning. Again, knowing more about the character or the situation than the words actually reveal can help the announcer/actor do a good job.

Being able to pantomime is a valuable tool for the TV actor. It may also help radio actors get the feel for what they are trying to project to the audience. As suggested in "Using the Body" in Chapter 1, clenching the fist or tensing the body as a whole helps put across an idea that comes as a result of such tension: being mad, being scared, etc.

Doing Character Types

As previously suggested, characters in 30- or 60-second dramas tend to be caricatures. Others are probably character *types* rather than fully developed characters that would appear in a play. How can an announcer play a character type for a commercial?

Let's look at some of the most common stereotypes.

- The old man or woman. Of course, many older people have ordinary voices. But, to do a caricature or stereotype, the announcer's voice could be coarse, weak, raspy, or breathy. An additional wrinkle you might add is toothlessness. This is achieved by wrapping your lips around your teeth, which does give a toothless sound. Another gimmick is the shaky voice. The person who is hard of hearing may speak extra loudly. Obviously, You will probably not use all of the techniques at once on the same stereotype character but you can apply several of these techniques at the same time. The more techniques applied, the older the character should become. Be careful, however, not to offend by making fun of the elderly. These are also good gimmicks to use the next time you need to mimic a witch.
- The child. Here voice placement is in the mouth. Use a fairly high pitch and slip in a hint of baby talk by substituting "w" for "l" and "ew" for "yew," as in "igh wuv ew" (I love you).
- The stuffed shirt. Place the voice in the throat as if for a gargle without actually producing the repeated gurgling. Use a blustery approach—bursts of speech in short phrases, often repeated. Use repetitive expressions such as "of course, of course," "really my dear," "my good man," or other such interjections.

In addition to these, there are other stereotypes that tend to be uncomplimentary and probably should not be used because advertisers do not want to offend prospective customers. There are techniques, however, that can be combined and used to create additional recognizable caricatures:

- Speaking very slowly might be used to suggest a person who is deliberate or perhaps not very bright.

- Speaking rapidly connotes a "slicker," one who is trying to put something over on others, or a person who is always in a hurry. Rapid speech in jerks and stops may indicate an extremely nervous person.
- Use an ethnic or regional accent—Jewish, British, French, Spanish, Russian, or black. An accent and speech rhythm done well can readily set your character apart.
- Purposely mispronounce certain vowel or consonant sounds; e.g., leave off the "g" in "ing" words or substitute the short "i" sound where the short "e" sound would be in standard English. This might be used to suggest one who is less educated or from another region of the country.
- Using a high-pitched voice with a whine can portray a character who's uncertain about almost everything.
- Using a breathy, raspy voice may suggest a mature person who is used to dominating those about him or her.
- Smiling whenever you speak may be used to indicate someone extremely happy or with a bright personality.
- Placing your voice in your head (speaking through your nose) might indicate a person with a speech impediment or a bumpkin.
- Only partially open your mouth as you speak. Keeping your teeth together or exaggerating the use of your lips to enunciate may also be used to create a distinctive voice.
- Speaking through clenched teeth can also indicate controlled rage.

Remember though, if the technique used makes you too difficult to understand, the characterization has little value.

Sometimes the script writer will write in words or expressions that make it easier to give the character a stereotypical sound. The older farmer may have sentences filled with "I reckon," "sure enough," "gonna," and "git."

There are many techniques that can be used. Listen to television, movies, and theatre as well as radio to pick out other mannerisms you can use to make your characters sound different from the other characters in the spot you are working on. Be careful, however, not to offend members of your audience with negative stereotyping.

APPLYING THEATRE TRICKS

The legitimate theatre has been around centuries longer than the electronic media. It is helpful to attend stage plays on a regular basis. Try out and act in theatrical productions when you have the chance. It does much to build the confidence and the technical know-how so important to the radio or television announcer.

As powerful and influential as theatre is, it is startling to realize that one television network presentation of *Hamlet* in the mid-1950s in the United States was seen by more people than had seen all of the previous performances of this classic in all of the theatres in all of the 350 years since it was originally performed at Stratford-on-Avon.

Use the tools of the theatre. Use them well. But never forget that you have one of the most important information media ever conceived at your command as a radio or television announcer.

EXERCISES

1. Mark the copy provided at the end of this chapter as recommended in previous chapters.
2. Follow the instructions for studying word lists as suggested in the previous chapter, this time doing word lists 7A and 7B. Be prepared to pronounce the words correctly, write the correct phonetic transcriptions when tested, and define the words when used in a sentence.
3. Read your marked copy for word lists at the end of this chapter onto your cassette tape to be handed in. You may also reread paragraphs from previous word lists to review. Your tape will be handed in for evaluation. Be sure that your marked copy for the current word lists is handed in with your cassette. See also exercise 4.
4. With another member of the class or a dramatically talented friend, read the dramatic commercials that follow. Repeat until they are ''the best you can do.'' Pay particular attention to timing. Your spot cannot be long. It may be up to two seconds short.
5. Read this chapter's word list copy and the dramatic commercials until you have done the best you possibly can, or until you have read for a full hour. When you feel that you have done your best, review the previous week's word list paragraphs or news for the balance of your hour tape, putting your best effort at the end for evaluation.
6. Bring your marked copy and dramatic commercials to class. Pick your best 60 seconds to be read ''live'' for the other members of the class. You may also be asked to read a character with another student. Study each part carefully and plan a possible character-ization.

BROADCAST VOCABULARY WORD LIST   Unit 7-A

1. putsch (n)—a swift, illegal government takeover

   _____   *pooch*

2. anti-semitic (adj)—hating the Jews

   _____   *an ti su me' tik*

3. antithesis (n)—exact opposite

   _____   *an tith' u sis*

4. apartheid (n)—the policy of strict racial segregation of South Africa

   _____   *u par' tight (or) u par' tayt*

5. apportionment (n)—dividing or sharing out according to a plan

   _____   *u por' shun munt*

6. referendum (n)—a proposed law up for a vote of the people

    _____   *re fur en' dum*

7. autocracy (n)—rule by one person

    _____   *aw tok' ru see*

8. autonomy (n)—self-governing; condition of self-rule

    _____   *aw ton' u mee*

9. president pro tempore (n)—a temporary chairman; acting president

    _____   *prez' u dunt proh tem' por ee*

10. Bundestag (n)—lower house of the German legislature

    _____   *boon' dus taug*

11. plebiscite (n)—a direct vote of the people to determine issues

    _____   *pleb' u sight*

12. plenary (adj)—a fully attended meeting of a group

    _____   *plen' ur ee (or) plee' nur ee*

13. parity (n)—equality in amount or status

    _____   *pair' u tee*

14. nuclear (adj)—relating to atomic energy

                                                 new' klee ur

15. pristine (adj)—of the earliest times; uncorrupted

    _____   *pris' teen*

16. dioxin (n)—a toxic chemical waste

                                                 digh oks' un

17. interferon (n)—a product of the immune system that fights disease

    _____   *in tur feer' on*

18. Perrier (n)—a brand of effervescent spring water bottled in France

    _____   *per' ee ay*

19. Falangist (n)—a member of the Spanish fascist party

    _____   *fu lan' jist*

20. cybernetics (n)—the design of mechanical-electrical units to replace human functions

_____   *sigh bur net' iks*

BROADCAST VOCABULARY WORD LIST   Unit 7-B

1. telegrapher (n)—one who operates a telegraph key

_____   *tu leg' ru fur*

2. photogenic (adj)—being an attractive subject for photography

_____   *foh toh jen' ik*

3. topography (n)—detailed mapping of features of a district

_____   *top og' ru fee*

4. photographer (n)—a person who takes photographs

_____   *fu tog' ru fur*

5. seismograph (n)—an instrument used to measure and record earthquakes

_____   *sighz' mu graf*

6. zoology (n)—the branch of biology dealing with the study of animals

_____   *zoh ol' u jee*

7. ornithology (n)—the branch of zoology dealing with the study of birds

_____   *or nu thol' u jee*

8. opthalmologist (n)—a doctor of medicine specializing in the eye

_____   *of thu mol' u just*

9. optometrist (n)—a person who tests eyes and prescribes glasses and contact lenses

_____   *op tom' u trist*

10. psyche (n)—the mental or psychological structure of a person

_____   *sigh' kee*

11. psychological (adj)—pertaining to the mind or mental process

_____   *sigh koh loj' i kul*

12. geologic (adj)—of or pertaining to the science dealing with the earth's surface

_____   *jee oh loj' ik*

13. ally (n)—a friend or close associate

_____   *al'   ligh*

14. ally (v)—to become a close associate

_____   *al   ligh'*

15. profuse (adj)—plentiful, overflowing, copious

_____   *proh   fyews'*

16. promulgate (v)—to announce or put into effect officially a law or decree

_____   *prom'   ul   gayt*

17. melee (n)—a violent free-for-all

_____   *may'   lay   or   may   lay'*

18. belfry (n)—a bell tower, steeple with bells

_____   *bel'   free*

19. cauldron (n)—a large kettle

_____   *kaul'   dron*

20. profuse (adj)—of great quantity, in great abundance

_____   *proh   fyews'*

WORD LIST PARAGRAPH   Unit 7-A

The president pro tempore of the legislature felt the new apportionment to be the antithesis of democracy. In the change from autocracy to self-government, he felt it important that the putsch leaders be punished. Not only was de facto apartheid being practiced, but anti-semitism as well.

The leader indicated that he thought a plebiscite necessary to determine the form of government. Though the Bundestag had been in plenary session in order to help create parity among the citizenry, a referendum appeared necessary before autonomy could be granted. The question was, did the governing body's constituency approve?

A Falangist group was gaining strength in the newly autonomous state. One of the greatest areas of concern was the dioxin pollution. It was hoped that a new

Perrier plant would be free of this drug and that cybernetics would come to the rescue. If not, one proposal suggested that interferon might ease physical deterioration of many of the residents.

WORD LIST PARAGRAPH   Unit 7-B

The telegrapher was about to promulgate a decree banning photography when he saw a photographer approaching. The photographer pointed out that the two most efficient ways to record the topography were with a camera or with a seismograph. The geologic formations were, in effect, photogenic. The process at the same time would allow certain research that would be of benefit not only to zoology, but particularly to ornithology as well.

Since the photographer had recently visited an ophthalmologist, after referral by an optometrist, he knew that physically he was up to the task.

The question arose, however, was he psychologically prepared? Was his psyche such that he could withstand a profuse flow of data and not become overwhelmed? When the facts were known, the telegrapher became the photographer's ally.

ACADIAN TRAVEL
30 SECONDS

Sound: MOTOR BOAT FADES IN & TO B. G.

Jacques: Billie Joe, how come those boats go so fast on Acadiana Bayous with nobody a-paddlin'?

B. J.:   Jacques, that boat has a motor. In Acadiana folks motor boat in many beautiful waterways.

Jacques: How come that gal has a rope and is trying to pull the boat back?

B. J.:   She's not pulling the boat back, she's water skiing. The motor pulls the gal and pushes the boat. Water skiing is a favorite pastime on Acadiana Bayous.

JACQUES: That girl looks a mite chilly wearin' nothin' but a couple of bandannas. Hope she don't have to blow her nose.

B. J.: That's a bikini, Jacques. Gals wear them swimming.

JACQUES: Billie Joe, I'm givin' up my ambition to be a brain surgeon. Gonna be a motor boater so's I can play tug-o-war with a gal wearing bandannas here on Acadiana Bayous.

B. J.: Cajun country and Acadiana Bayous mean fun for all.

CLASSICAL RADIO PROMO
30 SECONDS

FATHER: My little girl . . . a lawyer.

DAUGHTER: Oh, Daddy. Here, let's listen to some music.

SFX: CLICK OF RADIO BEING TURNED ON

FATHER: Don't turn on the radio.

MUSIC: CLASSICAL MUSIC B. G.

DAUGHTER: I thought you liked classical music.

FATHER: Um, I love the sound of good music, it's those radio stations I can do without.

DAUGHTER: You happen to be listening to _____ ,
(CALL LETTERS)

_____ .
(DIAL LOCATION)

FATHER: That's _____ ?
(CALL LETTERS)

DAUGHTER: It's _____ and it's a radio station, the station
(CALL LETTERS)

that provides the sounds of good music.

FATHER: If _____ sounds this good, I don't want to stop
(CALL LETTERS)

listening. Here, let's turn it louder.

DAUGHTER: Yes, with _____ you can.
                            (CALL LETTERS)

ANNOUNCER: Fill your house to the rafters with the sound of music

from _____ .
                            (STATION & DIAL LOCATION)

THE DOCSI CORPORATION
CONTINUITY[6]

DATE: March 6, 1991   WID: JP   SESSION DATE: 3/7/91
AGENCY: LUGGAGE CENTER
PRODUCT: ATTACHÉ CASES
TITLE: "BILL'S PROBLEM"   LENGTH: 60

WOMAN: I FIRST NOTICED BILL'S PROBLEM DURING THE FRITZEL

MERGER NEGOTIATIONS . . .

BILL: WHAT PROBLEM? I DON'T HAVE A—

MAN: BILL, PLEASE, WE'RE HERE TO HELP . . .

BILL: WHAT PROBLEM?

ANNCR: BILL HAS A PROBLEM.

BILL: WHAT PROBLEM!

ANNCR: A PROBLEM SO UGLY HIS CO-WORKERS COULDN'T GO ON

IGNORING IT.

MAN: THE FIRST TIME I NOTICED BILL'S PROBLEM WAS ON A

BUSINESS TRIP TO BUFFALO . . .

BILL: WHAT PROBLEM?

WOMAN: DIDN'T THE CLIENT NOTICE . . .

MAN: OH YES, THE CLIENT NOTICED TOO.

ANNCR: YES SEE, BILL HAS . . .

BOTH: AN UGLY ATTACHÉ.

BILL: I DO NOT!

WOMAN: (WHISPERS) HE'S IN DENIAL.

BILL: I AM NOT.

[6] Reprinted with permission of Dick Orkin, DOCSI, Inc.

ANNCR: YES, BILL'S ATTACHÉ IS AN EYESORE, A MESS, A DOG.

BILL: IT IS NOT.

WOMAN: OH BILL.

ANNCR: THANKFULLY . . . THERE'S HELP FOR BILL.

BOTH: THE LUGGAGE CENTER.

ANNCR: THEY'RE CALIFORNIA'S NUMBER ONE DISCOUNTER OF QUALITY LUGGAGE ATTACHÉS, LIKE SAMSONITE.

BILL: YOU REALLY DO THINK I HAVE A —

BOTH: CONFRONT IT BILL . . .

BILL: AN ATTACHÉ PROBLEM.

ANNCR: AT LAST A NURTURING ENVIRONMENT WHERE BILL CAN FIND THE RIGHT ATTACHÉ AT A DISCOUNT PRICE . . . THE LUGGAGE CENTER.

BILL: ALL RIGHT! I'LL GET A NEW ATTACHÉ!

MAN: ATTA BOY, BILL . . .

ANNCR: AT THE LUGGAGE CENTER, WE UNDERSTAND. WE CARE.

MAN: NOW LET'S TALK ABOUT THE TOUPEE, BILL . . .

BILL: THE TOUPEE STAYS!!

WOMAN: IT LOOKS LIKE A HAMSTER . . .

ANNCR: THE LUGGAGE CENTER. CALIFORNIA'S NUMBER ONE DIS-COUNTER OF LUGGAGE . . . AND ATTACHÉS. 16 LOCA-TIONS.

THE DOCSI CORPORATION
CONTINUITY[7]

DATE:	OCTOBER 16, 1990	WID:	RAO/CC
AGENCY:	CME		
PRODUCT:	JEEP WRANGLER		
TITLE:	LETTER #1	LENGTH:	60

DAN: DEAR FRANCINE AND FRED . . . JUNE AND I ARE REAL SORRY—

JUNE: SORRY SOUNDS WIMPY. SAY SHATTERED . . .

[7] Reprinted with permission of Dick Orkin, DOCSI, Inc.

DAN: SHATTERED WE MISSED YOUR DAUGHTER MYRA'S WEDDING. BUT WE DO HAVE A GOOD EXCUSE.

JUNE: EXCUSE IS DEFENSIVE. SAY REASON.

DAN: REASON. WE STARTED FOR SANTA ROSA IN OUR NEW JEEP WRANGLER . . .

JUNE: DON'T MENTION THE JEEP WRANGLER . . .

DAN: THIS WILL WORK. TRUST ME!

JUNE: HA!

DAN: NEW JEEP WRANGLER, THE WIND FLYING THROUGH OUR HAIR, TWO FREE SPIRITS HURLING DOWN THE HIGHWAY OF LIFE AS ONLY THE ONE AND ONLY FOUR BY FOUR JEEP WRANGLER CAN HURL. . . .

JUNE: DAN?

DAN: WE GOT LOST.

JUNE: DAN?

DAN: WHAT THEN?

JUNE: WHY DON'T YOU JUST GO AHEAD AND TELL THEM YOU WERE HAVING SO MUCH FUN IN YOUR JEEP WRANGLER SCOUTING THE WEST YOU MISSED THE TURN-OFF!

DAN: MOI? YOU WERE HAVING SO MUCH FUN RIDING ALONG SINGING "KING OF THE ROAD" YOU WEREN'T WATCHING THE MAP!

JUNE: AT LEAST I RECOGNIZED WE HAD PASSED SANTA ROSA AND WERE ENTERING SEATTLE!

DAN: OH, THIS IS SILLY! AFTER ALL, WE MAY HAVE MISSED THE WEDDING . . .

BOTH: BUT WE DID HAVE MORE FUN!

DAN: DEAR FRANCINE AND FRED . . . WE'RE SHATTERED WE MISSED THE WEDDING. BUT ALIENS TOOK US . . .

JUNE: ABDUCTED US FROM OUR JEEP WRANGLER . . .

DAN: ABDUCTED US . . .

> ANNCR: REDISCOVER AMERICA AND VALUE NOW, CALL 1-800-352-JEEP AND SEE YOUR CALIFORNIA JEEP AND EAGLE DEALER FOR THE JEEP VEHICLE YOU'VE ALWAYS WANTED. JEEP IS A REGISTERED TRADEMARK OF CHRYSLER CORPORATION.

THE DOCSI CORPORATION
CONTINUITY[8]

DATE: JUNE 20, 1991   WID: RAO/CC   SESSION DATE: 7/1/91
AGENCY: CME (IRVINE)
PRODUCT: JEEP CHEROKEE
TITLE: "MARTIN FLYING"   LENGTH: 60

SFX: DOOR BELL AND OPEN.

AL: YEAH?

WILLI: AL LAKUM?

AL: R-RIGHT

WILLI: IT'S ME, MARTIN FLINK.

AL: MARTY? I HAVEN'T SEEN YOU SINCE 7TH GRADE. BOY, I NEVER—

WILLI: LET ME CUT RIGHT TO THE CHASE HERE. . .

AL: OKAY. . .

WILLI: AUGUST 12, '61. SATURDAY. MATINEE. THE RIALTO. "LADDIE, THE FARM DOG!" RING A BELL?

AL: NO. . .

WILLI: YOU CRIED LIKE A BABY. SAID IF I NEVER TOLD THE GUYS. . .SOMEDAY YOU'D GIVE ME ANYTHING I WANT. . .

AL: (LAUGHS) OH, YEAH. . .RIGHT.

WILLI: WELL, I WANT YOUR JEEP CHEROKEE.

AL: (LAUGHS) (BEAT) ARE YOU SERIOUS?

WILLI: HEY, I ALWAYS WANTED A JEEP CHEROKEE. IT'S A LEGEND. YOU HAVE ONE. I WANT IT.

[8] Reprinted with permission of Dick Orkin, DOCSI, Inc.

AL: MARTY, THAT WAS THIRTY YEARS. . .

WILLI: I'VE BEEN MONITORING YOUR LIFE. . .UP TILL NOW YOU HAVEN'T HAD ANYTHING I WANTED.

AL: THIS IS STUPID. . .

WILLI: YOUR JEEP CHEROKEE HAS THE AVAILABLE FOUR WHEEL ANTILOCK BRAKING SYSTEM?

AL: YEA, BUT—

WILLI: I'M GONNA LOVE MY NEW JEEP CHEROKEE!

AL: IT'S NOT YOURS.

WILLI: HAS THE MOST POWERFUL AVAILABLE ENGINE IN ITS CLASS.

AL: LOOK, I'M NOT GIVING YOU MY NEW JEEP CHEROKEE AS HUSH MONEY. I WAS 12 YEARS OLD. I DON'T CARE WHO KNOWS I CRIED AT "LADDIE, THE FARM DOG."

WILLI: (BEAT) YOU DON'T?

AL: NO.

WILLI: WOULD YOUR WIFE CARE THAT I HAVE PICTURES OF YOU AND GAYLE HELDMAN AT YOUR 13TH BIRTHDAY PARTY PLAYING POST OFFICE?

SFX: DOOR SLAM.

WILLI: (SHOUTS) THEY'RE IN COLOR!

ANNCR: REDISCOVER AMERICA AND GET $1500 CASH BACK FROM CHRYSLER ON NEW JEEP CHEROKEES AT YOUR CALIFORNIA JEEP AND EAGLE DEALERS. CALL 1-800-352-JEEP. JEEP IS A REGISTERED TRADEMARK OF CHRYSLER CORPORATION.

NO PRESSURE, NO HYPE   "COCKTAIL PARTY"
CAMPAIGN II   SPOT #1 :60

HELENE: LOIS, THIS IS MY FIANCÉ, FRANK.

LOIS: WELL, HI FRANK. Y'KNOW HELENE NEVER MENTIONED WHAT IT IS YOU DO.

FRANK: WELL, I'M A. . .

HELENE: COULD YOU EXCUSE US FOR JUST A MINUTE. WHAT WERE YOU GOING TO TELL HER?

FRANK: I WAS GOING TO TELL HER THAT I'M A CAR SALESMAN AT BOB HARRIS FORD LINCOLN MERCURY.

HELENE: YOU CAN'T DO THAT. YOU KNOW HOW PEOPLE FEEL ABOUT CAR SALESMEN.

FRANK: BUT AT BOB HARRIS FORD LINCOLN MERCURY WE AREN'T LIKE OTHER CAR SALESPEOPLE. WE DON'T USE PRESSURE OR HYPE.

HELENE: JUST THINK OF SOMETHING ELSE.

SFX: STEPS BACK.

FRANK: WELL, ACTUALLY LOIS, I'M A MORTICIAN.

CROWD: OOOOOOO.

HELENE: COULD YOU EXCUSE US A MINUTE?

SFX: STEPS AWAY.

HELENE: COULDN'T YOU THINK OF SOMETHING BETTER THAN THAT?

FRANK: YEH, THE TRUTH, THAT I'M A RELAXED, FRIENDLY CAR SALESMAN FROM BOB HARRIS FORD LINCOLN MERCURY.

HELENE: ANYTHING BUT THAT, OK?

FRANK: OKAY. JUST KIDDING ABOUT BEING A MORTICIAN. I'M REALLY AN AUDITOR FOR THE IRS.

CROWD: OOOOOOOO.

HELENE: COULD YOU EXCUSE US A MINUTE. FRANK!

FRANK: WELL YOU SAID "ANYTHING ELSE."

HELENE: JUST USE YOUR IMAGINATION FRANK. . .

SFX: STEPS BACK.

FRANK: TO TELL YOU THE TRUTH LOIS, I'M A RUSSIAN SPY TRAVELING INCOGNITO. AND HELENE HERE IS A. . .

HELENE: (HYSTERICAL) HE'S A CAR SALESMAN OKAY! ! ! !

FRANK: FROM BOB HARRIS FORD LINCOLN MERCURY.

CROWD: OOOOOOOO

HELENE: (TALK OUT) I'M SO PROUD OF HIM AND HE'S ALL MINE.

ANNCR: COME TO BOB HARRIS FORD LINCOLN MERCURY FOR NO
          PRESSURE AND NO HYPE.

AMAZING RADIO
AUTOMOBILE CAMPAIGN 1
SPOT #1 "DANCE LADY"   LENGTH: 60 W/:15 SECOND LIVE TAG

ANNCR: DON'T YOU WISH EVERYTHING WAS AS EASY AS BUYING
          A CAR AT CEDAR RAPIDS TOYOTA?

SFX: TINNY FOX TROT IN BKG.

MAN: LOOK, I'M NOT SAYING YOU'RE A BAD DANCE IN-
          STRUCTOR. . .

INS: THERE ARE NO BAD INSTRUCTORS, ONLY BAD STUDENTS!

MAN: I CAN'T GET THESE STEPS. . .

INS: ONCE MORE. LEFT FOOT BACK, RIGHT TO THE SIDE, LEFT
          PIVOT UP AND SKIP!

MAN: LEFT FOOT FRONT. . .

INS: LEFT BACK, THEN RIGHT, THEN UP AND THEN BACK AND
          PIVOT AND SKIP. DO IT!

MAN: THIS IS SO COMPLICATED. BUYING A CAR AT CEDAR
          RAPIDS TOYOTA WAS A LOT SIMPLER THAN THIS. I WAS
          IN. I WAS OUT. (SNAP) LIKE THAT.

INS: THIS IS NOT COMPLICATED. TOGETHER.

BOTH: LEFT FOOT BACK, RIGHT TO THE SIDE, LEFT PIVOT. . .

INS: THAT IS A SKIP! DIDN'T YOUR MOTHER TEACH YOU THE
          DIFFERENCE BETWEEN A PIVOT AND A SKIP? WHAT IS
          THIS?

MAN: A PIVOT?

INS: OH, BOY. ANOTHER DYSFUNCTIONAL FAMILY! FROM THE TOP! LEFT FOOT UP, BACK TO THE SIDE. . .

ANNCR: THERE'S COMPLICATED, THEN THERE'S BUYING A CAR AT CEDAR RAPIDS TOYOTA. SELECTION, OPTIONS, SERVICE. ALL SIMPLE. CEDAR RAPIDS TOYOTA. WE'RE EASY. AND PROUD OF IT.

AMAZING RADIO
AUTOMOBILE CAMPAIGN I
SPOT #4 NOON IN SIBERIA   LENGTH: 30

ANNCR: DON'T YOU WISH EVERYTHING WAS AS EASY AS BUYING A CAR AT CEDAR RAPIDS TOYOTA.

MAN: I BOUGHT THIS WATCH HERE LAST WEEK.

CLERK: YEAH?

MAN: I'M HAVING TROUBLE SETTING THE TIME—

CLERK: THIS IS SET FOR NOON IN SIBERIA.

MAN: HOW DO I CHANGE—

CLERK: IF YOU MESS WITH THIS OSCILLATION COUNTER BEFORE YOU ADJUST THE CALENDAR RATCHET, IT'S GONNA BE NOON IN SIBERIA EVERYTIME.

MAN: BOY, BUYING A CAR AT CEDAR RAPIDS TOYOTA WAS EASIER THAN THIS. . .ONE, TWO! IN, OUT!

CLERK: REMEMBER: IF YOU'RE IN AN EASTERN OR WESTERN TIME ZONE, THIS WATCH DON'T WORK.

MAN: WHAT!

ANNCR: THERE'S COMPLICATED. THEN THERE'S BUYING A CAR AT CEDAR RAPIDS TOYOTA. SELECTION, OPTIONS, SERVICE. . .ALL SIMPLE. CEDAR RAPIDS TOYOTA. WE'RE EASY. AND PROUD OF IT.

**ACTIVE CLUB
30 SEC PROMO
HAUNTED HOUSE**

WITCH I   Double, double, toil and trouble—

WITCH II   Fire burn and cauldron bubble—

SFX   SQUEAKING DOOR

WITCH I   Visit the Active Club's haunted house.

WITCH II   Be scared like you've never been scared before—

SFX   FLAPPING OF WINGS, MOANING OF GHOSTS, AND
                 RATTLING OF CHAINS—AD LIB

WITCH I   Bats in the belfry . . .

WITCH II   Ghosts in the hidden passages . . .

WITCH I   Ghouls in the dungeon . . .

ANNOUNCER: Take the kids to the Active Club's haunted house this weekend
                 in the abandoned house at 117 Virginia Avenue near General
                 Medical Center, 5 to 8 nightly. All proceeds go to the Active
                 Park Improvement Fund.

WITCHES I & II   (COARSE LAUGHTER)

8

Interviewing

OBJECTIVES

Upon completion of this chapter the student should be able to:

1. Point out the differences for the audience of interviews on radio, on television, and in the print media.
2. Describe six traits and interview practices of the successful broadcast interviewer. List four possible purposes of an interview.
3. Explain three kinds of experience that enhance interviewer skill and credibility.
4. Explain how satellite technology has changed local news coverage for stations.
5. List and give examples of seven important criteria for interviewee selection.
6. Give examples of six general types of people who might fulfill your needs for a local news interviewee on almost any topic.
7. Give five avenues of research the interviewer might pursue to get needed information on an interviewee.
8. List and explain four things the interviewer needs to know about the interview topic.
9. Describe four qualities good interview questions should have.
10. Describe seven different types of interview queries.
11. Explain three techniques the interviewer can use to keep control of the interview.
12. Give three techniques the television interview director, producer, or interviewer can use to help the audience understand the proceedings.
13. List six points about the interview that should be explained to the interviewee in advance.
14. Describe how interviewers should respond to the answers to their questions.

A CRITICAL INFORMATION CHANNEL

Radio and television interviewing projects ideas and feelings differently than a similar written report does. When a story is written following an oral interview, the writer interprets what was said. The reader is denied the full impact of the discussion being reported. The readers cannot see the expressions on the faces of the interviewees as they utter their explanations, nor can readers hear the inflections in the voices of interviewees. The only encounter that might be more meaningful than a radio or television interview would be an in-person discussion between the interviewee and the audience member. Even that might well be less informative, if the audience member did not have the background necessary to carefully interrogate the interviewee.

Interviewing as done in the electronic media has become an art form. It is a skill that the news reporter is expected to perfect, and it is perhaps the most important skill of the talk show host. As with many other skills, the perfection of the techniques come from extended practice and encountering many different situations.

THE SKILLED INTERVIEWER

Experienced interviewers tend to display several common traits. In addition to having an appearance that evokes confidence on the part of the interviewee, good interviewers can be expected to display self-confidence and knowledge of the topic, and be dressed in an appropriate, conservative style. The seasoned interviewer has a pleasant, reassuring manner.

Interests

Most good interviewers have a broad background in many fields of endeavor. They have a good education, but perhaps more importantly, they are constantly working to keep abreast of the current news, current international and national problems, and proposed solutions to the world's ills.

Good interviewers are genuinely interested in people, in what makes them "tick," and in why they do what they do. Interviewers are interested in what's going on in literature, entertainment, and sports. They are always on the lookout for new information and new insights into the world around them.

Opportunities

Interviewers and news personnel have more opportunities than other station personnel may have to interact with leaders in international, national, state, and local affairs. Seldom does one do an interview without a short "getting-acquainted" session beforehand. As a radio or TV interviewer, you are somewhat of a celebrity yourself. So, it is fairly easy to interact on a nearly equal basis. Most interviewees want to project a positive image. It is much easier to do this during the on-air interview if they have established rapport with the interviewer.

Experience

The experience of meeting and conversing with dignitaries—along with the experience of actually interviewing such people—creates a feeling of confidence and ease of communication for interviewers. This not only adds to their credibility with those they interview, but also makes it easier to conduct interviews and provides a smoothness and polish to presentations that otherwise might be difficult to attain.

The interviewer needs to be on the lookout for guests' hidden agendas. (A hidden agenda is a list of objectives to be achieved that is different from objectives apparent or intended by the organizer of the event.) Handling forceful interviewees with hidden agendas can be a challenge. Having experienced these obstacles and having overcome them successfully also lends the interviewer confidence to handle any situation that might arise.

PREPARATION AND PLANNING

Can you brashly proceed to stick a microphone in someone's face and get a *good* interview? Probably not. In a rapidly developing news situation, it may be possible to get a few brief responses for color or human interest in your story, but certainly this is not an interview. Man-on-the-street "interviews" often tend to be nothing much more than an exchange of ignorance. However, sometimes answers from a large number of respondents can be judiciously edited to create a meaningful sequence.

"Be prepared" should be the watchword of the interviewer. Being ready for all contingencies requires careful research and planning.

Purpose

One of the first things to consider is, "What is the purpose of this interview?" Is it intended to be a humorous interlude or a "chatty" get-acquainted session? Are you seeking the considered judgment of an elder statesman? Perhaps the person has an exciting experience to relate. Maybe the person being interviewed has a storehouse of factual information that the world is waiting to hear.

The possible purposes of an interview, then, are to entertain, to acquaint, to persuade, or to provide insight. . .perhaps all four.

The use to which the interview is to be put can be an important factor in determining what questions will be asked and how. *Larry King Live* or a Barbara Walters special will necessarily differ from an interview for a documentary or for a news sound bite, and preparation will vary as well.

Especially for extended interviews, it is well to know as much as possible

[handwritten margin notes: Needs to usually so follow up lead Answers to reaterational queries]

about the interviewee and the topic so that as interviewer you can ask intelligent, relevant questions, and can follow up answers with additional probing queries.

If the interview is for television, it is possible that the presence of the camera may influence the response of guests, who are concerned with how they look. The camera or a microphone can make some guests restrained and unwilling to talk freely. For others, the effect can be quite the opposite. The person now has a visible platform from which to proclaim the "truth" as he or she sees it. For this reason it may be important to have researched your interviewees to find out their attitudes. *[handwritten: Find out Attitudes of Interview]*

The Situation

Where and under what circumstances the interview takes place may make your job as interviewer vary considerably. At a news conference, for example, you may or may not ask questions. Many times reporters try to pull news conference principals aside to ask slightly different questions so that their station has material that differs from the competition. Obviously, this is not always possible. If you've seen presidential news conferences on TV, you know that the questions are solicited from a variety of reporters and that usually no one can expect to have an exclusive story from the president. (This has not always been true. President John Kennedy, for instance, entertained individual reporters and "made a fetish of giving exclusive interviews."[1])

When you are reporting live from the scene of a news event, the on-the-scene interview has an urgency to it that often makes for exciting journalism. A remote broadcast interview may keep audience members on the edge of their chairs, or it may be boring. Probably, it is somewhere in between. The interviewees often reveal their winning strategy, their potential in upcoming events, or their insights into what the competition is doing that makes them superior. Some live reports, on the other hand, are not only mundane, but painfully obvious. If the person to be interviewed has nothing to say other than what is already easily seen, it is probably better left unsaid. Asking the proper questions often means the difference between an interesting response and one that is woefully boring.

A Matter of Taste

[handwritten margin notes: Poor Interviewing Question]

Of importance to consider also is the type of event being covered. If it is a tragic event, rules of good taste should be considered in the coverage. Asking the mother of an auto crash victim, "How does it feel to see your daughter smashed under the wheels of a truck?" might be classified under "cruel and unusual punishment." Certainly, it is in bad taste. At times it appears that a reporter or producer is trying to get an interviewee who will break down in tears for the "human interest" value. . .obviously also a matter of poor taste. If "capturing

---

[1] William L. Rivers, et al., *The Mass Media and Modern Society* (San Francisco: Rinehart Press, 1971), p. 134.

moments'' is one of television's strong points—and it is—try to be sure that the moments you help capture are in good taste.

Choosing the Interviewee

Sustaining an interview show can be a constant challenge. On the national scene, such hosts as Phil Donahue, Oprah Winfrey, and Sally Jessy Raphael have staffs that do nothing but line up guests. News shows too are constantly looking for experts on topics of the day. With news shows like *Nightline,* it can be particularly difficult for the interview booker when late-breaking events may cause a change in the show's nightly topic. Most topics on *60 Minutes* or *CBS Sunday Morning* have less demanding deadlines, though obviously they also use the interviewing technique.

Interview television shows abound: from the early-morning *Good Morning America,* to *Geraldo,* to the *Tonight Show, Arsenio Hall,* and *David Letterman,* and more all the time. Such shows need bodies with personalities attached, as do their competitors. Most shows offer transportation and a minimum $200 fee, though *Geraldo* has been said to have given up to $1,000 for a guest appearance. In spite of what they might say, there is competition to land the most desirable guests.

The television interview is also increasingly important on the local level. In-studio local interview programming is increasingly found on cable access stations and low-power television stations. Regular local broadcast television stations find that they can now do interviews more readily at a distance. Satellite technology makes it possible for a local angle on distant events such as national political conventions, where local delegates can be interviewed, thereby giving a local flavor to these events. No longer is interviewing on the national scene left exclusively to the networks. Interviewing by local stations is becoming more prevalent as technology makes more things possible.

Radio shows also draw large audiences and important guests. When the *Larry King Show* on the Mutual Radio Network was first presented nationwide from Washington, D. C. (and before additional phone company equipment was installed to handle the demand), there were so many callers to this middle-of-the-night show that phone service in the 301 area code completely broke down more than once. This area code includes the Pentagon and the CIA![2]

Most celebrities can just about choose the shows they want to appear on. Usually politicians choose the shows with the highest ratings.[3] Other celebrities may pick the show or host they prefer without considering the ratings. Often there is a quid pro quo (something in exchange for something), a special extra mention of the star's latest picture, for example, in exchange for the star's ''witty'' conversation.

Radio has networks devoted exclusively to talk shows. These shows often include a studio guest who is interviewed or call-in participants who may also ask

[2] Larry King with Emily Yoffe, *Larry King,* p. 60.
[3] Ron Givens, ''Talking People into Talking,'' *Newsweek,* July 17, 1989, pp. 44–45.

Figure 8–1 Telephone interviews on radio are a
Larry King forte.

(or be asked) appropriate questions. *Car Talk* hosts Click and Clack, the Tappit
Brothers (on PBS), are like the *Tonight Show* hosts in that they do their own
comedy bits to keep the audience interested. If the car talk of Click and Clack or
the private lives of *Tonight Show* guests are not really relevant for most listeners,
the one-liners the interview hosts insert and (often) the innuendo of their retorts
keep listeners amused. These interview shows tend to feature the interviewers
much of the time rather than the person being interviewed.

Local radio and TV also find the interview show relatively inexpensive to
produce. Thus, local issues and local celebrities make not only the 6 o'clock news,
but may also be the prime ingredients in early-morning, daytime, or late-night talk
shows.

Figure 8–2 Click and Clack, the Tappit brothers,
feature their own brand of humor on
NPR.

[handwritten margin notes:] T.V. focus straight on ——. T.V. not often things in the room.

Interview talk shows on radio may not have the highest ratings, but people who tune them in are concerned citizens who are "listening," unlike a general audience that is just "hearing" programming. Talk show hosts such as Rush Limbaugh and Bruce Williams draw large, involved crowds when they make personal appearances around the country. Music programming, in contrast, may be the background to whatever else a listener may be doing or thinking about. (This is why most radio ads need to be somewhat redundant and often feature shouting, hard-sell "personalities.") Many advertisers believe that interview show listeners are already tuned-in and listening, so they can treat the audience like intelligent human beings.

It should be apparent, then, that interviewing skills are increasingly in demand and that most radio or TV personalities will find that they will be called on at some time to do interviewing.

[handwritten margin notes:] Radio is secondary activity

Interviewee Criteria

What kinds of people make the most desirable interviewees? Obviously, it depends on the show, but what the interviewees have to say needs to be of interest or be entertaining to the audience. Things to look for in guests are celebrity, authoritative knowledge, personality, accomplishment, involvement in an unusual event, an impressive sense of humor, or an ability to entertain. If the guest can combine several of these attributes, the show has that much better a chance of sustaining audience interest.

A dee-jay may want to interview a known star with a new album or a hit single. It is probable that this star will be available if the dee-jay's show has high ratings and is in a major market (or is syndicated in several markets), because extensive exposure of the star and the music sells records. On the other hand, a new record release by a little-known performer may make this would-be star available for interviews to dee-jays in many more markets than is the star whose celebrity status gets him interviewed on *Entertainment Tonight* or the *Today* show.

News shows, of course, prefer to interview the principals (the people involved) in a news story, or family members, close friends, or recognized authorities on the subject of the news story. Also possible are others familiar with the event or less-known authoritative individuals (perhaps from the local area) who may have credibility because of previous similar experiences or other familiarity with the event. *[handwritten: Individuals tied directly to event useful.]*

Depending on the general appeal of the topic and the person's celebrity status, authors of new books often make "the tour" from talk show to talk show and city to city to get themselves and their books before the public.

Similarly, stars of just-released movies find their studios lining up guest spots for them on popular interview shows.

Professional team and college sports information directors may circulate the telephone number of the football or basketball team's coach for possible telephone interviews. Others offer a toll-free hot line with recorded comments by the coach ready to be recorded and inserted into sportscasts. Sometimes the local sportscaster can formulate questions that the coach appears to answer with his recorded comments.

On television, the in-person, on-the-spot, or in-studio interview is standard. An alternative is putting the interviewee in a studio in another city and interviewing him or her via satellite. Television demands pictures. In television the telephone interview is usually limited to low-budget news operations or to foreign coverage where TV satellite pictures are not available.

Local Interviewees

What should you look for in a guest for a local talk show or newscast? Celebrity status often is an important criterion here too, but your first consideration probably should be knowledge of the topic and ability to provide the needed information. Thus, the person should be not only knowledgeable, but able to communicate readily as well. These characteristics, along with the host's introduction and respect, can ensure the guest's credibility. A sense of humor is often an added bonus that can help keep the audience interested in an extended talk situation.

The person's time availability to do the interview must also be considered, especially on a talk show. Can you make the interview situation so rewarding (usually with prestige or recognition) that the person will want to take the time

Humor often an important element in long Interview.

Figure 8–3 Local shows often feature local interviews.

to be your guest? News and talk show interviewees usually will fit into these categories:

1. the principals involved in news stories or members of their families,
2. the witness of a newsworthy event or other persons with firsthand information about it,
3. the author of a new book that gives firsthand information and/or has been thoroughly researched,
4. college professors who teach in an area related to the topic,
5. a present or former elected official with responsibility in the topic area,
6. a practitioner or former practitioner; e.g., a lawyer, doctor, union official, auto mechanic, or anyone who might be considered knowledgeable because of experience in the field,
7. a president or past president of a local organization with interest in the area under discussion; a corporate representative (if a corporation is involved), preferably a corporate officer or manager, rather than a public relations person; other organizations that might supply appropriate personnel might include the Chamber of Commerce, Boy Scouts, City Council, United Way, farmers' co-op, etc.,
8. a performer or songwriter who has new material released (it might also be an anniversary or other landmark occasion relating to some of his works or works he respects),
9. the star, producer, or director of a new show or film, and
10. politicians who specialize in the desired topic area or represent a local constituency.

Before you make a selection of an interviewee on a controversial issue, preliminary research should reveal the person's known biases. (Two interviewees with opposing views make for an interesting show.) A person's reputation for exaggeration or complete honesty should also be considered. (If the prospect tends to misquote data, the interviewer needs to be prepared with the "facts.") Most people like the idea of being a radio or TV guest, but this is not a given. Thus, "Could you spare the time for an on-the-air appearance?" needs to be one of the first questions you ask on your initial contact seeking interviewees. Also important is the possible guest's schedule in relation to your scheduled air-time or deadline. You may have to settle for an on-the-spot interview rather than a studio appearance. With a documentary or news, this may actually be more desirable because it surrounds the authority with his or her own environment.

Research

The good interviewer needs to know enough of the background of the person to be interviewed to ask questions that relate to the interviewee's experience in relation to the topic to be discussed.

There are at least five major research avenues you can consider:

1. Get a résumé of the person to be interviewed. Most professional people will have an up-to-date résumé ready for such requests.
2. Ask questions of the person's colleagues and associates. Insights that otherwise

might be overlooked can often be gleaned from those who work with the interviewee every day.

3. Newspaper archives can be helpful. If the person has been in the news, newspaper indexes can reveal the public personage.

4. References to persons of national repute can usually be found in *Who's Who in America* or similar types of reference works. Many professions and geographic areas also have specialized listings of important people. Some people may be listed in more than one source.

5. The computer search invokes technology to search databases of various kinds. At least two kinds of searches are most often appropriate: one of the news media (Lexis and Nexis databases (where available) and one or more of the other library data sources.

The more you know about your interviewee, the better you are able to ask informed questions. Typically, it is well to know most of the kinds of things that appear on a résumé: essentially a person's accomplishments. The résumé may not indicate a person's hobbies or vested interests and biases, however. These too are important and probably can be found only by asking people who know the interviewee.

In addition to being fully informed on the interviewee, you also need to fully explore the topic of the interview. Only if you have been covering this particular issue for an extended period of time (and are yourself an expert) can you forgo this vital part of your homework.

Students sometimes make the excuse that they are conducting an interview representing the public, and so should come to the interview with no more knowledge than that of the average citizen. Nothing could be more incorrect. To ask intelligent questions, it is essential that you have a solid grasp of the topic and an understanding of your guest's background.

The types of things you need to know about the topic include:

1. The history of the topic, from previous important events to its current status.

2. The arguments usually offered both for and against various aspects of the topic.

3. The subtleties of the topic. Be wary of oversimplification—trying to distill topics to the "pure and simple." Restating an old Oscar Wilde aphorism, important topics are "seldom pure and never simple."

4. The leaders or advocates of the topic. At the local level one needs to know the local, regional, national, and, perhaps, international players in the topic's unfolding.

Most national programming organizations for whom an interviewer might work have researchers to do much of the digging out of data. At the local level, the responsibility may be up to you as interviewer. (See also research methods suggested for ad libbing in Chapter 5.)

The Questions

Do you prepare questions ahead of time? Absolutely. Do you necessarily ask all of the questions you have prepared or in the order in which you had intended to use them? Absolutely *not*.

build up questions slow

In a one-on-one interview you will want to ask easy questions first to build confidence in the interviewee and to give your listeners important background material. Gradually, you may increase the probing and confrontational quality of the questions if it is appropriate. A confrontational first question in some cases could end the interview before it really gets started if your respondent feels forced to "stonewall" or simply "take a walk." *—it not my result in "STONE WALL"*

If the interviewee is one of several who are being interviewed simultaneously and "live," the questioning may be of a probing nature from the start. In such a case (as on the PBS *MacNeil-Lehrer Report* or ABC's *Nightline*) the audience usually has been given background information before the questioning begins.

Chances are you will begin with one of your prepared questions. Remember:

1. Questions need to be concise and to the point.
2. Questions should come one at a time. Multiple-part questions can confuse not only the interviewee, but the audience as well. After all, the listener is the one for whom this exercise is being performed.
3. Try to avoid opinionated questions, those favoring either the position of the interviewee or those of his opponents (though it may be necessary to state an opponent's arguments in order to get specific points refuted).
4. If there seem to be several options as to the solution to a problem, try to make your listing of the options fair. Alert interviewees will correct you if you fail to fairly list the alternatives they favor, perhaps lessening your credibility.

Broadly speaking, there are only two types of questions: open and closed. Other types of questions are one of these types as well.

1. An *open question* is a question or a probe that cannot be answered intelligently with a single word or short phrase. It demands at least a sentence-length explanation.
2. A *closed question* can be answered easily with a single word or phrase. Alert interviewees will not let themselves be tricked by closed questions that force a "yes" or "no" answer where there are really more than two alternatives, or where either "yes" or "no" fails to thoroughly explain their position and puts them in a no-win situation. (See *leading questions*.)

In general, open questions are to be preferred because the interviewee is doing most of the talking with open questions. Your guest is there to explain one side of the question, not to confirm or deny the interviewer's concept of the topic. With closed questions, the interviewer spends most of the time framing the question and the not-very-talkative guest may respond with a single word. For example:

INTERVIEWER: I understand you've been in the United States for about a year.

How do you like it?

INTERVIEWEE: Fine.

INTERVIEWER: Have you had trouble adjusting to the American culture and American English?

INTERVIEWEE: Not really.

You can see that the interviewer has done his homework, but who is doing the talking? Not the guest. How much better the conversation would be with these questions phrased as open questions or statements of inquiry:

INTERVIEWER: Tell us about your first year in the United States.

INTERVIEWEE: It's been an exciting experience. I've been in . . . .

INTERVIEWER: Can you give us some examples of how life in the United States differs from . . . ?

INTERVIEWEE: The first thing I noticed was . . . .

A key to asking open questions is to start with a phrase such as:

- "How do you think . . . "
- "What is your opinion of . . . "

A *statement of inquiry* is one of the best ways to get an extended response. Though a statement of inquiry is a request for information that is not really a question, it obviously requires more than a single-word response. The most commonly used statement of inquiry is:

- "Tell me about . . . "

The tell-me-about technique is a favorite of Barbara Walters. Next time you see her do an interview, note how many times she uses this phrasing.
Closed question examples might be:

- "How long have you lived in . . . ?"
- "How old are you?"
- "Who is your favorite candidate in the . . . race ?"
- "Do you enjoy your work as . . . ?"
- "How are you?"

The last one is normally considered a closed question. The expected answer is "Fine." Probably only hypochondriacs would take the opportunity to relate all of their ills and make it into an open question.

It is true, of course, that open questions can be used by interviewees to go on at length on their favorite topic, telling much more than was asked for. (See "Controlling the Interview" near the end of this chapter.)

As we look at the interview process, we can see other question types that can be identified.

Follow - up Question

- The *follow-up question* is used by the interviewer to ask the respondent to elaborate on a previously discussed point by asking a clarifying question. This question may not have been on your prepared list.

To ask good follow-up questions, the interviewer must constantly *listen* to answers being made to the questions posed. There is a tendency to want to be mentally framing the next question. This can occupy the interviewer's mind to such an extent that there is little or no listening taking place. Listen. Your guest may be answering the next question or another question on your list. It is, of course, logical not to ask a question that has already been answered, though you've probably seen it done on national television by experienced interviewers who know better. This embarrasses not only the interviewer and the interviewee (who must repeat what he or she just said), but it embarrasses the alert segment of the audience as well.

- The *probing question* asks for specifics in such a way that the answer might incriminate respondents or get them ro reveal a secret.
- The *leading* or *loaded question* not only incriminates respondents but assumes their guilt. A favorite example: "Answer yes or no. Have you quit beating your wife?"
- The *catch-all question* is often used to complete an interview. Essentially it asks, "Is there anything more you have to say?" This is not only the fair thing to do, but is a way to maintain the good will of your guests. You may want this guest back at some future date. Nothing can be much more frustrating to interviewees than to have the message they wish to convey completely missed in the questioning and not have at least a quick chance to explain what they see as an important point. Have you mentioned the name of the author's book more than once and explained its content clearly? Did the star's movie get the mention intended? Did the guest get a chance to explain how listeners can contribute to the current United Way drive?

THE INTERVIEWEE'S NEED TO KNOW

Your guest has agreed to appear in your production. Be sure that he or she is fully aware of the circumstances of the interview.

- You've advised your interviewees of the *topic* so that important data is at their fingertips.
- A mutually agreed-upon *time and place* have been set.

- You have advised the interviewee *how long the interview is expected to be* and whether it is *live or taped*.
- You have explained *how the interview is to be used:* for a documentary, as a news insert, or as an extended feature.
- You have indicated to the guest *whether others are being interviewed* at the same time or as part of a documentary on the same topic.
- The interviewee has been advised as to *who the expected audience is to be* and the *expected coverage area*.

Not only is it courteous to advise interviewees of these circumstances, but it should make for a better interview and a better program.

Preliminaries

Before a TV remote interview, it is important that you scout the location to determine any modifications that might be needed to be made to get camera angles and to ensure proper lighting. If the interview is on the guest's home turf and you need to rearrange the furniture, draw the curtains, or set lights, be sure you advise your interviewee, and allow sufficient time for this setting up.

Consider Your Guest

You've set a specific time for the interview. Be on time. Your guest's time is valuable, and most people dislike having to wait. It is not only polite to be prompt, it shows your respect for the person who has taken time and agreed to serve as your interviewee.

If you have not previously gotten acquainted with the person to be interviewed, some small talk is appropriate. Your research may have revealed a hobby or civic activity that can be talked about to show your interest in the person as a *person*. To break the ice, talk about some of the special interests of your interview guest. If nothing else seems to present itself for discussion, you can always fall back on the weather. As you start the interview, and before you get into the questions, be sure to thank your guest for his or her time and willingness to appear on the program.

Consider Your Listeners

Proceed with your questions. Listen carefully to all that is said so that you are not asking questions already answered and so that you can *paraphrase* key ideas for your audience. Especially after long explanations or particularly complicated ideas have been expressed, try to paraphrase the basic ideas for your listeners and be sure that both you and the listeners fully understand.

Identify your guest and his or her expertise frequently during the interview so that those joining the show late can be enticed to keep listening. A periodic, very brief summary of what has transpired on the program can also be helpful to the latecoming audience. On TV, superimposing the guest's name and title may be sufficient to inform the viewers who join the show late. Be sure that your director has the name spelled correctly and that the person's title is ready to be slipped in from the character generator when appropriate. The name needs to be held long enough (at least 15 seconds) for viewers only partly watching to catch it.

Right along with listening to the person you are interviewing comes *responding*. Often your response as interviewer will merely be a nodding of the head to acknowledge that you understand. Repeating such phrases as "I see" without variation can get annoying to the audience. Change your phrase of confirmation if you think you need to respond verbally. Phrases such as "Tell me more" can help break a pattern.

Another helpful phrase is:

"Did I understand you to say . . . ?"

followed by succinctly paraphrasing the concept just expressed. Do not make it difficult to follow the interview. When your audience does not understand, they usually change stations. This is not a good way to build ratings.

Controlling the Interview

You should have a plan for your interview, providing background for your listeners, knowing where you want the discussion to go, and knowing how you intend to get there. Be sure that your guest *answers your questions*. Some guests will have planned ahead what they want to say, and they will give these prepared answers no matter what questions are asked. These people need to be pinned down to answer *your* questions. Again, it is essential that you *listen* to be sure that your questions are indeed being answered. If the guest is tending to ramble off into areas you do not want to get into, or launches into a subject ahead of time (before you have laid a foundation for it), try asking a series of closed questions. This sometimes can act as a damper on overzealous respondents. At other times, the zealot must be interrupted as politely as possible, perhaps by explaining the lack of background of the listeners, perhaps with the reference to an upcoming commercial break, or with an emphasis on the extreme time limitation for the interview.

Responding

If the answers you receive are legitimate but different from what you expected, your plan may change as you proceed. It was suggested at the beginning of this chapter that an interview might have several functions. It is possible that not only the plan of the interview but the function may change as well while it is in progress. If you as an interviewer consciously make this decision, that is fine. But do not let the interviewee make that choice for you. Keep in control at all times. If you have multiple guests and they get into a shouting match, it is up to you to be fair in allocating time equally on a question. Fairness is important in helping to keep a diverse audience.

When you have finished, be sure to thank your guest a second time. Remember, this person is doing you a favor, and it is important to be appreciative.

You need to be psychologically prepared for your interview. As in any other kind of announcing, it is important that you do your homework. Don't let a big name overwhelm you. After all, you are a celebrity too, at least in your local area.

Interviewing may be an art, but there are skills that can be learned to create a professional product of which you can be proud. The following books can serve as useful reference material:

Robert McLeish *The Technique of Radio Production,* 2nd ed. (London: Focal Press, 1988); and

Charles J. Stewart and William B. Cash, Jr. *Interviewing Principles and Practices,* 4th ed. (Dubuque, Iowa: Wm. C. Brown Publishers, 1988).

EXERCISES

1. Do an interview on your audio tape with another student in the class on a topic of his or her choice: a hobby, a hometown, this school, a vacation trip, etc. Limit the interview to five minutes. Follow the format below to demonstrate your ability to use the question types described. Make sure that you understand the question types and the format before proceeding with the interview. Turn in the tape as part of your regular taped assignment, as noted below.

INTERVIEW FORMAT FOR TAPED INTERVIEW

OBJECTIVE:

TOPIC:

THREE MAIN POINTS: 1.

                     2.

                     3.

1. GETTING ACQUAINTED (open or closed questions, probably about the weather).

2. THANK YOU STATEMENT.

3. STATEMENT OF INQUIRY. "Tell me about . . . ." (open question)

4. STATEMENT OF INQUIRY. "Tell me also about . . . ." (open question)

5. RECAPITULATE the first main point. "Did I understand you to say . . . ?" (closed question)

   6. SECOND MAIN POINT. "Why do (does) . . . ?" (open question)

   7. FOLLOW-UP QUESTION on second main point. (open or closed question)

   8. RESTATEMENT of second main point. (closed question)

   9. THIRD MAIN POINT; e.g., "How do you feel about . . . ?" (open question)

  10. SUMMARIZE third point and RESTATE points 1 and 2 (closed question).

  11. CATCH-ALL QUESTION. "Is there anything more . . . ?" (open question)

  12. CONCLUDING STATEMENT. "Thank you . . . ."

2. Follow the instructions for studying word lists as suggested previously, doing word lists 8-A and 8-B. Be prepared to pronounce the words correctly, write the correct phonetic transcriptions when tested, and define the words when used in a sentence.

3. Read your marked copy for word lists following this chapter onto your cassette tape. You may also reread paragraphs from the previous four word lists to review. Hand your tape in for evaluation.

4. Read this chapter's copy, doing the best you possibly can, or until you have read for 50 minutes. Put the interview described in exercise 1 and the oral questions of exercise 6 on the end of your hour tape.

5. Select a topic of current interest. Then select a person (such as the mayor, senator, professor, or other authority) with whom you might do an interview on that topic. Get the approval of your instructor on both topic and prospective interviewee. Research the topic in the library. Get information on the four types of things you need to know about the topic as listed in the chapter. Use research tools suggested in the chapter and previous chapters. Research the person. Get as much of the information on the following outline as possible. You will be asked to hand in the outline of your library research as well as the information sheet on your interviewee.

INTERVIEWEE INFORMATION

Interview Topic

Interview Purpose

Interviewee Name

Title	Age	Place of Birth

Education

Hobbies

Vested Interests (coporate ownerships, family holdings, etc.)

Other Areas of Expertise

History of Experience with the Interview Topic

Recent Actions in Respect to the Interview Topic (if any)

6. Record the following interview outline (doing your side of the interview only) onto your cassette tape. Use the information developed in exercise 5.

INTERVIEW OUTLINE

OPENING

      self-introduction

      informal conversation (if appropriate)

      topic preview

      interview plan briefing

      expression of appreciation

BODY

      background

      planned questions

      open questions

      appropriate closed questions

      follow-up questions

      repeat obscure explanations, or

      amplify unusual ideas, or

      paraphrase involved concepts

      additional factual questions

      catch-all questions

CLOSE

      review and summarize

      future projection of topic concepts

      pleasantries

      thank you

BROADCAST VOCABULARY WORD LIST   Unit 8-A

1. repatriate (v)—to bring or send a person back to his or her own country

    ————————————————   *ree pay' tree ayt*

2. repertory (n)—a theatrical company that performs a schedule of several plays; or a repertoire of such a company

_____   *rep'   er   tor   ee*

3. repertoire (n)—songs, plays, etc., that a performer or group is ready to do

_____   *rep'   ur   twar*

4. repercussion (n)—an effect or result of some event

_____   *ree   pur   kush'   un*

5. reprisal (n)—retaliation against an enemy for injuries received

_____   *re   prighz'   ul*

6. reprise (n)—in music, a return to the first theme, a repetition of an idea

_____   *ree   preez'*

7. repudiate (v)—to cast off or disown; reject as having no authority

_____   *ree   pyew'   dee   ayt*

8. reputable (adj)—held to be honorable, responsible

_____   *rep'   yew   tu   bul*

9. rescind (v)—to invalidate by a higher authority; annul; revoke

_____   *re   sind'*

10. wreak (v)—to inflict or execute punishment or vengeance

_____   *reek*

11. realtor (n)—a person in the real estate business and member of the National Association of Real Estate Boards

_____   *ree'   ul   tur*

12. realty (n)—landed property; real estate

_____   *ree'   ul   tee*

13. rapport (n)—a harmonious relationship

_____   *ru   por'*

14. rapprochement (n)—reestablishment of harmonious relations, as between two countries

_____   *rau   prohsh   mau(n)'*

15. asterisk (n)—a star-like design inserted to indicate a footnote or an omission.

_____   *as'   tur   isk*

16. encore (n)—a demand, as by applause, for repetition of a song or act

————————————   *on' kor*

17. hirsute (adj)—hairy; covered with hair

————————————   *hur' sewt* or *hur sewt'*

18. xenophobic (adj)—suspicious of foreigners

————————————   *zee noh foh' bik*

19. ptomaine (n)—poison in spoiled food

————————————   *toh' mayn*

20. beret (n)—a soft, brimless hat

————————————   *bu ray'*

BROADCAST VOCABULARY WORD LIST   Unit 8-B

1. disputatious (adj)—argumentative; contentious

————————————   *dis pyew tay' shus*

2. diva (n)—a distinguished female singer; a prima donna

————————————   *dee' vu*

3. docile (adj)—easily managed; tractable

————————————   *dau' sul*

4. drowned (past tense) (v)—suffocated by immersion in water or other liquid

————————————   *drownd*

5. ebullient (adj)—overflowing with fervor, enthusiasm, or excitement

————————————   *ee bul' yunt*

6. eccentric (adj) or (n)—deviating from the customary character or practice; irregular; or a person of this type

————————————   *ek sen' trik*

7. echelon (n)—a level of command, authority, or rank

————————————   *esh' u lon*

8. ecstasy (n)—an overpowering emotion or exaltation; rapturous delight

————————————   *eks' tu see*

9. effervescent (adj)—bubbling; gay; lively

_____ *ef er ves' unt*

10. efficacy (n)—the capacity for producing a desired effect; effectiveness

_____ *ef' i ku see*

11. electoral (adj)—pertaining to electors or election

_____ *e lek' tur ul*

12. elixir (n)—a panacea; a cure-all

_____ *e liks' ur*

13. emaciated (adj)—made thin by a wasting away of the flesh

_____ *i may' shee ayt*

14. emeritus (adj)—retired from active duty but retained on the rolls

_____ *ee mer' i tus*

15. eulogy (n)—a speech or writing in praise of a dead person

_____ *yew' lu jee*

16. ruse (n)—a deceptive action or device

_____ *rews*

17. ecstatic (adj)—a feeling of elation or rapture

_____ *ek stat' ik*

18. arbitrageur (n)—a trader who profits from price discrepancies in different stock or
   commodity markets

_____ *aur bi trauzh ewr'*

19. anathema (n)—a curse or denunciation, or one cursed or reviled

_____ *u nath' u mu*

20. vacillate (v)—to change from one belief to another, waver

_____ *vas' u layt*

WORD LIST PARAGRAPH   Unit 8-A

To repatriate the realtor seemed apropos. He had, after all, established rapport with the hirsute kidnappers and exchanged realty for the actors held hostage. One of the repercussions was that the country's repertory company had been able to perform neither an encore production nor its repertoire. Rather than to wreak vengeance on the xenophobic hostage holders, and to attempt to establish rapprochement with the outlaw nation, the reputable realtor declared it preferable to rescind the treaty that had prevented ptomaine yet had caused a reprisal. The legislature could not repudiate the deed, for the population wanted respite and continued the reprise for peace.

WORD LIST PARAGRAPH   Unit 8-B

The disputatious diva was ebullient over her plan to build a new opera house though the rest of the company seemed to vacillate over the proposal. In order to keep the diva at least slightly docile, the higher-echelon personnel of the company feigned ecstasy at the mention of the eccentric singer's proposal. An arbitrageur had promised some financing, but the anathema remained.

An emaciated ingenue prepared an effervescent elixir to make the diva forget her plan. The efficacy of the ruse was greater than anticipated. The diva found the elixir so ecstatic that she drowned her ambitions in the elixir, and a eulogy by reviewers for the star was the result. The electoral response to the whole affair was the voting of the diva to an emeritus position with the opera company.

9

The Sportscaster

OBJECTIVES
Upon completion of this chapter the student should be able to:

1. Describe five types of sportscasting a radio or TV sports announcer might engage in.
2. Know how best to rapidly get a team's background.
3. Explain five distinctive types of things sportscasters can do before each game to properly prepare themselves to participate in a play-by-play broadcast.
4. List requirements for a national network sports announcer and relevant areas of college study.
5. Explain the possible duties of a small- and medium-market sportscaster in radio or television.
6. List four situations where sports interviews might be important.
7. Describe the voice and language qualities expected of a sportscaster.
8. Explain three attitudes required for the consummate sportscaster.
9. List elements of play that need to be highlighted when doing play-by-play.
10. Explain three story elements that may need to be rewritten to make a newspaper story an effective broadcast piece.
11. Discuss microphone requirements for good play-by-play coverage.

The important factors in being a [sports] broadcaster are knowing the game, reporting it with enthusiasm, and being adaptable to situations that arise.[1]

THE SPORTSCASTER REGIMEN

So you want to be a sportscaster. . . . What does a sportscaster do? You've seen sportscasters on television and heard them on radio. The job consists of play-by-play announcing, providing color for a play-by-play event, interviewing sports figures, and reporting scores and results of athletic activities. These events may be local, national, and sometime international. At times a sportscaster may find it appropriate to engage in editorializing or informed discussion. Key skills include ad libbing, interviewing, and reading with a high energy level.

With the advent of cable, one can find several sporting events to watch almost any hour of the day or night. In addition to the national broadcasting and cable networks' transmission of sporting events, there are over a dozen regional cable sports networks as well as radio networks associated with every major college and professional sports team in the country.[2] Thirty or more sports channels can be projected as cable systems or direct broadcast satellites provide 150 or more television program options with the adoption of burgeoning video technologies.

Chances are that as a sportscaster you will be employed by a radio station, a television station, a network or other syndicating sports organization, or by a team itself. Most play-by-play reports are presented by two people, the actual play-by-play announcer and a color person.

The straight play-by-play announcer has a clearly defined role. Here Howard Cosell describes Keith Jackson's role during the first year of *Monday Night Football* on ABC:

> It was impressed on him time and again that he was to think of himself as a public-address announcer, slipping in and out, factually accurately, with the vital information—who made the tackle, who threw the ball, who caught the ball, how many yards were gained, what down it was.[3]

Though in television the picture tells much of the story and the announcer fills in the data and commentary, radio demands the same kind of information, but in the present tense—describing the action of the game as it is happening. Both need to provide the energy and enthusiasm that make games exciting. The sportscaster needs to get involved in the game enough to get his listeners involved as well. It is important, however, not to let emotions supersede good judgment. Derogatory

---

[1] Ken Coleman, *So You Want to Be a Sportscaster* (New York: Hawthorne Books, 1973), p. 7.
[2] Sandy Widener, "Rooting for the Home Team," *Continental Profiles*, August 1990, p. 38.
[3] Howard Cosell, *Cosell* (Chicago: Playboy Press, 1973), p. 310.

remarks about opposing players or teams, officials, or coaches need to be avoided, even if made "only in jest" or indirectly.

Play-by-play announcers need to keep their eyes on the ball in order to report the game. If radio sportscasters are faked out by a deceptive play, they should admit it to the listeners, some of whom may be watching on television or listening to their radios in the stands. The public address announcer in the background can also give away what really happened.

The color person does background on the teams and players, and describes the "color" of the game, the related game activities, and crowd behavior. (See also ad libbing, Chapter 5.) The color person also provides a second pair of eyes on controversial plays as well as educated insights and statistics about the game or previous encounters of the teams or players.

In football, other pairs of eyes may be provided by two spotters, usually one spotter for each team, and a statistician. Spotters' duties consist of pointing out names of players on a chart. In addition, they may pass notes to one of the sportscasters, perhaps identifying other local personnel, highlighting local traditions, and explaining any unusual aspects of the playing arena. The football statistician (as the name suggests) keeps track of such things as downs, yards from scrimmage, yards penalized, and the like. In addition to quarterly statistics, the statistician can be expected to pass notes to the play-by-play announcer or color person regarding the game's progress statistically. Similarly in basketball, the statistician keeps track of fouls on each player, his or her scoring, foul shots, three-point baskets, etc. In baseball, the statistician should be able to report hits, scoring, runs batted in, players left on base, etc. Most sportscasters have forms they expect the statistician to fill out as the game progresses.

The five-person play-by-play crew is the ideal setup for football. Spotters and a statistician may also help complete your crew for other sports as well, though for basketball or hockey, where the game is particularly fast, their help may be limited.

Dedication

Perhaps in no other broadcast specialty is such devotion required, because the specialization requires constant updating and because the competition is intense. If you are the average rabid sports fan devouring every tidbit of information about your favorite stars, your favorite clubs, and their competition, you are only half-way toward the special dedication and preparation required, because you need to try to comprehend the entire sports scene if you are to be a broad-based sports reporter. Both over the long haul and each time you get ready for a game, careful and thorough preparation is required.

If preparation is important for the dee-jay before going on the air—and it is—it is doubly important for the sportscaster. Broadcasters need to try to get to a team practice if they can—to meet the players individually, so that players are recognized instantly, and so that the sportscaster has a feel for the athletes' performance styles. The well-prepared sportscaster also memorizes the names and numbers of team members (both sides) when preparing for play-by-play. In basketball, where the announcers may be close to the action, it is suggested that in addition to the number, sportscasters note a physical characteristic unique to each team member, so that if the player's number is partially covered, he or she can still be readily identified.

You need to know both teams' histories, especially their records against each other. Obviously, you also need to know the current status of each. Probably the fastest way to learn the facts is to talk to the team publicity people and the coaches. At the top of the college publicity team is the sports information director (SID). Members of a team's publicity organization are usually readily available to radio or television talent who cover their games. The sports information people's primary purpose is to provide current data and statistics that the sportscaster can use. Studying this material can be important in helping sports announcers thoroughly prepare for their assignments.

Education

You need to know sports. You need to read about sports, listen to sports, view sports, and participate in sports. You probably need to be a sports addict to do a good job. In most phases of broadcasting, you can sometimes "fake" it by reading a script in a knowledgeable manner. This is not usually true in sports. Sportscasters need to "eat and breathe" the various activities they cover.

Today's sportscasters are expected to perform as if they have a college education. Unless you are a sports celebrity in your own right, a college degree is something you can expect employers to require. Obviously, a college degree requires more than sports participation or study. There may be courses in the coaching and physical education departments at your school. Of course, announcing, ad libbing, and interview skills, as discussed earlier, are basic. Perhaps most critical, however, is a broad educational background.

The good sportscaster needs the skills and understanding gained in courses in statistics, sociology, vocabulary, and psychology. (Is sports psychology available at your school?) Also of importance may be political science, history, law, and biology. (A sports medicine course would be right to the point.) An ability to use a foreign language (especially Spanish) may well be an extremely important skill as more Hispanics join the sports scene. As with authorities in any field, successful sportscasters need a wide understanding of the world around them so that they can relate the day's sportscast to society's broader problems and needs.

A SPORTSCASTER'S DUTIES

The duties of sportscasters vary with the size of the market, the size of the station, whether it is radio or TV, and the particular sports emphasis a station may wish to project.

Radio

At the small radio station the sportscaster may be a jack-of-all-trades, and may be expected to be a master of several. Chances are that unless you yourself are a sports celebrity, you'll start your career in such a small station, doing high school play-by-play on the weekends and daily sports summaries mostly from the wire services. In addition, you may also serve in sales, programming, or news.

At a small station when a play-by-play announcer is first starting out doing high school ball, he or she may or may not have the luxury of a press box. The announcer may be on the roof of the stadium (if it has a roof), in the grandstand or bleachers, even (heaven forbid) slightly elevated on a vehicle in the end zone. Similarly, at the small town station other duties may preclude the sportscaster from a chance to get acquainted with team members or the teams' records and formations as a regular part of his or her paid duties. If you really want to do sports, and are in a small market, you may very well be spending some of your own time trying to prepare to do a reasonable job of calling a game.

If you work yourself up to a slightly larger market, and the radio station has a talk, news-talk, or flexible multi-faceted format, you could end up preparing a sports report as a segment of the news or even as a freestanding program. This may consist of little more than compiling scores from the news wires and running down scores of local high schools and other locally important scores. Sports editorializing is not a common occurrence except perhaps on a telephone call-in show, where the sportscaster is asked for an opinion on a specific sports topic or sports happening.

Interviewing (also discussed in Chapter 8) could be the focal point of a sports report show or be part of a news item on a newscast sports story. Almost always sportscasters doing local play-by-play try to get an appropriate guest for half-time in football, basketball, and many other sports, for rain delays, or between double-header games in baseball. Going back to the studio for musical fill, especially during half-time at a game, is a real "cop-out." In such an instance, listeners who may have started looking for the game late may think that it is not on at all.

As interviewees, coaches usually have much to say, though they may not always be available. Players also can make good guests, though they may be less at ease. A good technique to help players relax (particularly on television) is to get them to demonstrate something for you: how they hold the bat, the football, the basketball; a successful stance they use; or any similar, appropriate technique they use that might be of interest to fans or other players. The demonstration can get the nervous player's mind off of the camera and the mike to make for a more relaxed interview.

The use of good interview skills can also help put the players at ease. Your questions may range from opinions on today's game to "How did you get started in the game?," "Who has most influenced you in your career?," or "Tell us about your most exciting moment playing the game." If possible, give your guest a copy of most of the questions ahead of time so that he or she will have a chance to think about the answers. It is not only thoughtful on your part, but also makes for a better interview.

Some sportscasters build a file of newspaper or magazine clippings of feature stories or interviews with sports personalities they might interview some day. If these get used, fine. If they do not, busy sportscasters still have added to their knowledge of the game.

Where there is play-by-play, you can expect a color person as well. This may be your lot. If so, even more research and study may be required for you to do the kind of a job that will advance you to a larger market or to doing play-by-play.

Television

Another entrée to the sports job ladder may be as "flunky" at a television station. This type of job could develop from a sports internship through your college. The strength of union organization in the market may determine the number of different tasks you may be allowed to perform as an intern, but it is a foot in the door. Local television is much like local radio: the size of the market and the station's desired sports emphasis determine the sportscaster's role.

Commonly, the primary function of a local television sportscaster is to report for the news at 7 p.m. and 11 p.m. Eastern and Pacific times (6 p.m. and 10 p.m. Central and Mountain times). Included in these reports are interviews with local sports celebrities and national figures, if they should pay a visit to your town.

Above all, it is important to keep the ratings up. One of the requirements for a properly enthusiastic sports reporter is to understand that sports buffs are really in the minority. Studies show that as few as 15% of TV viewers watching the news are particularly interested in sports. One of the duties of the sportscaster, then, is to satisfy the sports fans without boring the other 85% of the audience.

This may be done with unusual action replays, play-of-the-day features, "Weenie of the Week" (Glenn Brenner, WUSA-TV, Washington, D.C.), or participation by the sportscaster himself in some of the sports he covers, which may include everything from fishing to auto racing.

One enthusiastic Midwestern sportscaster captivated his audience by personally participating in a different sport each week. He was a boxer, a basketball player, a wrestler, a golfer, and so on. He took some pretty hard knocks. When playing with the professionals and top amateurs in the area, he invariably lost. The audience could relate to this and consequently, his ratings soared. He soon was able to move to a larger market.

Play-by-play of local college sports often falls to an independent station in the market. It is possible that this station does not emphasize other local news, but a meet-the-coach (or coaches) show is usually part of the mix. Coaches are generally extremely easy to interview, but (as suggested in the interview section) it is important that the interviewer keep control of the session. Highlight video tapes of the previous week's game are an important component of the interview show, so the sportscaster in this instance may find it necessary to be able to edit video tape skillfully and to possess the skills necessary to put a complete show together.

The top rung of the sportscasting ladder tends to be reserved for the network sportscasters, who often present some of the most important games of the week, no matter which team is playing. Obviously, constant prepping is required to keep abreast of each team that may be on the schedule and to justify a sportscaster's top spot in the profession.

Most major league baseball clubs hire their own sportscasters who travel with the team. The pressure on this person to learn about new teams may not be quite so intense, yet obviously, this sportscaster spends much time in preparation as well. Here the advantage is being able to be in regular contact with team members and coaches. The need for constant preparation means that sportscasters must love their jobs, or they will soon burn out.

THE VOICE BEHIND THE MIKE

In radio, the voice is a *sine qua non* (an essential without which there is nothing). In television, pictures may be essential, but the voice is not far behind. As a sportscaster, your personality and stimulating voice are important keys to holding an audience (and thereby your job).

Voice Quality

A deep, sonorous bass voice probably never has been a sportscaster requirement. In fact, early sportscasters often were raucous and grating in their styles. Today, the sportscaster needs a strong voice to be able to sustain hours of talking. The voice needs to be well modulated for a similar reason: so that the fans will want to listen for hours and not be annoyed by an untrained presentation.

Language Use

Sportscasters need a good vocabulary with the right words to describe the action. They need to be able to use words to describe what they see and (on TV) what their audience is seeing. They need to develop expressions that are flexible, build suspense, and create the excitement of the game, as well as get from one play to the next. The sportscast becomes more interesting and even more entertaining if the announcer has a vibrant control of the language. Like any desirable trait, language use can be overblown, as some critics have accused Howard Cosell of doing.

Reading and Copy

If there is one thing that the exercises in this text are expected to do, it is to develop your reading skills so that a presentation sounds conversational even

Figure 9–1 Sportscaster looks over his script while tape is running. The blank blue background facilitates chroma key.

though the material is being read. To be sure, much of the presentation of the sportscaster is ad libbed. For a color person or a sports reporter, however, reading skills are paramount.

It has been pointed out that wire copy needs to be carefully scrutinized before it is used in an on-air presentation. Sports news releases from sports information offices may take the form of newspaper articles. Newspaper stories sometimes are done in a style resembling oral English; sometimes not.

The traditional newspaper story lead tries to put who, what, where, when, and why all in the first sentence. This can lead to extremely long and complicated sentences. Oral style calls for short sentences. Some simple editing by the sports-caster often can correct this problem. Sports stories may be expected to have a "beginning, a middle, and an end," much like a broadcast news story (Chapter 4) or a commercial (Chapter 6).

Also important is to whom certain facts or statements are attributed. Newspapers often put attributions at the end of the first sentence. This is called trailing attribution. This can lead to false impressions on the part of the listeners. For ease of audience understanding, attribution needs to come at the beginning of the information that is ascribed to another source. For instance, say:

Coach Brown says the team is looking fine.

rather than:

The team is looking fine, according to Coach Brown.

Many newspaper news releases start with a dateline (the name of the city where the story is written or the action has taken place). The dateline is seldom

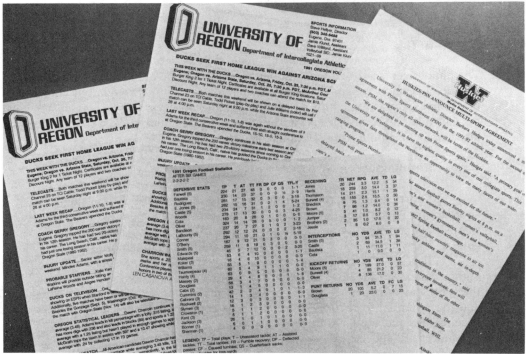

Figures 9–2 & 9–3 Publicists help by supplying data for athletic teams.

used by broadcasters. If the place is important but is not included in the lead, the sports news item that starts with the newspaper dateline "Los Angeles, California" can be started orally with "In Los Angeles, ..." Then the story can continue.

It is always important to use correct pronunciation to maintain credibility. This may be somewhat difficult for the novice sportscaster because of the many unusual names that sports figures seem to have. While wire copy may give pronunciations (sometimes incorrect), the copy often does not, and the sportscaster needs to *know*. If an announcer only does sports part-time, this may be a challenge. It is wise to make friends with other sports reporters in the area, so that you can ask them when questions arise as to the pronunciation of names. As with news, it is also good to listen to respected national announcers who report about personalities you may run across in your stories.

News releases intended for print may contain other extra data that will be confusing to the listener unless it is inserted as a separate sentence at another point in the story. For example, the story might say, "The game is being played in Arlington Stadium (41,284)." This last number, of course, is the seating capacity of the named ball park. This statistic may or may not be of particular importance to the story. It is probably up to you to decide when you are previewing the story whether you want to use that fact, and where in the story it will go if you do. Chances are that a good announcer will also round off the number to "41-thousand," or maybe even "more than 40-thousand," to simplify the information the listener is expected to assimilate.

ATTITUDE AND STYLE

The announcer's attitude is not something that can be hidden from the audience. The dedication of the sportscaster may not always show through, but you can bet that a negative attitude will be obvious to the observer. The sportscaster must display not only enthusiasm and confidence, but humility as well. All of these attributes contribute to the announcer's style.

Enthusiasm

Sports winners result from enthusiasm. If there is one quality that a sportscaster needs above all others, it is enthusiasm. Since enthusiasm is catching, this is an important way to hold an audience. As Marv Albert has said, "The genius of any broadcaster is to make even a quiet game exciting."[4]

It is true: not all games are exciting. How does the sportscaster sustain enthusiasm in the face of a dull game? It is not easy. Is it the job for an actor? No, the sportscaster is not acting. He or she is truly enamored of the game, the talent, and the potential for action. Here is where solid knowledge can help. Recalling other games and similar situations can help sustain that enthusiasm so essential to the successful sportscast.

[4] Steve Albert, "Introduction," in Marv Albert, *YESSS!* (New York: Signet, 1979), p. xv.

Confidence and Humility

In addition to being enthusiastic, sportscasters must display confidence and obviously be authorities on the game they call and the teams they call the game for. With the knowledge necessary to be an authority, it is difficult not to let confidence slip into egomania, but nothing is much more repulsive than announcers who revel in letting their audiences know how smart they think they are. If the announcer is truly knowledgeable, he or she has discovered that the more you learn, the more you discover you don't know—the key to humility.

Style combines the elements of knowledge and humility. It also includes how an announcer explains the action. Often, certain catch phrases will become part of a sportscaster's style. One Seattle baseball sportscaster in the 1940s had a distinctive way of using tone and voice pattern to proclaim, "It's a . . . double play." Fans were rooting for one of the teams to make a double play so that they could hear the verbal trademark. There are seldom many double plays in any game, so that trademark did not get overused. On the other hand, it is easy to fall into using the same expressions repeatedly to such an extent that they can grate on listeners' nerves. Be sure that the style you develop generates excitement without becoming even slightly obnoxious. Remember, no matter how good you've become in a job, you can always improve. And be warned: no matter how long you have been on a job, there is always somebody waiting to step in, somebody who thinks that he or she can do the job better than you can, and may get a chance to prove it.

Also, remember that it is just a game. The sun will rise tomorrow no matter who wins, or how good a job a sportscaster does in reporting a game. Remember too, fans tune in to hear the game . . . seldom to listen to the voice of the sportscaster.

Criticism

A direct result of egomania is second-guessing the officials, the players, and the coaches. Be careful of criticizing officials. Yes, call attention to what you may think is an error in judgment or a misperception of the action. Point it out. Explain it. Then, drop it. A constant harangue can be as annoying to most of your audience as any other too-often repeated phrase or concept.

Players, coaches, and officials are all doing what they think is right. The players and coaches want to win. The officials want to be correct. There is no conspiracy against anybody. It is just a game.

THE CHALLENGE OF RADIO

Since radio came first, many of the traditions of broadcasting sports originated with radio. Radio still presents an exciting challenge, allowing the announcer to create the proverbial "theatre of the mind." Sportscaster Marv Albert holds a particular affection for the power of radio in reporting basketball. He says:

I've always felt something special about broadcasting basketball, especially on radio. That's because in radio broadcasting of a basketball game the announcer is everything. He is the eyes and ears of his audience, which must depend on him totally to know what's going on. And, because of the geography of the court, the game can be captured so well. Frontcourt, backcourt, left corner, right corner, circle, key, or lane. Those are all places on the court, part of the map the broadcaster uses to describe the location of the ball.

With basketball, I feel the most important quality for a broadcaster to have is consistency. The listeners get to know the consistency of the call, and they can follow the game because they know the geography.[5]

Albert also likes to give the score after each basket. This is especially important, many think, on radio. Watching in person or on television, you can observe the scoreboard or see the score flashed on the screen. With certain TV directors who do not insert the score on a regular basis, the TV sportscaster may want to insert the score after every basket. In radio, voice is the only way you can pass the information along. To the fans following the game closely, as well as to those who are only half-listening, the score is really what the game is all about.

The team names (as well as the players' names) need to be used regularly on radio, and even on television if their uniforms do not immediately name both teams. Otherwise, those listeners who may have tuned in late or are not familiar with team members' names cannot figure out who is doing what to whom.

Comparing Radio and TV

The difference between doing a game on radio and a game on television is essentially the difference between describing the game for a "blind" audience and describing it for a seeing one. The seeing audience is almost insulted if the TV sportscaster describes every move and pass, yet for the "blind" radio audience, vivid and complete description is required for listeners to fully grasp the action. A clear, well-balanced audio signal is important for both media.

Mike Placement

There should be at least three microphones for any sportscast: one for each announcer and one for crowd reaction. It is important that each of these sound components be on a different *potentiometer* (volume control) so that proper balance can be maintained between announcers and crowd reaction, and to be sure that there is enough field noise to demonstrate the game's excitement. It is important that reaction sounds from the field not be allowed to be so loud that the listener has to strain to hear the play-by-play. *Automatic volume control* (AVC) raises background sounds when there is a break in what the announcer is saying, maintaining a roar from the crowd that is constant and always at the same intensity. AVC is to be avoided in a sportscasting situation because it makes increased crowd participation meaningless. The constant clamor may also be irritating to listeners.

[5] Marv Albert, *YESSS!* (New York: Signet, 1979), p. 3.

Instant Replay

Instant replay is a great device for getting another view of the touchdown or pass reception, of a step out of bounds, or of a foul being committed. The director determines when replays are to be shown. Some directors get so carried away with using the technology that they can interrupt the flow of the game. Flow, of course, is important to tell the story of what is going on. Some experts say that the announcer should be watching the monitor and describe the game from the monitor. It is, after all, what the fans at home are seeing. Sometimes it is difficult to pick up the players from the small screen when you can see more clearly by looking directly at the action. When the sportscaster gets carried away and forgets to describe what the home audience is seeing on its sets, the omnipresent earpiece (a device inserted directly into the announcer's ear and that the producer has at his or her disposal) can be used to alert the sportscaster to watch the monitor. The considerate producer uses the earpiece sparingly, because it can really put a strain on the play-by-play person who needs to describe the game and listen to directives at the same time.

The play-by-play and color commentator need to be able to work together hand in glove. Each needs to pick up the other's rhythm and have a feel for what the other is going to do. Often the play-by-play announcer will nod to the color person when color inserts are desired. Play-by-play means instant description. If the color person's background or description material overlaps some of the action and the crowd roars approval or disapproval, the play-by-play must cut in so that the home audience can be told immediately what happened, even if it is relatively unimportant. The home audience must be constantly informed as to what is going on or they'll feel cheated. If the game proceeds while a replay is being shown, it is up to the sportscaster to fill the audience in as if describing via radio, because the audience has momentarily lost its view of the game.

SPORTS SUMMARY

For those dedicated souls who really want to devote their lives to being sportscasters, here are a few pointers:

> Watch sports on television.
> Listen to sports on radio.
> Go to as many games as possible.
> Devour newspaper accounts of sporting events.
> Get to know sports information people.
> Get acquainted with players and coaches.
> Build a library of sports books and periodicals.
> Study sports literature and statistics.
> Look at and ingest the record books.
> Learn the rules of each game you want to call.

Study the announcing styles of national sportscasters.

Discuss sports records, game plans, and personalities with others more knowledge-able than you.

Sportscasting takes a dedicated, alert, enthusiastic, knowledgeable per-son. Is that you?

EXERCISES

1. Mark the copy provided at the end of this chapter as recommended.

2. Follow the instructions for studying word lists as suggested previously, this time doing word lists 9-A and 9-B. Be prepared to pronounce the words correctly, write the correct phonetic transcriptions when tested, and define the words when used in a sentence.

3. Read your marked copy for the word lists onto your cassette tape to be handed in. You may also reread paragraphs from the four previous word lists to review. Your tape will be handed in for evaluation.

4. Read this chapter's word list copy until you have done the best you possibly can, or until you have read for a half hour. When you feel you have done your best, proceed to reading the sports copy at the end of this chapter on the balance of your hour tape. Again, repeat until "perfect."

5. Find a sporting event on TV (football, basketball, or baseball). Turn off the audio and do the play-by-play for five minutes or more. You will find that you have a better presentation if you know something about the teams playing. You probably can get enough color material for a five-minute segment if you first find a preview of the game or articles about one or both of the teams in a newspaper or sports magazine.

6. Read the list of scores at the end of this chapter onto your tape. Strive for variety in your presentation. Especially try to insert a variety of verbs: "The Yankees *beat* the Mariners . . . the Colts *slaughtered* the Giants," etc. Reading a list of any kind is difficult to enliven. Repeat the list several times, getting the variety necessary to hold an audience.

7. Contact the sports information office on your campus for recent releases. Also, check the local newspaper for sports items. Then, rewrite the news releases and newspaper stories and read a second hour on tape.

8. Bring your marked copy and list of scores to class. Pick your best 60 seconds to be read "live" for the other members of the class.

9. Be sure that the assigned material (the best you can do) is at the end of your tape since your instructor will pay particular attention to this to evaluate your improvement.

BROADCAST VOCABULARY WORD LIST:
ACCENTING THE CORRECT SYLLABLE   Unit 9-A

1. imminent (adj)—likely to occur at any moment; impending

   ———————————————   *im' i nunt*

2. emollient (n)—a substance that is soothing, especially to the skin

   ———————————————   *i mol' yunt*

3. impetuous (adj)—as with a sudden, impulsive action

_____   *im   pech'   yew   us*

4. bourgeois (adj)—describing a member of the middle class

_____   *boor   zhwau'*

5. cache (n)—a hiding place, especially in the ground, also a storage place for computer
   data

_____   *kash*

6. entourage (n)—a body of personal attendants

_____   *on'   tu   rauzh*

7. entrepreneur (n)—a person who organizes, manages, and assumes responsibility for a
   business or other enterprise

_____   *on   tru   pru   nur'*

8. superfluous (adj)—beyond what is needed

_____   *sew   pur'   flew   us*

9. envelop (v)—to wrap in or cover; to surround entirely

_____   *en   vel'   up*

10. epitaph (n)—a commemorative inscription on a tomb

_____   *ep'   i   taf*

11. epitome (n)—a person or thing that is typical of or possesses to a high degree the
    features of a whole class

_____   *u   pit'   u   mee*

12. impotent (adj)—lacking ability or power

_____   *im'   pu   tunt*

13. errant (adj)—deviating from the regular or proper course; erring

_____   *air'   unt*

14. indefatigable (adj)—untiring; not able to be tired out

_____   *in   di   fat'   i   gu   bul*

15. inclement (adj)—severe or stormy, as in weather

_____   *in   klem'   unt*

16. defense (sports) (n)—the attempt to prevent the opposition from scoring

———————————————   *dee' fens*

17. defense (all non-sports uses) (n)—protection against attack

———————————————   *di fens'*

18. library (n)—a book storage and access facility

———————————————   *ligh' brer ee*

19. athlete (n)—one who participates in sports

———————————————   *ath' leet*

20. eminent (adj)—prominent, outstanding

———————————————   *em' u nent*

BROADCAST VOCABULARY WORD LIST
More Gazetteer   Unit 9-B

1. Al Fatah—Palestine guerilla organization

———————————————   *al fu taw'*

2. Alitalia—Italian airline

———————————————   *al i tal' yu*

3. Antilles—island chain in the Caribbean; part of the West Indies

———————————————   *an til' eez*

4. Cristobal—city in the Panama canal zone

———————————————   *kris toh' bul*

5. Eurasian—person of Asian and European descent

———————————————   *yur ay' zhun*

6. Greenwich—city in Connecticut; observatory in England from which longitudes and
   time zones are measured

———————————————   *gren' ich*

7. Guadalajara—city in Mexico; town and province in Spain

———————————————   *gwaud u lau haur' u*

8. Guadaloupe—French islands in the West Indies

———————————————   *gwaud lewp'*

9. Guinea—country in West Africa

   _____   *gin'   ee*

10. Louisville—city in Kentucky

    _____   *lew'   u   vul*

11. Martinique—French island in the West Indies

    _____   *mar   tun   eek'*

12. Mojave—desert in California

    _____   *moh   hau'   vee*

13. Nepal—mountain kingdom in central Asia

    _____   *ne   paul'*

14. Reading—cities in Massachusetts, Ohio, and Pennsylvania; also in England

    _____   *red'   ing*

15. Reuters—British news agency

    _____   *roi'   turz*

16. Sarajevo—city in Bosnia (formerly Yugoslovia)

    _____   *sar   u   yay'   voh*

17. Sault Sainte Marie—Canadian and U.S. port cities and canals

    _____   *sew'   saynt   mu   ree'*

18. Thames—river that flows through London

    _____   *temz*

19. Worchestershire (n)—an English county; also a flavoring sauce

    _____   *wews'   tur   shur*

20. Yosemite—California national park; famous waterfall

    _____   *yoh   sem'   u   tee*

WORD LIST PARAGRAPH   Unit 9-A

The indefatigable entrepreneur was truly a bourgeois gentleman demanding an encore from his impotent entourage. The defense of liberty was based on a cache beneath the library where a bestial rogue had a clandestine rendezvous with a prince livid with anger because of the inclement weather.

While the entrepreneur was the epitome of valor, the warm emollient and the cool parfait had made him impotent and unable to further exploit the athlete's defense. If the gendarmerie were to envelop the site, capture would be imminent and an epitaph would be all that would be left of the indefatigable, errant, bourgeois gentleman.

WORD LIST PARAGRAPH   Unit 9-B

The Eurasian guide offered several tour choices. One was a visit to the Antilles including Guadaloupe and Martinique, then a jet hop to Guinea.

An American vacation could include the City of Reading, Pennsylvania, and Yosemite National Park, as well as the colorful Mojave Desert in California. Further south, the agent suggested Guadalajara and Cristobal.

Middle American spots of interest might include the canals at Saulte Sainte Marie and the Kentucky Derby at Louisville.

European high points were pointed out by Reuters to be the Greenwich Observatory on the Thames and the quaint countryside in Worchestershire.

From Britain one might take Alitalia to Sarajevo. Nepal was not considered a viable vacation spot at the time because of extended Al Fatah bookings.

Where in the world do you want to go?

SPORTS COPY

TULSA, Okla.—USL's Ragin' Cajun football squad had problems in the second quarter of its 1990 season, but Cajun head coach Nelson Stokley is hoping that a half-time intermission will give his team a chance to regroup for the second half.

The Cajun squad, after a one-week break for an open date, will kick off that second half of the 1990 campaign here Saturday when USL takes on the Golden Hurricane of the University of Tulsa. Kickoff is scheduled for 2 p.m. (CDT) in Skelly Stadium (40,385) on the Tulsa campus for the seventh football meeting between the two schools.

The Cajuns (2-4) have lost four straight contests after opening the season with back-to-back wins, and Stokley said that last week's open date came at a perfect time for his club, which kicks off two straight weeks on the road this Saturday.

Stokley said, ''The open week helped us rest up mentally and emotionally and get charged up for the second half, and it helped us heal up some of our wounds and give our injured players another week of rest.'' Stokley continued, ''Hopefully we'll be back and ready to play.''

The Cajuns don't have a monopoly on hard luck this weekend, though, as the hometown Golden Hurricane (1-6) comes into the contest on a five-game losing streak. Tulsa fell to Louisiana Tech 35-21 last Saturday for its fifth straight loss, and the Hurricane has also lost two in a row at home for the first time since 1987.

LAFAYETTE, La.—The Lady Cajuns softball team concluded its fall season with three wins in the USL round robin held Sunday at Lady Cajun Park.

USL had defeated Southern Mississippi 12-0, Nicholls State 1-0 in nine innings, and Southeastern Louisiana 6-1.

''Our play kind of surprised me,'' USL head coach Yvette Girouard said. ''Our pitching and defense were outstanding. I knew all along that our hitting would be great.''

Sophomore Kim Heath and freshman Kyla Hall split the pitching duties with Heath defeating USM on a two-hitter and Hall shutting out Nicholls State on a five-hitter. The tandem split the SLU game with Heath allowing SLU's only run of the day on a wild pitch. Hall came on in the fourth and struck out five in four innings.

Leading the hitting was junior outfielder Dorsey Streamer, who hit .462 with six hits in 13 at bats. She also stole four bases and scored four runs.

USL opens its 1991 season Feb. 20, hosting Northeast Louisiana in a 6 p.m. doubleheader.

DATE: Saturday, October 26, 1991   KICKOFF: 12:30 p.m.
SITE: Husky Stadium   CAPACITY 72,500

THIS WEEK: Two long-time Northwest rivals, Washington and Oregon, square
off in a Pacific-10 Conference game in Husky Stadium on Saturday. Kickoff will
be at 12:30 p.m.

LAST WEEK: Unbeaten California gave the Huskies all they could handle last
Saturday before a final desperation pass with no time remaining went awry in
Washington's 24–17 win in Berkeley. Washington appeared to have put the game
away with just under two minutes remaining when Jay Barry (Northglenn, Colo.)
raced 13 yards for an insurance TD. However, the Huskies were called for holding
and were pushed back 10 yards to the Cal 23. After a Cal sack of Billy Joe Hobert
(Puyallup, Wash.) moved it back to the 25, sophomore Travis Hanson (Spokane,
Wash.) missed a 42-yard field goal which would have upped the margin to 10
points. Cal took over and drove to the Huskies' 22 as time was winding down. A
desperation Mike Pawlawski pass was incomplete with no time left, but both
teams were penalized (UW/offsides; Cal/holding), giving the Bears one last shot.
However, Pawlawski's bid for a possible tying TD was off the mark near the Husky
end zone as he looked for Brian Treggs. Junior Beno Bryant's 65-yard score early
in the final period proved to be the game winner for Brian Treggs. Junior Beno
Bryant's 65-yard run by Cal's Lindsey Chapman with one second left in the third
period was the longest run of the year against Washington, which had gone into
the game boasting the nation's top run defense. Chapman's tally helped knot the
score at 17 after Washington had built a 17–10 halftime lead on a 35-yard pass from
Hobert to Mario Bailey (Seattle, Wash.), a 23-yard Hanson field goal and a nine-
yard run by Barry. Cal's first half points came on a 59-yard pass from Pawlawski

to Sean Dawkins and a 50-yard field goal from Doug Brien. In addition to his miss from 42, Hanson also missed a third quarter attempt from 34 yards.

THE SERIES: Washington will be meeting Oregon for the 85th time, the most of any UW opponent in history. The Huskies hold a 51–28–5 lead in the series and they have won the last two games between the two long-time Northwest rivals. The series stands at 23–10–2 in Husky Stadium and Don James has a 13–3 record against Oregon and an 11–3 record against Rich Brooks. The only loss by a Don James' squad to Oregon in Husky Stadium came in 1980, 34–10, which was the team's only loss in Pac-10 Conference play that year.

THE LAST MEETING: Washington solidified its hold on the Pac-10 Conference lead with an impressive show of defensive force in a 38–17 win over 19th ranked Oregon. The Huskies moved to 5–1 overall and 3–0 in league play with the win. Greg Lewis rushed for a then career-high 169 yards on 23 carries as Washington broke open a game that saw them lead by just four points at the half, 14–10. An 11-yard run by Mark Brunell followed and upped the Huskies' margin to 21–10 after three periods and then Mike Dodd added a 27-yard field goal to make it 24–10 early in the final period. Four minutes later, Brunell connected with Orlando McKay on a 45-yard score and Washington's lead was now 31–10. Oregon countered moments later when it marched 58 yards in three plays for a score, but the Huskies put the game away when they drove 80 yards in eight plays for an insurance score by Beno Bryant. Washington held the Ducks to just seven yards rushing while gaining 278 themselves.

DUCK TRAVEL PLANS: Oregon will arrive in Seattle on Friday afternoon and the Ducks have a workout scheduled in Husky Stadium at 3:00 p.m. They will be housed at the Bellevue Hyatt Regency on Friday evening.

1991 OREGON FOOTBALL (MF91-1020-08)
GAME SEVEN—Oregon (3–3, 1–2) vs. Washington (6–0, 3–0)

Saturday, October 26 (12:30 p.m. PDT)
Husky Stadium, Seattle, Wash.

BROADCAST: Oregon Sports Network, 12:00 p.m. PDT (Jerry Allen and Mike Jorgensen)

DELAYED TELECAST: Prime Sports Northwest (Cable), Monday, 8:00 p.m. PDT (Don Polet and Todd McKim)

DUCK HOTLINE: 503-346-3121 (Actualities with Coach Rich Brooks)

THE GAME'S THEME. . . . Oregon's next assignment on the heels of its checkered past brings to mind every cliché associated with unenviable situations. The Ducks come off their first idle mid-season Saturday in six years to face one of the best teams on many recent schedules. Oregon continues its search for the suitable replacement after a season-ending injury to its starting quarterback. The Ducks' error-prone offense has its first opportunity to make corrections against one of the nation's tight-fisted defenses. Rich Brooks appears in no humor to celebrate the occasion of presiding over more games than any Oregon coach in history. The Ducks try to avoid possessing a losing record for the first time in four years.

THE COACHES. . . . Oregon Coach Rich Brooks passes the legendary Len Casanova for games coached as the Ducks begin the stretch run of his 15th season as the Ducks' head coach. Brooks has redirected Oregon's football program during the second half of his career, owning a 47–39–0 (.546) mark in the last eight years to hike his career mark to 71–88–4 for a .448 winning percentage. Casanova has the longest tenure among Oregon's head coaches with 16 seasons, encompassing a total of 163 games. Washington's Don James, Terry Donahue of UCLA, and

Oregon's Brooks have the longest current employment records in the Pacific-10 Conference. James has started his third decade as a head coach and 17th season at Washington. He has won more Pac-10 games than any coach in history and boasts a 138–54–2 record at Washington. Brooks is 3–11 vs. Washington and James and the Huskies' coach owns a 13–3 mark against Oregon, including a 7–1 mark in games at Seattle.

CONFERENCE CALL. . . . Coach Rich Brooks will be available to any interested news media member each Wednesday via conference telephone call. Just notify the sports information office by 4:30 p.m. Tuesday and call the Darome Connection in San Francisco (415-896-1609) at approximately 10:30 a.m. There is a 30 minute time limit, but Coach Brooks will stay on the line to answer as many questions as possible. Brooks is available in person at practice at other times.

THE SERIES. . . . Oregon and Washington square off for the 85th time and the schedule between the neighboring rivals regains some sanity after the Ducks' third straight meeting in Seattle. Because the teams were not paired several seasons ago, administrators made arrangements to fill the void, but it wasn't accomplished without bartering with future games. Washington played twice in a row in Eugene and the repayment was the relocation of the 1990 contest to Seattle. The home team has a five game winning streak, dating back to Washington's 1986 triumph in Eugene. The Huskies hold a 51–28–5 edge in the series with five straight victories in Seattle as well. Oregon last won at Husky Stadium in 1980 when Washington was ranked 13th nationally. A year ago both teams were rated when they met in Seattle, only the second time that had ever happened. Seventeenth-ranked Washington was just beginning its ascent in the national polls and No. 19 Oregon had cracked the Associated Press' top 20 teams for the first time in two years. The series returns to Eugene (Oct. 17) next fall for the first time since 1988.

AP-NP-04-11-90 1857CDT (+ V17301NT—

R S AP-EVENINGSPORTSWATCH (TW   04-11 0314
∧AP-EVENING SPORTSWATCH (TWO TAKES) <
   BY BOB KIMBALL

   KENT HRBEK (HUR' -BEK) STARTED THE JOB AND MINNESOTA'S
PITCHERS FINISHED IT THIS AFTERNOON AT THE OAKLAND COLISEUM.
THE TWINS' SLUGGER CRACKED A THREE-RUN HOMER IN THE TOP OF
THE FIRST INNING IN A 3-TO-0 VICTORY OVER THE ATHLETICS. KEVIN
TAPANI (TAP' -UN -NEE) AND THREE RELIEVERS COMBINED A SEVEN-
HITTER AS MINNESOTA SALVAGED THE FINAL OF THE THREE-GAME
SERIES. ALSO IN THE AMERICAN LEAGUE TODAY, BOSTON'S DWIGHT
EVANS HOMERED AND, IN THE LAST OF THE TENTH INNING, DROVE IN
THE WINNING RUN, TO LEAD THE RED SOX OVER DETROIT 3-TO-2. THE
TIGERS HAVE LOST TEN STRAIGHT GAMES TO THE BOSOX DATING BACK
TO LAST JUNE. THE SAN FRANCISCO GIANTS OPENED DEFENSE OF THEIR
NATIONAL LEAGUE PENNANT WHEN RICH REUSHEL (RUHSH' -IL), JEFF
BRANTLEY AND ATLEE HAMMAKER TEAMED ON A THREE-HIT, 8-TO-0
WIN OVER ATLANTA IN THE FIRST GAME OF A TWI-NIGHT DOUBLE-
HEADER. REUSCHEL—THE LEAGUE'S OLDEST PLAYER AT 40—WENT THE
FIRST FIVE AND TWO-THIRDS INNINGS. THE GIANTS AND BRAVES WERE
RAINED OUT LAST NIGHT, NECESSITATING THE TWINBILL. OIL CAN
BOYD'S NATIONAL LEAGUE DEBUT WITH THE MONTREAL EXPOS CAME
UP A WINNER. THE RIGHT-HANDER—OVER FROM BOSTON AS A FREE
AGENT—GAVE UP FOUR HITS AND THREE RUNS IN SIX INNINGS TO HELP
THE EXPOS DOWN THE ST. LOUIS CARDINALS 6-TO-4.

   AND A COUPLE OF LOCAL BOYS MADE GOOD IN NEW YORK, WHERE
THE METS BLANKED PITTSBURGH 3-TO-0 ON A COMBINED SIX-HITTER.
FRANK VIOLA WENT THE FIRST SEVEN AND TWO-THIRDS INNINGS
BEFORE JOHN FRANCO FINISHED UP FOR THE SAVE.

AP-NP-04-11-90 1858CDT <+V 732INT—

R S AP-EVENINGSPORTSWATCH-TA 04-11 0205 /\AP-EVENING
SPORTSWATCH-TAKE 2

EDDIE SUTTON HAS RETURNED TO COLLEGE BASKETBALL AS
COACH OF OKLAHOMA STATE. THE COWBOYS TODAY NAMED THE EX-
KENTUCKY COACH TO REPLACE LEONARD HAMILTON, WHO TOOK THE
MIAMI OF FLORIDA JOB OVER THE FINAL FOUR WEEKEND. SUTTON
PLAYED COLLEGE BALL IN STILLWATER IN THE LATE 1950S BEFORE
BEGINNING HIS COACHING CAREER.

NEXT STOP FOR SEAN HIGGINS—THE N-B-A. THE SIX-FOOT NINE-
INCH JUNIOR TODAY MADE OFFICIAL HIS WISH TO LEAVE MICHIGAN IN
FAVOR OF PRO BASKETBALL. A HAIRLINE STRESS FRACTURE IN THE
FOOT SUFFERED IN JANUARY HAMPERED HIGGINS, WHO HELPED THE
WOLVERINES TO THE 1989 NATIONAL CHAMPIONSHIP.

SEVEN N-B-A PLAYERS OWE THE LEAGUE OFFICE A TOTAL OF TEN-
THOUSAND 500 DOLLARS FOR THEIR PARTS IN RECENT ON-COURT
SCUFFLES. PHOENIX GUARD MIKE MCGEE DREW THE HEAVIEST
FINE—THREE-THOUSAND DOLLARS AFTER HE POKED NEW JERSEY'S
PURVIS SHORT IN THE BACK OF THE HEAD. SHORT ALSO DREW A ONE-
THOUSAND PENALTY, WHILE OTHER FINES WENT TO XAVIER MCDANIEL,
TODD LICHTI (LEK' -TEE), PATRICK EWING, CHARLES OAKLEY AND
CHARLES BARCLAY.

SECOND-ROUND WINNERS AT THE JAPAN OPEN TENNIS
CHAMPIONSHIPS INCLUDED IVAN LENDL, AARON KRICKSTEIN AND
BRAD GILBERT. AND IN WOMEN'S TENNIS, STEFFI GRAF (GRAHF) PLAYS
THE SECOND MATCH AFTER A TWO-MONTH INJURY LAYOFF WHEN SHE
FACES ANDREA TEMESVARI ON AMELIA ISLAND, FLORIDA.

AP-NP-04-12-90 0925CDT <+

R S AP-4THSPORTSMINUTE   04-12   0193
∧AP-4TH SPORTSMINUTE

PITCHERS MARK LANGSTON AND MIKE WITT OF THE CALIFORNIA
ANGELS COMBINED ON A NO-HITTER LAST NIGHT AS THE ANGELS BEAT
SEATTLE 1-TO-NOTHING. LANGSTON WENT SEVEN INNINGS AND WITT
FINISHED THINGS UP. THE COMBINED NINE-INNING NO-HITTER IS
JUST THE FIFTH IN BASEBALL HISTORY.

BASEBALL FANS IN CHICAGO WILL BE TREATED TO A
DOUBLEHEADER TODAY AS THE CUBS ENTERTAIN PHILADELPHIA. IN
OTHER AFTERNOON ACTION IN THE NATIONAL LEAGUE, PITTSBURGH
PLAYS AT NEW YORK AGAINST THE METS, IT'LL BE LOS ANGELES AT SAN
DIEGO AND ATLANTA ENTERTAINS SAN FRANCISCO.

THE AMERICAN LEAGUE CARD HAS TWO AFTERNOON GAMES.
CLEVELAND IS AT NEW YORK AND BOSTON PLAYS AT DETROIT.

THREE TEAMS CAN ADVANCE TO THE SECOND ROUND OF THE
STANLEY CUP PLAYOFFS TONIGHT. ST. LOUIS LEADS TORONTO THREE
GAMES TO ONE AND THE BLUES CAN WRAP THE SERIES UP WITH A WIN
TONIGHT. LOS ANGELES SKATES AT CALGARY AND THE KINGS LEAD BY
THE SAME MARGIN, AND WINNIPEG WILL ATTEMPT TO FINISH OFF
EDMONTON WITH A GAME ON THE OILERS' HOME ICE THIS EVENING.

V071901A-X

R S AP-LA-LOUISIANASPORTS   04-12—0286
∧AP-LS-LOUISIANA SPORTS

HERE'S THE LATEST LOUISIANA SPORTS NEWS FROM THE
ASSOCIATED PRESS.

FOGGY JOCKEY

(LAFAYETTE) - A LAWYER FOR JOCKEY SYLVESTER CARMOUCHE SAYS HE WILL APPEAL HIS CLIENT'S TEN-YEAR SUSPENSION. CARMOUCHE WAS SUSPENDED FOR ALLEGEDLY HIDING HIS LONG-SHOT MOUNT IN THE FOG, LETTING THE REST OF THE FIELD PASS BY, THEN RACING HOME TO A 24-LENGTH VICTORY.

(-DASH-)

THE RACE IN QUESTION OCCURRED JANUARY ELEVENTH AT DELTA DOWNS IN VINTON. CARMOUCHE'S ACTIONS WERE CONSIDERED BY THE LOUISIANA RACING COMMISSION YESTERDAY (WEDNESDAY) IN LAFAYETTE. COMMISSIONER JEFFREY KALLENBERG SAYS HE DOESN'T KNOW HOW CARMOUCHE DID IT, BUT HE KNOWS HE CHEATED. THE VOTE TO SUSPEND CARMOUCHE WAS 7-1. MEMBER JAMES BRADFORD VOTED NO AFTER HIS MOTION TO SUSPEND CARMOUCHE FOR ONLY FIVE YEARS FAILED.

SOUTHERN SIGNINGS

(BATON ROUGE) SOUTHERN BASKETBALL COACH BEN JOBE SAYS QUICK HIGH SCHOOL SIGNINGS ARE FOR BIG SCHOOLS, NOT HIM. YESTERDAY (WEDNESDAY) WAS NATIONAL SIGNING DAY AND JOBE HAD NOTHING TO REPORT.

(-DASH-)

JOBE SAYS HE'S NEVER SIGNED A PLAYER ON THE FIRST DAY OR DURING THE FIRST FEW DAYS. HE SAYS HE ALSO CAN'T REMEMBER SIGNING ANYONE AT THE EARLY SIGNING PERIOD IN NOVEMBER. HE SAYS PART OF THE REASON IS THAT SOUTHERN CAN'T AFFORD A FULL-TIME RECRUITER. JOBE SAYS HE'S LOOKING AT ABOUT 38 POTENTIAL PLAYERS AND WILL BE LUCKY TO GET THREE TO FIVE SIGNEES FROM THAT GROUP.

HERE ARE TODAY'S FINAL SCORES FROM THE BALL PARKS:

NBA

FINAL   ATLANTA 106 MILWAUKEE 94

FINAL   DETROIT 98 NEW JERSEY 93

FINAL   CHICAGO 107 CLEVELAND 86

NATIONAL LEAGUE

FINAL   TEXAS 11 TORONTO 5

FINAL   BOSTON 3 DETROIT 2—10 INNINGS

FINAL   MINNESOTA 3 OAKLAND 0

FINAL   MONTREAL 6 ST. LOUIS 4

FINAL   N.Y. METS 3 PITTSBURGH 0

FINAL   KANSAS CITY 2 BALTIMORE 1

FINAL   CINCINNATI 5 HOUSTON 0

FINAL   1ST GAME SAN FRANCISCO 8 ATLANTA 0

FINAL   2ND GAME ATLANTA 4 SAN FRANCISCO 3

FINAL   SAN DIEGO 3 LOS ANGELES 1

FINAL   CALIFORNIA 1 SEATTLE 0

N-H-L STANLEY CUP PLAYOFFS

N. Y. RANGERS 6 N. Y. ISLANDERS 1

WASHINGTON CAPITALS 3 NEW JERSEY DEVILS 1

BOSTON BRUINS 6 HARTFORD WHALERS 5

BUFFALO SABERS 4 MONTREAL CANADIENS 2

10

The Audio
and Video Studios

OBJECTIVES
Upon completion of this chapter the student should be able to:

1. Explain the basic functions of the audio control console and the video switcher.
2. Describe the use of the audio console keys and pots and a video switcher's fader and special effects wipes.
3. Explain reasons to use the audition side of the audio board, the use of the preview, and mix busses on the TV switcher.
4. Describe the use of two aural and two visual monitoring devices for audio signals and the oscilloscope monitors for TV.
5. Describe the three basic microphone pickup patterns and the use of the television zoom lens.
6. List and describe three types of transducers used in microphones in modern radio and name the element used for picture pickup in TV.
7. Describe five different styles of microphone mountings and three types of camera mounts.
8. Explain the recommended announcer microphone use.
9. Note three basic differences between CD players and turntables.
10. Explain three advantages of multi-track recording for audio and explain possible uses of multiple tracks on video tape.
11. Compare reel-to-reel audio tape physical editing to video tape editing.
12. Describe the physical attributes that should make cartridge tapes ready for instant playing.
13. Describe a method of record cueing.
14. Describe how the board operator can be sure of consistent audio levels.
16. Describe three possible uses of the computer in three different departments of a radio or television station.

THE CONTROL CENTERS

The heart of any radio or television station is the *control center*. At the central switching facilities the station's broadcast signals come together before final release.

While they may appear to be quite different in design, all broadcast audio consoles perform basically the same functions in much the same way. Though somewhat more complex, video switchers, too, tend to have much in common. Learning about one audio board or video switcher then gives you insights on how others work. However, even those audio and video switching units in different stations that appear to be almost identical may be wired slightly differently by different installing engineers. But since the operating principles of all audio consoles are essentially the same, and video switchers are also similar in operation, techniques to use equipment at one production studio can be adapted to other switching devices—even those that may appear to be quite different.

FUNCTIONS

The audio console and the television switcher have much in common, including five basic functions. Each one handles its respective signal type: selecting, processing, monitoring, mixing, and routing. *Processing* in a radio station console consists primarily of amplification of the signal. The much more complicated video signal must be synchronized, stabilized, and enhanced through a series of complicated devices as well as being amplified.

Very weak audio signals in the form of electrical energy may be fed into the audio control console (or audio board, as it is also called). For example, microphone signals are so weak that they need to be amplified more than other inputs to the console. The microphone signal is boosted first through what is called a pre-amplifier (or pre-amp). Most other signals fed into the control console are at line level. After being routed, audio signals are amplified to maintain a proper level. TV signals are amplified at several points in the routing to and from the switcher.

Mixing entails combining signals from several sources, which are then amplified and become the output of the audio or video system. Audio sources that might be combined can be either digital or analog or both (assuming that proper interfacing equipment is available). *Digital* refers to the changing of information into on-off computer language that does not deteriorate with copying. The older *analog* technology duplicates an image of the information and tends to lose some of its clarity with each generation of reproduction. Signal sources include recordings from a computer's memory, audio or video disc, or tape; the output of a transducer (microphone or camera); or the output from a satellite, microwave, or a "telephone" line. Additional video sources include *still-frame storage units* (which resemble an electronic collection of immediately accessible slides) and *character generators* (electronic typewriter keyboards which allow the typing of

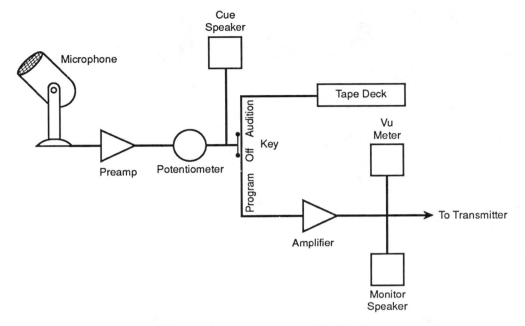

Figure 10–1 The microphone requires a preamp to get to line level.

many sizes, shapes, and colors of lettering on a television screen). *Note:* Output from a source becomes input to the board or switcher. A signal is "output" or "input" depending on its relationship to the device being discussed.

At times the switcher may merely serve to route and amplify a signal. That is, there is no additional mixing taking place. An example of routing-only would be a network show that comes into the switcher and then is fed directly to the transmitter (after enhancement processing).

Both the television switcher and the audio board are capable of several types of selection and mixing. Both may select a signal at full strength or fade it in gradually. Both may fade one signal in while another is being faded out (called a *dissolve* in television; a *cross-fade* in audio production).

In addition, television technology can provide an almost unlimited variation in modifying and creating picture elements and transitional techniques thanks to *digital video effects (DVE)* processing.

POTENTIOMETERS

When you look at most audio control consoles, you see a row of knobs or slide controls that control the level of amplification of each input to the board. These volume controls are called *pots* (short for *potentiometer*). Sometimes you will also find that pots are referred to as *gain*, as in "riding gain" (defined as carefully

Figure 10–2 Slide rule controls show the level of each potentiometer.

monitoring input and output levels). To the uninitiated, audio pots may be simply *volume controls*. Additional names for the potentiometer are *fader* and *attenuator*. (Though the volume control appears to amplify the signal by degrees, it is actually reducing the already amplified signal, working much as the rheostat on a dining room chandelier.) As a rule, a pot controls the volume of each program source.

The comparable television potentiometer is seen as a *fader arm* (or *bar* or *lever*), which reduces (or appears to intensify) television signals channeled through its circuits. Most of the buttons on all but the smallest video switchers represent input sources that can be selected.

KEYS

Selecting an audio source is usually done by using the *key,* which may be considered the simplest way to route an audio signal. On most audio control consoles, a three-way switch or series of push buttons over most pots gives you a choice of

Figure 10–3 Some operators prefer round potentiometer controls.

where to send the signal being controlled by that pot. With a three-way switch, the left position is *audition,* the center position is *off,* and the right position is *program.* Signals routed through the program circuitry usually go to the transmitters and out over the air, or in a production studio, into a tape recorder. Where push buttons serve the key functions, an additional button may provide the option of routing the signal to a telephone line or elsewhere.

Keys are normally left in the center or off position when not in use. Even though there might currently be no input to the console on this circuit, it should be in the off position. If a network key is left in program after a network feed has finished and input has ceased, the operator may be surprised a few minutes later when a 1000 cycle tone or another program comes down the line and probably out over the air.

The *audition circuits* (the audition side of the audio board) provide a separate selection, monitoring, mixing, amplifying, and routing facility. They may be used to audition (listen to in advance) other programs or recordings, or to actually do audio production or recording while another program from the network, a tape, or another source, is airing on the program side of the board.

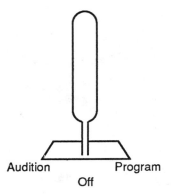

Audition   Program

Off   **Figure 10–4** The key directs the output of each source.

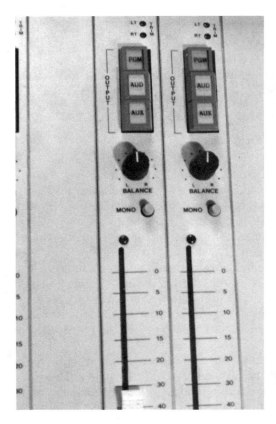

Figure 10–5 When push buttons serve the key functions there may be additional options.

Figure 10–6 Sizes may vary but most video switches perform the same functions.

Similarly in the television studio, the *preview monitor* allows production personnel to view in advance the next picture to be routed to "line out" (the video tape recorder, the transmitter, etc), though (unlike in audio) only one TV show can be produced at a time through the video switcher.

An audio *delegation switch* may select which of two or more sources is directed to a given channel to be switched to program or audition. For example, a station may use programming from more than one network. A delegation switch may determine which network is being fed to the network input on the board. In a sense, all of the source buttons on the video switcher are delegation switches, selecting a signal to be aired or recorded.

MONITORING DEVICES

How does the operator know what's going out over the air or being recorded? The signals must be *monitored*. An audio signal is visually checked with the VU meter or peak program meter, and aurally with headsets and monitor speakers. A television signal is viewed on TV screens at each step in the system, and on oscilloscopes such as a wave form monitor and a vectorscope.

The VU Meter

The audio control operator can see how loud the output of the board is by observing the *VU (volume units) meter*. The VU meter has a prominent position

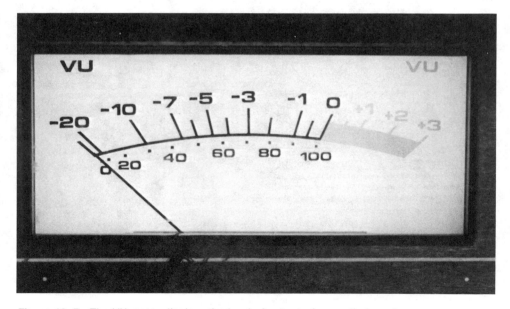

Figure 10-7   The VU meter displays the level of output of an audio board.

on the control console, displaying the signal strength after it has passed through the board's amplification. Fulfilling the VU function on some consoles is a series of light-emitting diodes (or a plasma display). Stations may differ slightly in what they have determined to be the "correct" level reading, but usually acceptable levels displayed on the VU meter are between 60 and 100 percent average modulation. As the needle peaks into the red (over 100 percent), the signal may distort. The signal can be expected to distort especially if the needle is "pinned" by excessive loudness. (*Pinning* refers to a signal so loud for so long that the VU needle lies on the pin that limits the needle's maximum swing, or lights up all of the light-emitting diodes for an extended period.) Most transmitters now have limiters that restrict overmodulation, but pinning is nevertheless not recommended practice because it can also damage the VU meter itself. The limiter on the transmitter is an emergency device like a fire extinguisher—in most cases not recommended for everyday use.

The VU meter measures the "average" signal being monitored. The scales displayed are in volume units and percent modulation. On the other hand, the *peak program meter* (as the name suggests) indicates the signal peaks, and displays the signal intensity in decibels. Some consoles may have both visual measuring systems, but the VU meter is more common in the United States. The peak program meter is more popular in Europe.

Oscilloscopes

While a dee-jay may monitor the VU meter in audio production, an engineer is usually expected to be monitoring TV's *oscilloscopes,* which in many ways are analogous to the VU meters of audio production. The *waveform monitor* is used to keep the white and black picture elements in balance, so that the brightest elements of the signal do not exceed the 100 percent level that the system can successfully handle.

A *vectorscope* monitors color components and allows them to be adjusted for maximum quality of the primary and secondary colors.

Headsets

Headsets connected to the audio console allow the operator to listen to a particular source or the output of the board while the board microphone is open, or to cue records or tapes without the sound being picked up by the mike or heard by an in-studio audience. Headsets are particularly useful to gauge balance between speech and music when the board operator is speaking on the microphone over music. The tendency for many beginners is to maintain the music level and try to talk over it. Music levels need to be considerably lower than the voice level if an announcer expects the audience to understand and pay attention to the copy being read or the comments being made. Since the VU meter cannot show balance—only total loudness—the headsets are extremely important to the announcer who is balancing voice and music, as they are to the sportscaster who needs to balance his or her descriptions with the crowd noise or other ambient sounds.

In television, headsets are used primarily for intercom communication between the director, the camera operators, the engineering staff, and other production persons. For the operator of a boom microphone (described later in this chapter), it is especially helpful to have the output of the microphone being positioned or the audio board in one earphone and the director's intercom in the other. Some intercom systems may be set up this way with audio board and director commands in separate earphones for everyone on a headset.

Monitor Speakers

Both in radio and television, the *monitor speaker* is usually used to listen to what is going out over the air when a control room microphone is not open. If the mike is open and the monitor speaker is "on," feedback can result. (*Feedback* is the high-pitched squeal that occurs when a system retransmits its own signal.) To avoid this feedback, audio control consoles are equipped with a *muting relay,* which automatically turns off the monitor speaker when the mike is opened.

Figure 10–8 Student rides gain as he listens in the headset.

Figure 10–9 There is a monitor for each source on the video switcher.

Feedback can also result if a caller on the air from a telephone at home has a radio playing loudly and tuned to your station.

Monitoring of the video system is done by television monitor screens on each camera. Usually there is a larger monitor on a stand in the studio for floor directors and/or talent. On a news set this is often a smaller video monitor recessed in the top of the news desk. In the control room, there is a monitor for each camera as well as the previously described preview and line monitors.

In addition to the audition side of the audio board for auditioning sources, there is an additional circuit that is used to cue records and tapes. When the pot knob is at its lowest amplifying point (usually ''0''), the knob may be turned down an additional notch and clicked into *cue*. Use of the headset or a separate cueing speaker allows the operator to listen to the beginning of a record or tape without the sound going out over the air. Again, a muting relay turns the cue speaker off when the mike is open to prevent cueing on the air. The headset is not usually controlled by the muting relay.

SOUND AND VIDEO SOURCES

The audio or video switcher operator selects, monitors, mixes, amplifies, and routes both recorded and live sounds and images. To be fed into the switcher, sounds or images must be changed into electrical impulses by microphones or cameras.

Microphones and Cameras

Microphones and video cameras can be classified by pickup pattern, by transducer type, and by physical mounting.

Pickup Patterns   There are three basic audio pickup patterns: the cardiod, the omni-directional, and the bi-directional or figure 8.

The *cardiod pattern,* as the name suggests, is somewhat heart-shaped. Viewed from above, the primary pickup pattern is roughly the shape of a valentine heart with the microphone pickup at the point of indentation at the top of the heart. This is the basic uni-directional pattern. This pickup pattern can be modified to be even more directional, with the ultimate narrow configuration being realized into a shotgun mike. The observer will see ports along the sides of the elongated tube, which is the physical shape of a shotgun mike. These ports pick up sounds from unwanted directions that are in turn cancelled by these same sounds arriving at the transducer a fraction of a second later at the mike's primary pickup point. The ports on a uni-directional microphone should not be covered in any way, including by the hands of a performer holding the instrument.

The *omni-directional* (or non-directional) mike picks up in "all" directions from the transducer. It is the mike most commonly used in remote locations by TV or radio news personnel who want to pick up the background sounds (or *ambient noise*).

The microphone with a *bi-directional* pickup pattern, which worked extremely well for radio drama, is no longer as popular as it once was. As suggested by the name, the primary pickup pattern of the bi-directional microphone is from two sides. When viewed from above, this pattern can be represented by a figure 8.

The picture size and magnification of a video camera (analogous to the microphone pickup pattern) is determined primarily by the lens adjustments. The zoom lens has an infinite number of possible magnification options within the lens's range. This range may vary considerably on various video cameras.

As high-definition television becomes standard, a change in the picture aspect ratio may be expected to be related to the newer wide-screen standards. The *aspect ratio* refers to the vertical units (inches, millimeters, etc.) compared with horizontal units of the picture. The standard film (and therefore the standard TV) aspect ratio has been three units high by four units wide (e.g., 9 by 12, 15 by 20, etc.).

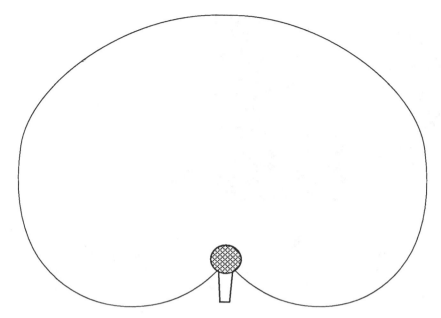

Figure 10–10 Uni-directional is a variation of the cardiod pickup pattern.

Figure 10–11 The shotgun mike is comparable to a zoom lens on a TV camera.

Figure 10–12 Covering up the ports of a uni-directional mike will change its pattern.

Extremely high magnification lenses tend to distort size relationships, as you have probably noticed in a televised baseball game when the pitcher, batter, and catcher are picked up in one shot. Similar distortions can be seen when the president addresses joint meetings of the houses of the U.S. Congress. The long lens makes the vice president and the speaker of the house appear to be the same

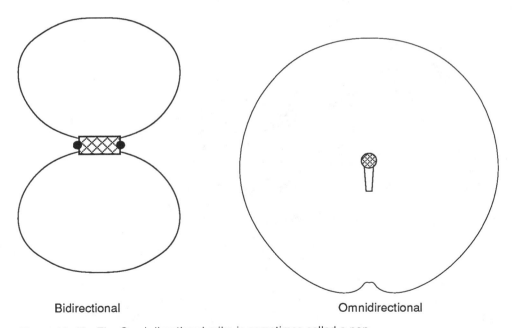

Bidirectional   Omnidirectional

Figure 10–13 The Omni-directional mike is sometimes called a non-directional mike. The bi-directional mike picks up equally well from two sides.

Figure 10–14 A close-up using a wide angle lens tends to distort the image.

size as the president who, being closer, should be larger. Another distortion occurs when a wide-angle lens (which picks up an extra-wide view) is used for a close-up shot of a person. The effect can be gruesome, as seen in many shots of Ernest, Vern's borrowing neighbor (of television advertising and movie fame).

Transducer Types A *transducer* changes one form of energy to another. In a microphone, the change is from sound wave energy to electrical energy. There are three basic types of transducers used in broadcast microphones.

The *moving coil* (or *dynamic*) microphone is one of the most popular microphones. It has a good frequency response. The important factors most buyers look at, however, are its relatively low cost and its durability. The moving coil stands up well to relatively rough handling and performs well in difficult environments, such as a windy day. A wind screen of acoustic foam further cuts wind noise. Colored wind screens may match similar colors on control knobs and wiring to help avoid sound engineering mixups.

Gaining in popularity is the *condenser* microphone because of its high frequency response and versatility. The condenser mikes may be extremely small, and some offer a variety of pickup patterns. A possible disadvantage is the requirement of a supplementary power supply, usually in the form of a battery. The microphone is available with a "phantom" power supply, a tap into a studio power circuit for use in a studio configuration. In many instances there is a battery between the microphone and the control console that must periodically be replaced for continued service.

One of the old standbys is the *ribbon* microphone, which tends to enhance voices to give them a slightly more mellow bass sound. It is often preferred for studio consoles where it can be permanently mounted and enhance the sound of most announcers. The instrument is more fragile than mikes with other transducer types, and must be handled carefully, so the ribbon mike is seldom used for remotes.

The transducer or pickup element in the video camera changes light values into electrical impulses. Older video cameras use vidicon or other pickup tubes as transducers. Newer "chip" cameras use smaller, more rugged *CCDs* (*charge coupled devices*) as transducers. The smaller CCD has allowed the addition of the video tape recorder to the portable camera, combining into one lightweight unit equipment that had formerly been heavy and cumbersome.

Mountings Sometimes microphones are referred to by the particular housing into which the transducer is mounted. The floor stand mike, the table mike, the lavalier and clip-on mikes, the headset mike, and the boom mike are the most commonly used in broadcasting. The names of the mounts generally describe the mounts themselves. (A *lavalier* is a pendant worn around the neck. A *boom* is a mobile unit with an extendable arm for holding or manipulating a microphone or camera.)

Cameras may be mounted on dollies or booms for studio use or sporting events. In the field, tripods are often required for picture stability. In news reporting, the video camcorder (combined camera, microphone, and video tape recorder in one unit) is often mounted on the camera person's shoulder.

Microphone Use

No matter what the pickup pattern, transducer type, or mounting, most microphones are used in much the same way.

When testing a mike, you should *not* blow into the instrument or tap on it. To do so may damage its sensitive inner elements. When taking a level to

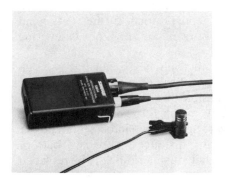 

Figure 10–15 A lavalier (which can hang around the neck) is more often a clip-on. The battery pack for a condenser mike can clip onto a belt.

Figure 10–16   The boom mike should pick up without being seen.

Figure 10–17   Interviewers and singers often prefer a hand-held mike.

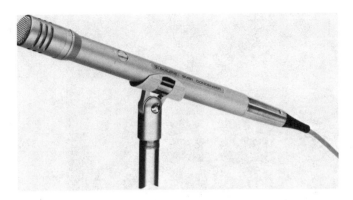

Figure 10–18 A mike stand may sit on a desk or on the floor.

determine the proper potentiometer adjustment, read copy or speak for an extended period of time in the normal manner you will use when on the air. Saying "hello, hello, hello" does not give enough time (nor is it probably at the correct level) for an engineer to take a reading. "Recite the alphabet" or "count backwards from 25 to 1" are the types of requests the floor director may make to get a proper level. If you have a script, the proper level can be expected to be achieved from reading that copy.

To produce the best sound, use your diaphragm and project your voice as if you are talking to someone across the room. With most microphone types the announcer should be 8 to 11 inches from the microphone. As previously noted, the distance can be measured with a standard piece of paper.

There are a few subtleties of microphone use that can be handy to know when you are using a mike with which you are not familiar. Rather than talking directly into a ribbon microphone, speak across the mike at a 45-degree angle to avoid possible excess *sibilance* (hissing of the "s" sound). Popping may result from *plosives* ("b" and "p" sounds) being projected directly into a moving coil mike. The previously noted foam wind screen helps overcome this problem, as well as the sounds made by the wind on location or the rapid movement of the mike when it is hand held or on a boom. Some microphone models have built-in pop filters that may also help solve the problem. Another problem that may occur with a moving coil mike is the *proximity effect:* the closer the sound source, the more the bass sounds are enhanced. Some mikes have a bass roll-off switch, which results in the *attenuation* (reduction) of the sounds below a certain frequency. Of course, the proximity effect may be used to advantage by some announcers in situations where a heavier voice may be desirable.

Some microphones that do not suffer from proximity effect may still have a bass roll-off switch. It can be used to reduce low-frequency sounds such as fans or air conditioners or construction or heavy traffic sounds on remotes. The bass drum at a football game or parade can be overpowering if the announcer has no way to control the pickup of sounds at the lower end of the frequency range.

Figure 10–19 The flexibility of this small remote audio mixer is somewhat amazing.

The low-cut filter built into many remote mixers can also effectively remove overpowering low-frequency pickup.

Disc Players

Since the beginning of radio, the disc recording has supplied much of the music heard on the air. The early 78 rpm records are seldom heard on the air today. The 45s and 33 rpm records still are aired, but many stations have converted to all compact discs.

Turntables

With the traditional turntable, record cuts are selected and the record must be cued to avoid *wow-in* (sound starting before the record gets up to speed). This is discussed later under audio techniques.

Though the frequency response of the tone cartridge through which the signal must pass is probably as high in fidelity as the rest of the chain of broadcast station components, and as most non-digital receivers can reproduce, the psychology of the quality of the compact disc seems to be dooming the studio turntable to oblivion.

CD Players

The compact disc (CD) is the current technology for the playback of music. The operator simply inserts the disc into the player, selects the desired cut, and sits back while the disc plays—the selected cut on the disc has been cued electronically. The quality is superb. With a laser light beam picking up the digital information (compared with the physical contact of a stylus on discs of earlier technology), it is obvious that the compact disc is subject to almost no wear from playing, though, of course, improper handling can result in damage to a CD. Avoid fingerprints—always handle all discs by their edges.

The compact disc reproduces sounds recorded digitally by using computer language, a series of "ons" and "offs." The sound is clearer, less distorted, and so pure that it has been described as sounding almost unreal. Of course, the sound that the radio or television station transmits still has analog components; until digital transmitters and receivers become a reality, the pure sound and fidelity of the compact disc cannot be realized by the home or auto listener via radio. One advantage of a disc format is that it can be started at any point without fast-forwarding through other material, as must be done with tape.

The video disc has found a place in computerized television instruction, where individualized programmed learning can be utilized. Because of the rapid, easy access to disc information, a student can be given additional televised information almost instantly when needed.

Audio and video discs have similar benefits, though video disc technology has not caught on to any degree in commercial broadcasting in the present formats. It seems probable that some form of video disc will emerge, though it may be as a computer "hard disk."

TAPE MACHINES

Tape technology came out of World War II and revolutionized the ability for radio producers to record programs. The original tape was on reel-to-reel machines. Cart machines were developed to overcome cueing problems for spots. The cassette has been slow in being accepted by radio broadcasters, though it has become the standard for most video tape.

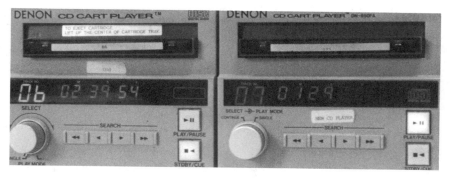

Figure 10–20   The compact disk uses digital technology.

Video tape uses the same basic theory of the magnetic storage used for audio tape. It came onto the market in the mid-1950s, resulting in many industry changes as the technology was perfected.

Reel-to-Reel

Reel-to-reel audio tape decks may be used to record on several parallel tracks simultaneously. On multi-track audio, there is often a track for each performer on tape up to two inches wide. Each track can be edited, enhanced, and blended into the whole. Quality of performance previously unattainable is now possible. What is true of music is also true of commercials, audio drama, and special effects. Multiple-track video tape recording of audio is done primarily on video cassettes, which have largely replaced video reel-to-reel tape.

For news, audio tape (which has been recorded on one track only) may be physically cut (using a razor blade in a specially designed holder) and reassembled, saving only those words and sounds that are to be aired with the story. (See physical editing, later in this chapter.) Audio tape editing by computer is a more exacting, less tedious method.

Figure 10–21 A multitrack audio tape reel-to-reel deck has a VU meter for each track.

Video tape editing cannot be done satisfactorily by physically cutting and splicing the tape. Video tape editing is done by selective duplication of materials from one tape to another. More advanced systems use time code numbering of each frame. An edit decision list is fed to a computer, which then carries out the editing process.

Reel-to-reel audio tapes are recorded at varying speeds, depending on the content and the quality required. The 15 inches per second (ips) speed is preferred for editing, because it is easy to find edit points. At the other extreme, some reel-to-reels can be played at such a slow pace that by reversing the direction of the tape and switching to the other tracks as the tape continues to play, an entire week's programming can be recorded on one standard tape. This is valuable as a reference in case of defamation lawsuits and the like, or when questions come up as to whether a commercial presentation was aired properly.

Cart Machines

Audio cart machines allow for a "tight" board where program elements happen rapidly or even at the same time, an aspect extremely important in many of today's formats. The continuous loop of tape on the "cart" recues itself for instant play each time (unless a hurried disc jockey somehow stops the tape instead of letting it recue). Carts may be recorded with one short message that repeats each time the cart is played, or a cart may contain several spots that play in rotation. A cart inserts a cue tone on a separate channel each time the recorder is set to record. The cue tone at the beginning of the recording is a signal for the cart machine to stop when the continuous loop of tape returns to that point. The next time that cart is started, it is precisely at the beginning of the intended message. As a rule, cart machines do not have erase heads as other tape recorders do. A bulk eraser is used to *degauss* (erase) all previous recording and cue tones to prepare a cart for recording.

Cassette Recorder/Players

The audio cassette recorder has become the note pad of the electronic journalist (as well as of the newspaper reporter). For an interview or an on-the-scene report of a news event, the extremely portable audio cassette recorder has become almost essential. With it audio broadcast quality is available in an extremely small unit. Unless special equipment is available, however, the cassette does not lend itself well to editing. If it is necessary to edit an interview, the tape usually is *dubbed* (copied) to reel-to-reel tape. Most recorded video is recorded on video cassettes, and may range from a 10-second spot to an hour-long or longer program.

Digital Audio Tape

The clarity and frequency response of compact discs is also available on tape. Stations can record network programming as well as local production for

Figure 10–22 Cart machines may be stacked to preserve space.

later airing in digital-quality high fidelity. When *digital audio tape* (DAT) systems were introduced they were relatively expensive, but as with most new technology, as demand has increased, the prices are tending to come down. Digital audio tape is becoming a broadcast standard; digital video tape lies somewhere in the future. As noted earlier, it promises completely faithful reproduction and no deterioration of the image, as happens each time video is rerecorded (dubbed) or re-edited.

PATCH BAYS

In addition to modifying the routing of signals using the audio board's keys and delegation switches, routing may be achieved with patch bays (patch panels).

Figure 10–23   An audio cart resting on a bulk eraser. Cart machines have no
                 eraser heads.

Traditional Plugs

A *patch panel* is a series of outputs and inputs that can be accessed with
patch cords, which change the intended routing of the audio or video signals. If a
component such as a recorder is disabled, another unit may be brought up on that

Figure 10–24 Comparing a digital cassette with a standard audio cassette.

channel on the video switcher or audio console by patching the other unit into the disabled unit's patch panel input.

Patch cords may be double-pronged or single-pronged depending upon the design of the system.

Electronic Patching

Patching may be done with a *routing switcher*, an electronic patch panel that allows any output to be routed to any or all inputs in the system without the use of patch cords.

AUDIO TECHNIQUES

Among the techniques that the board operator should master are cueing records and keeping levels in balance.

Figure 10–25 A patch panel allows many signal routings.

Cueing

Cueing records allows records to get up to speed before the music is heard. One way to cue records is to choose the desired cut on the record. Put the tone arm needle on the record before the beginning of the cut. With the pot of that channel in "cue" on the console and the turntable in neutral, turn the turntable clockwise until a sound is heard. Then turn the turntable counterclockwise one-third to one-half a turn ahead of the beginning of the sound. (Using the record label for a reference point is easier than trying to keep your eye on a spot on the unmarked record groove). Select the proper turntable speed, take the pot out of cue, and the record is ready to play.

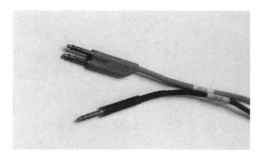

Figure 10–26 Patch cords may be single- or double-pronged, depending on the patch panel.

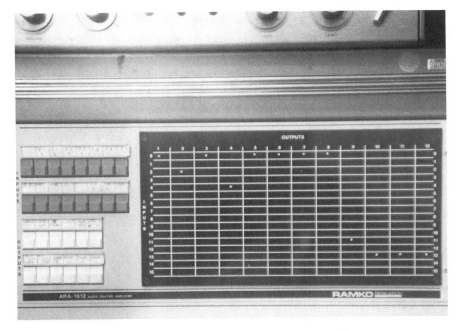

Figure 10–27 The routing switcher is an electronic patch panel.

Figure 10–28 Cueing a record.

Balancing Levels

One of the most common errors of beginning board operators is failure to watch the VU meter in maintaining output levels. There is a tendency to listen to the control room monitor, which may or may not correlate with what is being sent out over the air. If you fail to carefully watch the VU meter and ride gain, various programming elements may be too loud or too soft. Levels must be carefully monitored in the headset when you are speaking over music. As noted earlier, novices tend to have the music so loud that the announcer's voice is overwhelmed. When you are doing a *voice-over* (VO), you must keep the music level low, and in most cases the voice is the primary element that activates the VU meter. The same levels that the radio dee-jay or TV audio person must keep in balance are also an essential consideration in documentary and corporate television programming, whether on audio or on video.

Packaging

Packages are usually thought of as stories that are to be used in a newscast, though packages may be commercials or other program elements such as short features. A *package* is a short recorded segment that should have a beginning, a middle, and an end; or as your speech teacher probably said, an introduction, a body, and a close. A package tells a story and needs to have a single focus with all elements interrelating.

Physical Editing

An audio package may be put together by physically editing the audio tape on a reel-to-reel tape. By carefully listening to a tape, you can determine which elements you wish to save and which parts should be eliminated. Those parts to be eliminated may be physically cut out using a razor blade and a cutting block. If certain parts are to be moved around, these may also be cut out and saved. Special adhesive tape can be used to put the tape back together in the proper order. The process is simple, but you must take care to be sure that the elements are correctly reassembled, with the adhesive tape on the non-recording side of the audio tape. As pointed out earlier, physical patching of video is not a practical operation.

COMPUTER USES

The computer is becoming more and more a part of the production studio. Tape editing, news story access, and effects (for commercials and news stories) all can be expected to be more easily done with the aid of a computer.

Computer Editing

Several methods of computer editing for audio are being used. One system allows the editor to see the analog version of the sound being edited on the computer screen. In other cases, the ear determines where the cuts and assembly points should be. In each case, the tape is not physically cut; rather, it is rerecorded on the edited version of the tape, as previously described for video tape editing. Digital rerecording can be done without loss of quality. As digital tape becomes standard, computer digital editing can be expected to become standard too.

Computerized Newsroom

In the computerized newsroom, a computer data bank receives all wire copy as it comes from the wire services as well as stories that are written by reporters at the station. Stories are selected by the news editor on a computer terminal, modified as he or she sees fit, and grouped together to create the newscast that is read in the studio by the announcer from a computer screen, or is projected onto a teleprompter. The only paper involved is the hard copy that newscasters have on the set for emergencies and possible copies for camera people, directors, and other technical personnel.

Automation

Automation has been around since the 1960s, but as the computer has been perfected, so too has automation become more reliable, more flexible, and perhaps more functional. Interestingly, some stations that had switched to automation have found that a real, live dee-jay is preferred by listeners. Many stations have thus switched back to live announcers, though the computer assists that provide programming elements at the operators' fingertips help give stations a consistent, upbeat sound. In many television stations, a number of operations are similarly automated—with commercials inserted at station breaks automatically, for example.

EXPERIENCE

In spite of the magic of digital and the wonder of the computer, nothing seems to create a feeling of professionalism more than the experience and intelligent understanding of announcers with broad educational backgrounds, who are carefully planning what their next ''ad lib'' will be, or the next manipulation that will be required for the effect they wish to achieve using the marvels of modern technology. Professional announcers help provide the distinctive sound of top radio and television operations.

EXERCISES

1. Record a TV talk segment of about five minutes. Edit it down to two minutes. Be sure that you have a beginning, a middle, and an end. Save it on tape. Then edit it down to be used in a 30-second package. If you have not mastered editing skills at this point, view a similar tape and write out a description of your editing decisions. An additional option will be to edit this as an audio package.

2. Record an ad lib description of a campus event. Edit it down to make a 60-second audio package. Add additional narration if necessary.

3. Edit a piece of instrumental music down to a 30-second bed for a commercial. Use the beginning and the end of the cut. Record over the bed, striving for good balance between voice and music.

4. Record a 15-minute dee-jay segment. Avoid any dead air by anticipating when elements of programming are to occur, sometimes overlapping voice and music. Listen for balance.

5. Prepare a three-minute newscast to be performed before a studio or classroom camera.

BROADCAST VOCABULARY WORD LIST   **Unit 10-A**

1. bursar (n)—financial officer at a university

   _____   *bur' sur*

2. matriculate (v)—to enroll or become enrolled in a university

   _____   *mu trik' yew layt*

3. alma mater (n)—the school one attended or song of a school

   _____   *al mu maw' tur*

4. alumnus (n)—male graduate or former student

   _____   *u lum' nus*

5. alumni (n)—plural form of *alumnus*; may refer to both men and women

   _____   *u lum' nigh*

6. alumna (n)—a female graduate or former student

   _____   *u lum' nu*

7. alumnae (n)—plural form of *alumna*

   _____   *u lum' nee*

8. cavalry (n)—soldiers on horseback

   _____   *kav' ul ree*

9. faculty (n)—the instructors at a school

   _____   *fak' ul tee*

10. coup d'etat (n)—an attempted government takeover

   _____   *kew du taw'*

11. cum laude—with praise

   _____   *kewm lau' day* or *kewm lau' du*

12. defamatory (adj)—slanderous or libelous

   _____   *di fam' u tor ee*

13. microscopy (n)—the use of microscopes

   _____   *migh kros' ku pee*

14. plagiarism (n)—using someone else's material as your own

   _____   *play' jur iz um*

15. stipend (n)—payment for work or services

   _____   *stigh' pund*

16. honorarium (n)—a monetary gift to a professional for services that do not traditionally require payment

   _____   *on ur air' ee um*

17. tenure (n)—holding of a position over an extended period

   _____   *ten' yur*

18. pedagogy (n)—the art or study of teaching

   _____   *ped' u goh jee*

19. colleague (n)—a fellow professional

   _____   *kol' eeg*

20. sabbatical (n)—academic leave, usually for study, research, or travel

   _____   *su bat' i kul*

BROADCAST VOCABULARLY WORD LIST
GAZETTEER   Unit 10-B

1. Des Moines—city in Iowa

   _____   *du moin'*

2. Gloucester—city in England

   _____   *glos' tur*

3. La Jolla—city in California

   _____   *lu hoi' yu*

4. Le Havre—port city in France

   _____   *lu hauv' ru*

5. Leicester—English city, also a breed of sheep

   _____   *les' tur*

6. Lima—largest city in Peru

   _____   *lee' mu*

7. Lima—city in Ohio

   _____   *ligh' mu*

8. Sorbonne—part of the University of Paris, France

   _____   *sor bon'* or *sor   bun'*

9. Ankara–capital of Turkey

   _____   *ang' kur u*

10. Bordeaux—French seaport

    _____   *bor doh'*

11. Cannes—city of French film festival

    _____   *kan'*

12. Iraq and Iran—middle Eastern countries

    _____   *i rauk' i ran'*

13. Tanganyika—lake in central Africa

    _____   *tang u nyee' ku*

14. Pontchartrain—lake in Louisiana

    _____   *pon' chu train*

15. Cayuga—one of the Finger Lakes in New York State

    _____   *kigh yew' gu*

16. Yangtze—Chinese river (fourth longest in the world)

    _____   *yang' see*

17. Tigris-Euphrates—river system in Turkey, Syria, and Iraq

    _____   *tigh' gris - yew fray' teez*

18. Oahu—one of the Hawaiian islands

    _____   *oh wau' hew*

19. Majorca—Spanish island in the Mediterranean

    _____   *mu yor' ku*

20. Hokkaido—northern Japanese island

    _____   *hohk kigh' doh*

WORD LIST PARAGRAPH   Unit 10-A

After paying her fees at the bursar's office, the young woman was ready to matriculate at her new alma mater. An alumna of the institution had recommended a course in microscopy. Certainly, the tenure of the professor teaching the course suggested that the pedagogy was outstanding. She had won awards from her colleagues for the research she had engaged in during her sabbatical, and an alumni award with a stipend attached was also forthcoming. Many nurses were alumnae of the program and had awarded an honorarium when the honored professor presented a program for them.

Meanwhile, across campus, a student had committed a virtual coup d'etat by presenting research on the history of the U.S. cavalry. A history professor suggested plagiarism and made other defamatory remarks. But the student was able to prove his veracity and became an alumnus graduating cum laude.

WORD LIST PARAGRAPH   Unit 10-B

Travel, they say, is broadening. Most of us will try to travel when the weather is mild. You may want to visit Des Moines in the spring or fall because the summers are hot there. In England, Gloucester and Leicester tend to be rainy and a bit on the cool side, even in the summertime. The beautiful city of Lima, Peru, is enjoying a moderate winter while the similarly named Lima, Ohio, is sweating out the summer heat. Although farther south, La Jolla is on the shores of the Pacific, which tends to moderate its climate.

Traveling to France to study at the Sorbonne, students will usually land at Bordeaux or Le Havre. The film festival at Cannes is a must-see for most American students and usually takes place when the weather is mild. If you plan to see the Middle East you may end up in Iran or Iraq, perhaps by way of Ankara. Avoid the summers in these desert countries at all cost.

Large bodies of water, such as lakes, tend to offer moderate climates, often year-round. From tropical Tanganyika, to semi-tropical Lake Pontchartrain, to the cooler climate of the Finger Lakes and Lake Cayuga, the traveler can always find a desirable climate in which to enjoy lake scenery.

11
Radio Formats

OBJECTIVES
Upon completion of this chapter the student should be able to:

1. Explain the meaning of the term *format,* and note the difference between a generic format and a specialized format.
2. Describe programming practices in early radio.
3. Name the "first" radio format and explain why it may be so considered.
4. Define MOR and note its place in the history of formats.
5. Describe three vintage format types and demographics of each.
6. Explain play lists and play wheels.
7. Draw a play wheel that might be used by a news format and one for a vintage format of your choice.
8. Give the anecdotal story which describes the origination of the top-40 format.
9. Explain the evolution of AOR, the objective behind the progressive format, and indicate the types of music played.
10. Describe the programming of the first all-news and the first news-talk stations. Give the call letters and location of each station.
11. Explain the regulatory and technical events that led to the proliferation of beautiful music stations. Describe the format's present status.
12. Describe the primary reason for the popularity of the country format.
13. Explain the limitations and advantages to the advertiser of the classical music format.
14. List and describe the four factors that kept radio viable when television came on the scene.
15. Describe the urban contemporary format and its evolution.
16. Describe the radio formats which seem to appeal to a broad range of age groups.

EARLY PHILOSOPHIES

"People don't listen to stations. They listen to programs." This was the pitch of a salesman for KRSC, a minor radio station in Seattle during the 1940s. The reasoning went, "When 'we' have the ball game on our station [the Seattle Rainiers of the old Pacific Coast League], we're number one."

It is still true today. People tend to listen to programming on radio and watch programs on TV. People usually tune to a station for its programming, rather than to a station regardless of what may be on. Certainly there are exceptions—people get in the habit of tuning to a particular station, and just leave it on. With radio, this usually means that the type of programming the listener prefers is what is featured. On broadcast television, however, the listener more probably tunes for a specific program that is scheduled. Before television remote controls, and before the multiple choices of cable or a satellite dish, people in fringe reception areas may have had only one dependable signal, and they may have gotten into the habit of watching one channel. Much the same was true in 1920s radio.

NETWORK DOMINATION

Spearheaded by David Sarnoff and Owen Davis, the National Broadcasting Company broadcast the first major national network programming in 1926. Coast-to-coast broadcasting on a regular basis followed in 1928 after NBC had split into the Red and the Blue networks. What was to become CBS evolved from the Columbia Phonograph Radio Network in 1928 when entrepreneur William Paley took over the money-losing organization.[1]

Network radio development continued until World War II. Network programming tended to dominate the airwaves, yet there were some independent stations in the metropolitan markets that programmed primarily recorded music. This was in spite of the fact that multiple types of programming were expected by the FRC (Federal Radio Commission), which had come into being with the Radio Act of 1927, and the FCC (Federal Communications Commission), which succeeded it as a result of the Communications Act of 1934.

PROGRAM LENGTH

The federal regulators originally set up a required station identification every 15 minutes or every half-hour, depending on the length of the program. Programs usually ran 15 or 30 minutes. Rarely did programs on network stations extend to a full hour. It took a special FCC dispensation for the hour-long *Lux Radio Theatre* to have a station ID between the second and third acts (at 40 minutes after the

[1] Sydney W. Head and Christopher H. Sterling, *Broadcasting in America*, 6th ed. (Boston: Houghton Mifflin Co., 1990), pp. 45–46.

hour). All programs began and ended on the hour, or a 15-minute increment thereof, in the "golden age" of radio (the 1930s and 1940s). This tradition remains today on TV, though the 15-minute increment has largely given way to the 30-minute time slot, and most radio stations have one continuous program. With the time slotting on television, listeners can change stations and not miss the beginning of a show they want to hear on another channel.

THE '20s

Westinghouse (originally a manufacturer of railway air brakes) saw a way to sell radio sets made by its emerging electronics arm by providing programming for potential set owners. Westinghouse's KDKA was the first licensed commercial station in the United States, going on the air in time to cover the Harding-Cox presidential election in November 1920. (An earlier presidential election coverage by radio had come in 1916, when Lee De Forest broadcast the Wilson-Hughes contest. Using a newspaper, the *New York American,* as his source of information, De Forest incorrectly announced Charles Evans Hughes to be the winner.)

Some Program Firsts

The high points of early radio programming often were remotes of special events. A second Westinghouse station, WJZ in Newark, made history with the first broadcast of the 1921 World Series, between the New York Giants and the New York Yankees.[2] RCA's WJY Hoboken pioneered with the first major heavyweight prize fight to be broadcast: the Dempsey-Carpentier battle[3] (though KDKA is also given credit for this sportscast.)[4]

Early radio inventor and promoter Lee De Forest had done the first broadcasts of the Metropolitan Opera in 1911, though there were few radios to carry it. In fact, for many years the basic mass media function of radio was unrealized, radio being viewed primarily as a means of point-to-point communication much as the telephone or telegraph, but without wires (thus its early name, the wireless).

The Station Deluge

The excitement generated by one commercial station going on the air in 1920, followed by a few more in 1921, made it apparent to many people that radio was to become a future source of great political and economic power. In addition, owning a radio station became an important status symbol. In 1922, over 500

---

[2] Erik Barnouw, *A Tower in Babel* (New York: Oxford University Press, 1966), p. 84.

[3] Ibid., p. 80.

[4] Lawrence W. Lichty and Malachi C. Topping, "History of Broadcasting and KDKA Radio," in *American Broadcasting* (New York: Hastings House, 1975), p. 108.

stations went on the air, including 72 operated by educational institutions, 69 by newspapers, and 29 by department stores. Twelve stations went on the air under the auspices of religious groups.[5]

Early Programming

Early educational stations attempted various instructional programming, including farm and home information. This was often combined with news and classical music for a combination that might be considered a format (if one that might seem somewhat incongruous today). Several of the educational stations survive today: KOAC Corvallis (at Oregon State University), WHA (University of Wisconsin in Madison), and WOI (Iowa State University in Ames, Iowa).

Stations pioneered by newspapers, such as WMAQ—founded by the *Chicago Daily News*—did not program news or news-talk predominately (as has been done by that same station in the 1990s). Department stores certainly were not conducting a home shopping service like today's television shopping networks.

Format Pioneers

While state college–owned stations featured the classics, stations owned by religious groups had their own formatting ideas. Religious station programming began with preaching and religious music, much as is heard on many stations of this type today. Radio has been a popular way to "spread the gospel," almost from the birth of radio as a mass medium. We probably could say that religious radio was first with the modern concept of a single type of programming. The first important voice broadcast by Canadian Aubrey Fessenden on Christmas Eve in 1906 included religious music—Handel's *Largo* and Gounod's *O Holy Night*. The first remote from a church by a commercial station was the church service broadcast by KDKA in 1920.[6] Though stations broadcast whatever programming they could muster in the early 1920s, there was little thought of program specialization as we think of it today (except in the realm of religion, where stations were owned by church groups).

The McPherson Tiff One of the problems of early broadcasting technology was that of frequency stability. Stations would often drift from one frequency to another. As engineering improved, so too did the enforcement of standards. Tests for frequency compliance by the federal regulators became critical in the struggle to create and maintain order on the airwaves. A popular evangelist of the 1920s was Aimee Semple McPherson, who founded the Church of the Four Square Gospel in Los Angeles. McPherson's church operated a radio station with a transmitter whose signal tended to wander up and down the dial. McPherson was repeatedly warned to improve the station's engineering. When the Commerce

---

[5] Erik Barnouw, *A Tower in Babel* (New York: Oxford University Press, 1966), p. 4.
[6] Ibid, p. 71.

Department (which then was in charge of regulation) ordered the church's station sealed so that it could no longer broadcast because of frequency shifts, the response from McPherson was the following telegram:

> PLEASE ORDER YOUR MINIONS OF SATAN TO LEAVE MY STATION ALONE STOP YOU CANNOT EXPECT THE ALMIGHTY TO ABIDE BY YOUR WAVE LENGTH NONSENSE STOP WHEN I OFFER MY PRAYERS TO HIM I MUST FIT INTO HIS WAVE RECEPTION STOP OPEN THIS STATION AT ONCE[7]

Secretary of Commerce Herbert Hoover stood firm. It took better engineering before the station returned to the air.

The religious format is probably the one format that has existed little changed in some cases almost from the inception of radio broadcasting as a mass medium.

Classics vs. Jazz Just as religious zealots of the '20s thought that their message would convert the unchurched, classical music enthusiasts believed that a steady diet of serious music would convert radio's newly musically aware listeners into classical buffs.

> It was assumed that given adequate air time the inherent superiority of classical music would put an end to the growth of "jazz."[8]

One mail survey showed classical music 33 percent more popular than jazz.[9] Perhaps the survey methods of the 1920s were less accurate than those used today. It goes without saying that an early mass media assumption, the so-called "inoculation" theory (which held that large doses of propaganda would create or change attitudes), failed to work with either religion or classical music.

THE '30s AND '40s

Some stations excelled in certain types of broadcast programming in the 1920s and 1930s, though most radio stations tended to try to be all things to all people. As late as 1946, the Federal Communications Commission, in a report to the industry, laid out seven kinds of programming that stations were expected to include in their daily broadcasts. These included:

[7] Sydney W. Head and Christopher H. Sterling, *Broadcasting in America*, 6th ed. (Boston: Houghton Mifflin Company, 1990), p. 48.

[8] Frank Biocca, "Media and Perceptual Shifts: Early Radio and the Clash of Musical Cultures," *Journal of Popular Culture*, 24, 2, Fall 1990, p. 9.

[9] Ibid.

Figure 11–1   Studio sound effects often helped create "theater of the mind."

Entertainment, Educational, Religious, Agricultural, Civic (including fraternal, Chamber of Commerce, Charitable, and other non-governmental civic content), Governmental, . . . and News.[10]

Entertainment in the form of former vaudeville comedians, dramas, news, sports, quiz shows, and concerts made up the broadcast evening in much the same competitive spirit as television, which was to follow. Soap operas (often developed by the soap companies or their advertising agencies) filled many of the daytime hours on network radio in the 1930s. In January 1940 there were 55 hours weekly of sponsored daytime drama.[11] This was, in effect, a daytime format in itself.

[10] Charles A. Siepmann, "Public Service Responsibility of Broadcast Licensees (The Blue Book)" (Washington, D.C.: Federal Communications Commission, 1946), in Frank J. Kahn, ed., *Documents of American Broadcasting,* 2nd ed. (New York: Appleton, Century-Crofts, 1973), p. 175.

[11] Ibid., p. 176.

Live Performance

At one point in the 1920s, the Federal Radio Commission restricted radio stations with the most favorable frequencies from playing music from records. Live programming was deemed superior. Certainly recording technology had neither high fidelity nor stereo available. But even after the live music edict had been compromised early on, the national networks still clung to the concept that live music and other live programming were far superior. Only live programming was presented on the NBC and CBS networks, which dominated radio programming at the time. The two major networks owned or had affiliated with most, if not all, of the high-powered stations in most U.S. markets.

The two NBC radio networks and the CBS radio network became dominant in the late 1920s and did not relinquish this control even when the Mutual Broadcasting System, which was a cooperative organization owned by its members, became a national force in the 1930s with over 500 affiliates. When NBC was forced by the government to divest itself of one of its two networks in 1943, the NBC Blue Network became the American Broadcasting Company (ABC).

Recorded Programs

Continuing even into the 1940s, shows produced live in New York were done a second time live for the West Coast audience, so network shows were always live. In 1946, after the birth of ABC, that fledgling network was trying to attract highly rated shows. Recording quality had improved with the advent of audio tape, and Bing Crosby wanted to record his weekly program. Only ABC was willing to accept this stipulation, making the *Bing Crosby Show* the first recorded network show and the most important entertainment offering of the newest network.

Non-network stations programmed mostly recorded music, often with news on the hour or half-hour. Exceptions were stations that carried local professional sports. They would often build part of their programming around their live sportscasts. The Federal Communications Commission emphasized that:

> The *entire* listening public within the service area of a station, or of a group of stations in one community, is entitled to service from that station or stations . . . . *If . . . the station performs its duty in furnishing a well-rounded program, the rights of the community* have been achieved.[12]

Even in 1946, however, the FCC was beginning to entertain the concept of station specialization. The Blue Book also stated:

---

[12] Ibid., p. 173.

In metropolitan areas where the listener has his choice of several stations, balanced service to listeners can be achieved . . . by a number of comparatively specialized stations which considered together offer a balanced service to a community.[13]

Middle of the Road

The result of the FCC programming rules tended to be that most stations played an assortment of music, not with a play-wheel, play-list regularity (discussed later in this chapter), but rather within programs featuring one type of music or the music of one performer. The programming might include a 15-minute or half-hour show from records of country-western music, or of Fred Waring and "over half a hundred Pennsylvanians."

The popular format of the mid-1940s tended to be "middle of the road," which has been called music of moderation—not too much country, not too many top hits, not too many old favorites, not too much of anything. MOR, as it became known, combined conservative music programming with news, radio personalities, probably some sports, and maybe some talk feature programming, though call-in talk shows did not become popular until the 1960s.

'50s AND '60s CHANGES

After World War II and the arrival of television as a mass medium, many radio stations dropped their network affiliations and started to develop their own identities. The collapse of radio was predicted, as major drama and comedy shows moved from radio to television. Radio networks had little to offer but news, which many radio stations thought that they could do just as well and much more cheaply themselves using the news wire services. The FCC relaxed programming diversification requirements under pressure from radio stations struggling to survive. U.S. radio stations were no longer expected to carry all of the seven categories of programming.

Origins of Youth Formats

The current concept of *format* is traced by some historians to two deejays from Omaha's KOWH, Todd Storz and Bill Steward. They were sitting in a bar in 1954. Patrons kept playing the same currently popular music over and over. The idea seems to have struck both of them at about the same time: the two deejays suddenly realized that what they were hearing could be a radio format, and "top 40" was born.[14] Listen to the music that jukebox patrons play. The same few pieces do tend to get most of the play, and they do repeat over and over. A wireless jukebox proved to be what many listeners wanted.

---

[13] Ibid., p. 175.

[14] Michael Keith, *Broadcast Voice Performance* (Boston: Focal Press, 1989), p. 36.

Radio Changes

Several changes saved radio from the prophecy of the predictors of doom, who saw television in the process of completely destroying radio. The changes had to do with both technology and programming.

Technology   Foremost technologically was the invention of the *transistor* which was smaller and lighter, but performed the function of vacuum tubes. No longer were radios confined to the living room, where they had been replaced by the television set. Multiple sets appeared throughout the home, and car radios became standard equipment. More significantly, however, were the portable sets that went to the beach and the ball game. Battery receivers were truly portable for the first time. Radio gained the capability of becoming a constant companion.

The second technological improvement that brought radio new fans was *stereophonic transmission.* Beginning in 1961, FM not only had increased fidelity but also offered stereo to attract listeners.[15]

A third technological improvement was that of *recording quality* with the advent of CBS's long-playing 33 $\frac{1}{3}$ rpm one-record ''albums'' and RCA's single-play 45s. The need for live performance to preserve music quality had lessened considerably. All in all, the technologies of radio made significant strides during the '50s and '60s.

Programming   At about the same time, the FCC ruled that AM and FM stations in major markets that had carried the same programming simultaneously had to be programmed separately. This almost doubled the total number of radio listening options in some cities. Specialized programming was one of the immediate results. This, in turn, led to a rapid increase in the demographic studies of radio audiences, and sales personnel often found it easier to sell the specific audience created by specialized programming.

Of the several changes, however, perhaps the most significant was the advent of the popularity of rock and roll. Rock managed to infiltrate the top-40 formats and become youth's symbol of revolt against the older generations. Many teenagers forsook TV for the rock of radio. Rock music may have been the primary element that caused the phoenix of radio to rise from the ashes.

THE RULES CHANGE

After World War II and the mass migration of national advertisers to television, the FCC continued to relax radio rules. The only station ID required became the one on the hour. Even this was relaxed to on the hour or within three minutes before or after. Many stations (particularly those playing contemporary hits) made

---

[15] John Bittner, *Broadcasting and Telecommunication: An Introduction,* 3rd ed. (Englewood Cliffs, N.J.: Prentice Hall, 1991), p. 72.

a point of playing a top hit record that continued past the top of the hour and giving their ID at three minutes after. Since other stations were probably giving an ID and starting news or other programming changes right on the hour, listeners to the contemporary hit stations missed the natural programming break, and were not tempted to tune away on the hour to another program that had already started.

Of course, another way the hourly ID was disguised was by identifying the station between every musical piece or between each group of selections. In addition to the tune-out factor being somewhat overcome, this ID reiteration also implanted the call letters of the station in the minds of the listeners so that when they were called by a survey organization, they could readily remember the call letters.

GENERIC FORMATS

After the 1950s and 1960s, most radio stations tended to have just one continuous program, be it a specific kind of music or extended talk. Both music and talk often varied only to the extent that the program host was different. That one continuous program had become what is referred to as a *format*. Stations are often classified by generic format, or broad general category of programming; e.g., adult contemporary (AC), easy listening (EL), urban contemporary (UC), religious, contemporary hit radio (CHR), album-oriented rock (AOR), oldies, talk or news-talk, and ethnic (mostly Spanish language). Most formats are variations of these basic types.

Specific Formats

A station's format, however, is more than just the type of music played or the fact that a station airs nothing but news. A station's specific format is that collection of production elements that makes a station unique: announcers' style, grouping of programming and spots, the play lists, and the rotation and frequency at which songs are played and repeated.

For a radio station to maintain a consistent sound that attracted and held listeners, it was theorized that there needed to be some consistent pattern to the programming. Play lists and the format clocks (or music wheels) were the answer.

Play Lists

A *play list* usually consists of about 20 to 25 songs that are repeated periodically within the format so that listeners establish favorites, or regularly get to hear the favorites they may have already selected. A station often has a variety of play lists that get varying amounts of play at various times of the day. A top-40 station might have a short top-10 or top-20 list, a second-20 list, a recent list (up to six months old), and golden hits (up to two years old). Songs from each play list get a certain amount of play at specific times during the hour.

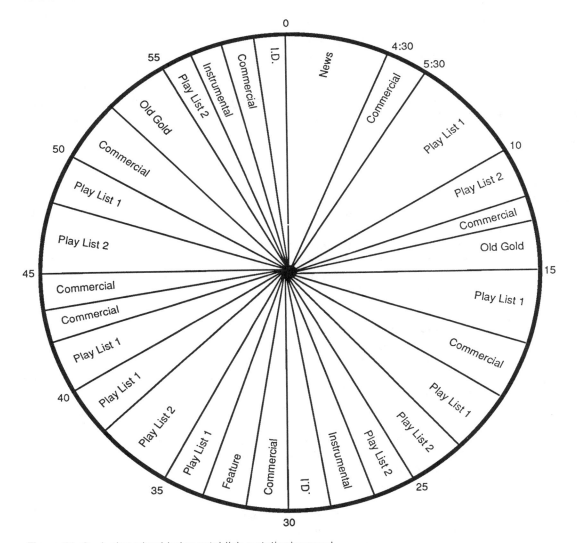

Figure 11–2 A play wheel helps establish a station's sound.

Play Wheels

Who designed the first play wheel is unknown. Probably several programmers came up with it simultaneously, as happens with inventions whose times
have come. The idea is simple and is used in many, if not most, formats.

The music rotation, programming, and advertising elements can be displayed on a *play wheel* or *hits clock*, indicating at what time during the hour a song

from a specific play list or other program element is aired. News-talk stations also have clocks with rotation of news types: national-international, regional, local, sports, commentary, etc. While music stations may not explain their rotation clock, news stations often do. Many cable TV viewers are probably familiar with the hourly schedule of the CNN Headline News cable network. Stations generally set a pattern and follow it on an hourly schedule, though the clock rotation often varies at different times of the day to please the slightly different audiences that the station hopes to attract.

THE '50s AND '60s FORMATS

The idea of formula radio was developed in the 1950s. It continued to grow in the '60s, as various demographic groups were identified and as alternatives to top 40 were developed. In the '50s and '60s, the most popular format in most markets was top 40. As that designation seemed to gather some negative connotations, the name became contemporary hit radio, the term by which this format is recognized today.

Contemporary Hit Radio (CHR)

Contemporary hit radio (or top 40) is the radio format that appeals to the youngest of the avid music listeners. It is fast-paced, and it is the format that is the most repetitious.

Many of the original top-40 stations featured local news and gaudy vehicles with their call letters emblazoned thereon. They would roam the streets, monitor police radio frequencies, and sometimes arrive on the scene before the police, providing instant on-the-scene news coverage. Most of the station vans in later years became remote sites for at-the-sponsor's-place-of-business dee-jay parties.

Characteristic of the CHR format is a rapid pace: no dead air; often two sounds at once (as if to make sure). *Pacers* consist of very short, upbeat musical interludes—sometimes with sound effects and reverb or other effects. These are often added to keep up the frantic pace. WOW Radio in Omaha bragged that they played more music than anyone else. Indeed they did, by speeding up normal 33 rpm records to 35 rpms, raising the pitch slightly, and giving the station a really upbeat feel. Each record, of course, got through almost 10 percent sooner. So the station really did play more music.

A CHR station might have a request line that took requests that never got aired specifically—because nine times out of 10 these requests were already in the rotation and the listeners would hear their "requests" if they just kept listening. Though the specific request might not be inserted into the format, the station could be expected to carefully tabulate each request that came in as a basis for future programming decisions.

Figure 11–3 CD storage makes selection easy.

"Top 40 came out of middle-sized markets, and out of middle America."[16] It revolutionized radio, with many imitators around the country and abroad. It was also the catalyst for many other formats.

Adult Contemporary

Many of the polls have shown adult contemporary as tops nationwide, not in the number of stations but in the number of total listeners. AC usually plays established current rock hits (except no hard or acid rock). It aims at the 24- to 39-year-old demographic, which is generally most desired by advertisers. Music is usually played in sweeps (several pieces without a break) and commercials are often in "spot sets" (several spots clustered together). Adult contemporary is also known as "soft rock," "light rock," and "easy hits," suggesting that it is really a version of top 40; it is modified to appeal to a slightly older age group, but involves many of the same programming elements.

[16] David T. MacFarland, "Up from Middle America: The Development of Top 40," in Lawrence W. Lichty and Malachi C. Topping, *A Source Book of the History of Radio and Television* (New York: Hastings House, 1975), p. 402.

Album-Oriented Rock

One of the most intense reactions to top 40 was a rock format that did *not* play the most popular rock hits. This was called progressive rock. When it evolved in the '60s and early '70s, stations using this format played long and often unknown album cuts, and may have had play lists with hundreds of selections. Announcers were "laid back," and might even allow pauses between music and voice. Almost every aspect was opposite of top 40. The stations often featured acid or psychedelic rock. The appeal was to a male demographic, ages 10 to 34. Though the format has more or less merged into other genres, the elusiveness of the adult male listener means that the format still has adherents and is quite popular in some markets.

Progressive rock has softened to album-oriented rock (AOR), and while many of the traditions still exist, the stations airing this format today sound much like AC, since many of the relatively unknown cuts of the past are now more familiar. AOR stations have updated their play lists, but many of the old progressive artists also have a wider acceptance, making AOR a less distinctive sound and more acceptable to a wider audience.

Easy Listening–Beautiful Music

Easy listening has been called "beautiful music," "elevator music," "wallpaper," or "background music." In a way, it was an outgrowth of the technology and FCC regulations of the times, and was another of the revolts against top 40. When FM stations first went on the air, they were primarily owned by the major AM stations, which took out the licenses and squeezed the new stations into their AM studios at minimum expense. The new licenses were taken out as "insurance policies" (just in case the new medium should catch on) and, of course, to keep the competition down as much as possible by using up the available frequencies. The easiest way to program these new FM stations was to simulcast the same programs that were presently on the AM station. In most cases this was what the established stations did.

So, unless you were a classical music buff living in a major metropolitan area where a classical FM station had come on the air, there was little incentive even to purchase a set capable of receiving FM.

In the mid-1960s the FCC ordained the non-duplication rule, which said that stations that had been simulcasting in markets over 110,000 must separate their AM and FM programming. Automation technology had started to prove its worth, and it was obvious to many station operators that the beautiful music format lent itself well to the new circumstances. The beautiful music format had been laid out by Gordon McLendon at KABL in San Francisco in 1959. Many stations across the country had had programming segments of soft, lush, relaxing, slow music often preceded with the admonition, "Now lean back and listen to. . . ." As "beautiful music" became "easy listening," it seemed to find a niche among older listeners as it played lush arrangements of show tunes and standards that had been popular when these listeners were in high school and college. Easy listening has been one of the top-rated music types in many major markets from time to time since the definition of easy listening/beautiful music.

As the population ages, easy listening is undergoing changes. Some broadcasters are theorizing that the baby boomers will never acquire a taste for easy listening and so are leaving the format, but as the president of Bonneville Broadcasting System points out, this "ignores the fact that in every generation instrumental music presentations attract a significant share of the audience."[17]

He continues:

> Easy listening speaks to the needs of a particular kind of person, well educated, upscale but traditionally oriented and conservative. . . . Easy listening is an adult coping mechanism which complements and compensates for busy lives in chaotic urban environments. . . . Listeners use easy listening music as a mood enhancer to reduce tension, relax and to cope with the world (or the traffic) around them.[18]

According to the National Association of Broadcasters:

> It appears that the easy listening format is walking a fine line, attempting to add personality and new product to attract older adult contemporary listeners without alienating the current set of easy listening loyalists.[19]

THE '70s AND '80s

Although disco came upon the scene in the early '70s, and even topped the ratings as a format in New York during one ratings period, it did not have enough substance to be sustainable. Audiences soon became tired of the monotonous beat, especially when they were not on the dance floor. Disco evolved into urban contemporary, a new variation of previous formats with more staying power and broader overall appeal. One of the most interesting changes of direction, which seemed to climax in the 1980s and 1990s, was the rebirth of musical hits from the past.

Urban Contemporary

Suddenly there was disco, and disco was king. Then, just as suddenly, disco was passé. Many of the stations that had adopted a disco format continued the idea of a dance beat and danceable music by evolving into an urban contemporary format.

Urban contemporary usually was and is basically an amalgam of black musical types: rock and roll, soul, rhythm and blues, jazz, and—later—rap. Of

[17] James Opsitnik, "Monday Memo," *Broadcasting,* November 5, 1990, p. 24.
[18] Ibid.
[19] Ed Cohen, "Easy Listening Radio: A Survey of Programmers," *Research & Planning Info-Pak,* National Association of Broadcasters, February 1988, p. 3.

course, most of these music styles had existed long before the disco craze. In fact, in the '40s WVON (Voice of the Negro) in Chicago (and a few other stations in predominantly black population areas) had discovered that by catering to a black audience they could dominate the ratings. The only station in America's second-largest market playing black programming in a metropolitan area that was 50 percent black could not help but be in a dominant position. As with the discovery of a market position for any product, it did not take long for other stations to see what was happening and join in the success. Advertisers were reluctant to appreciate the buying power of the audience at first. Today, urban contemporary which is essentially black radio, often has high listener ratings. Gospel is another of the variations of black radio.

In markets where there is a large Spanish-speaking population, Latin music often becomes part of the mix of the urban contemporary format.

When an artist who has become famous for one particular type of music *crosses over* (has a hit in another genre), a performer and his or her music can be on the play lists and popularity charts of more than one format. Many of the most popular stars sing one of the types of music played by urban contemporary stations, and their recordings are often heard both in CHR and AC stations as well.

Urban contemporary has continued to grow in popularity as more of the top recording artists perform in one of the many black and Latin traditions. In some of America's largest markets, urban contemporary format stations periodically dominate the ratings.

Vintage Radio

A vintage radio station is a station that plays music of an earlier time, which appeals to a demographic of older consumers. The station that plays music of the 1960s (in 1995) can expect a 45-and-older audience, with an emphasis on the 45-to-55 age group. If the choice is 1950s music, the demographic (in 1995) is expected to be age 55 and up, while 1940s music should attract still older listeners. During the 1970s, when a large portion of the population was of high school and college age, the emphasis was on serving this demographic group, the "baby boomers." As they aged, becoming "yuppies," the focus changed to these older listeners who became the largest demographic group. The decade of the 1990s has seen a decided swing toward programming of music of much earlier eras.

Michael Keith has divided vintage music into at least three categories.

> *Oldies,* its offshoot *Classic Hits,* and *Nostalgia* are distinct format genres collectively referred to as *Vintage* and sharing an affinity for the hits of the past. Whereas Oldies stations base their play lists on the chart toppers of the late 1950s and 1960s, Classic Hits stations draw from the 1960s and 1970s. . . . Nostalgia goes back even further, focusing on the popular tunes of the 1940s and 1950s.[20]

[20] Michael C. Keith, *Broadcast Voice Performance* (Boston: Focal Press, 1989), p. 66.

Keith credits Bill Drake and Chuck Blore with the development of "golden oldies" formats in the 1960s and Al Ham with "nostalgia" (also referred to as "Big Band") in the 1970s. "Original hits" stations may go back into the 1930s, and sometimes even earlier, for show tunes and other so-called standards, musical offerings that have gained lasting acceptance. Earlier standards would include the works of Irving Berlin, Jerome Kern, or Rogers and Hart, for example.

Talk Formats

The first all-talk station was KABC Los Angeles, which went all-talk in 1960, using telephone call-in as the basis for listener involvement and conversation.[21]

The first all-news format was developed by Gordon McLendon for a Mexican station, XETRA. "Extra news over Los Angeles" directed its powerful 50,000-watt AM signal to San Diego and Los Angeles, not too many miles from the border. When XETRA made significant inroads in the ratings, there were soon imitators who had the means to do it better. Though independents looking for better ratings followed first (WNWS Chicago, WINS-AM New York), it wasn't long before many CBS network O & Os (owned-and-operated stations) were converting to all-news. They had the (then) vast resources of CBS News to draw on. Stations like KCBS San Francisco, KNX Los Angeles, and WBBM Chicago were soon "all-news, all the time."

All-news is probably the most expensive of the radio formats. It requires not only reporters on the scene for local events, but a variety of news anchors and constant rewriting and updating on stories to hold listeners. It is indeed a far cry from the BBC news reader in the mid-1930s who is reported to have stepped to the microphone at news time to report: "There is no news tonight."

While the all-news stations were being born, KGO San Francisco, an O & O of the ABC network, was pioneering another kind of all-talk radio. Built around drive-time news blocks, the news/talk format included telephone talk show hosts of outstanding capability. Using thoroughly researched topics, the talk show hosts seemed to be geniuses with uncanny insight and a wealth of information. KGO had a 50,000-watt AM signal, directional north and south (in effect making it 100,000 watts in these two directions). The innovations of this station had tremendous influence, especially on the West Coast. Nationwide, stations embracing the news/talk format far exceed the all-news configuration.

Another version of the all-talk formats is what Keith calls news plus. The majority of news-plus stations program adult music, such as nostalgia, easy listening, or adult contemporary, around the news and talk features that represent their primary product.[22]

---

[21] Michael C. Keith, *Radio Programming* (Boston: Focal Press, 1987), p. 99.

[22] Ibid, pp. 99–100.

TIMELESS FORMATS

Some formats seem to appeal to diverse ages and have not evolved primarily from the top-40 tradition. Much as there are formats for older listeners and for younger listeners, so too are there formats that seem to be relatively ageless. Religious, country, and classical music formats tend to be less defined by age than by socioeconomic background.

The religious and country music formats appeal primarily to the blue-collar worker. Classical (or more properly "serious") music appeals more generally to those of elite background or that have been educated in the traditions of the upper classes. Financial status is an important factor, but it is gentility or having a formal music education that seems to be a hallmark of classical music listeners.

Religious Formats

In the 1990s, a broadcast ministry is increasingly popular with churches and ministers because it not only spreads the gospel but also is often an effective fund-raising method. On most commercial radio stations the listener pays indirectly for the service by purchasing the advertised products. On religious radio, there may be direct fund solicitation in addition to help pay for the programming. Stations may be owned by religious organizations, or they may be commercial enterprises like most other stations, selling advertising and air time to religious groups or other advertisers seeking this demographic.

Many of the older religious stations are on the AM dial, but the FCC considers a station run by a non-profit organization to be educational, so the section of the FM dial reserved for educational broadcasters continues to grow in the number of religious broadcasters. There are close to 500 religious stations on the air nationwide.

> In some of our cities, the number of [religious format] radio and television stations have [sic] grown far out of proportion (it would seem) to the population and Christian financial strength of the market.[23]

Religious is a generic format, but there are really many religious formats within the genre. In addition to fund-raising and ownership differences, there are also different programming philosophies. Religious stations may be almost all-talk, with preaching the main programming feature; or they may be primarily music, playing the popular categories of religious rock (sometimes called "Jesus rock"), religious adult contemporary, and religious western music with play lists, play wheels, and many of the style characteristics of sectarian radio.

---

[23] E. Brandt Gustavson, "Seventy Years with the Gospel Message," *Religious Broadcasting,* March 1991, p. 10.

Country

The fastest-growing format in the 1980s and 1990s, and the format with the most stations, has been country. Country stations for many years were found primarily in the Midwest and the South, though there were perennial old country favorites, like the "Sons of the Pioneers" and Gene Autry, who had nationwide fans.

During the 1930s, "Saturday night barn dance" was a generic program type found on major stations from Nashville to Shreveport, and from Chicago to Hollywood. In many instances, these programs were so popular that they were the precursor of all-country programming on radio and, in the 1980s, the all-country Nashville cable network. In many cases, country has long been the choice of the local audience, especially in small Midwestern and Southern towns. The stations that first played mostly country probably were not consciously creating a format, they were just trying to please their blue-collar audiences. Country music has been called

> a penetrating and revealing self-portrait of the blue-collar working class . . . truth set to music . . . and white man's blues.[24]

When country singers cross over to CHR, country also gets listeners formerly in the CHR audience.

For many years country and western, as it was called, drew the disdain of the elite. A Playboy magazine superbunny expressed this sentiment when she said that she thought country music was

> for Okies or people who didn't have enough intelligence to appreciate rock music.[25]

Much as early critics touted classical music over jazz, mainstream popular hits were deemed to be of greater aesthetic value than country music. As country music gained in popularity, the network programmers seemed to try to force it back into its "proper" niche. The *Hit Parade* show, the top-rated popular music show of the 1930s and 1940s, failed to acknowledge the existence or the popularity of the genre, playing only hits that fit its standards.

Like those using other formats, country music stations have adopted the play list and play wheel concepts. So much good country music has been produced in the 1990s that there is not room enough for all of it on the play lists, according to Larry Daniels, president of Country Radio Broadcasters. Daniels sees greater fragmentation of the format "in the directions of traditional, rock, and contemporary country" as a result.[26]

[24] Charles Gritzner, "Country Music: A Reflection of Popular Culture," *Journal of Popular Culture*, 11 (1978), p. 863.

[25] Ibid., p. 861.

[26] Lucia Combo. 1991. "Nashville Notes: The Country Radio Seminar." *Broadcasting*, vol. 120, no. 9., p. 46.

The Classical Tradition

Although the classical music buffs of the 1920s failed to convince the majority of the population that music in the classic European tradition was the most desirable, the music elite had had their chance. At

the very beginning of network radio in the 1926–27 season, classical music had a slight edge over popular [music] forms in the overall amount of air time.[27]

Persons educated in the classics usually tend to find this music the type, or at least one of the types, they prefer.

As with the state or university stations that initially programmed farm and home programming and classical music, public broadcasting stations tend to feature music based on the European classical tradition. Most of the 1,500 FM educational stations carry some classical music programming. The Texaco Metropolitan Opera Network, the longest-running network program on radio, is carried on public radio stations as well as on commercial classical format stations.

Though commercial classical format stations are few in number, and primarily limited to major markets, these stations have devoted followings and boast demographics of high-income, educated listeners usually available nowhere else in radio.

Some stations across the country have prospered using the classical format, among them WCRB (FM) Boston, which broadcasts the Boston Symphony and Boston Pops around the world. WFMT (FM) Chicago was the first radio ''superstation,'' and is heard on cable systems in 44 states. KING (FM), a commercial classical station in Seattle, pulled a rather astounding 3.2 share in a 1990 winter ratings book.[28]

WQXR in New York embarked on a classical format in the 1930s. With the advent of FM, the station expanded to this medium as well. Initially, FM stations not simulcasting an AM signal programmed primarily classical music. FM enthusiasts claimed that only FM had high fidelity, was free of static, and could broadcast silence. (AM transmission aways had a background hum.) With the advent of FM stereo in the 1960s, there was an additional enhancement to attract audiences to the superior sound of the frequency modulation band.

FM ceased to be the fine arts band as the effects of the FCC's mid-1960s non-simulcasting rule went into effect. Later, the advent of satellite network transmission provided higher-frequency response than conventional telephone lines of earlier network interconnection. This meant that more of the popular music types became network programming with FM sound quality.

It is interesting to note that classic jazz has also found a home in segments of programming on classical stations, as have some kinds of folk music.

---

[27] Frank Biocca. ''Media and Perceptual Shifts,'' *Journal of Popular Culture,* 1990, p. 11.
[28] John K. Major, ''Singing Classical Praises,'' *Broadcasting,* October 15, 1990, p. 26.

FORMAT ANNOUNCING STYLES

It would be convenient to say that one particular style of announcing is always found with each of the formats discussed. Of course, this is not the case. There is no one formula applicable to all stations of one genre. There may not be even two

Format Announcing Styles

Format	Announcing Style	Pitch	Age	Pace
Adult contemporary	personality	medium	mature	chatty, conversational
Album-oriented rock	innovative, one-to-one	medium	young adult	fresh, relaxed, intimate
Classical	knowledgeable, authoritative	low	mature	slightly formal
Contemporary hit radio	high-energy, upbeat	fairly high	youthful	frantic, rapid
Country	bright and cheery	natural	mature	friendly, neighborly
Easy listening	warm, relaxed	low, intimate	mature	low-key, conversational
Middle of the road	informed personality	low, resonant	mature	relaxed, no dead air
News-talk	earnest, high-energy	medium	adult	variety
Religious	honest, forthright	richly resonant	mature	restrained enthusiasm
Sports	enthusiastic	fairly high	adult	rapid, excited
Urban contemporary	energetic, with-it	wide range	adult	upbeat, festive
Vintage	recreational, fun	low to mid-range	mature	up-tempo, conversational

Based on Michael C. Keith, *Radio Production: Art and Science* (Boston: Focal Press, 1990), pp. 163–224.

independently programmed stations that follow exactly the same guidelines. So, obviously, announcer profiles will differ as well. There does tend to be a style of announcing that goes with each genre, however, and it appears in the table above.

MANY, MANY FORMATS AND CONTINUING EVOLUTION

The formats discussed here have many variations and modifications. Although some of the variations of the religious format have been noted, there are probably few, if any, stations that adhere to the strict confines of a defined generic format. Urban contemporary varies considerably across the country, depending on the ethnic makeup of the population. Contemporary hit radio and adult contemporary vary from station to station, depending upon the results of station research and the instincts of the program directors. Types of music tend to go through popularity phases, often the result of artists from one genre crossing over into another.

Spanish-language radio continues to gain in popularity as the Spanish-speaking population increases and continues to become more affluent. Most non–English language stations offer a wide variety of programming types, combining music with news and talk to provide "something for everyone" in that non–English speaking community. Spanish stations tend to play music that comes from the place where most of the local population originated: Cuba, Mexico, Central America, etc. As more Spanish stations enter the market, their formats tend to become specialized, much like other U.S. stations.

Ethnic stations spring up wherever there is a sizable, distinct ethnic population. Native Americans, for example, have stations across the contiguous United States and in Alaska.

As long as the United States promotes the free enterprise system in its broadcasting industry, programmers will continue to strive to find an advantage by changing the formula being used to attract an audience. Generic formats will continue to be created and existing formats continue to be modified. The sounds of radio can be expected to continue to change.

EXERCISES

1. Listen to the radio stations in your area. Determine and list the format of each station. Determine if each station's format seems to be a generic type as described in the chapter, or if it is so distinctive that you feel it should be listed in a subcategory. Indicate whether AM or FM.

2. If you are in a major metropolitan area with more than 20 radio stations, pick 20 stations that provide a representative mix with at least one of each of the formats listed in the chapter. Make a list and indicate the distinctive quality or style as you hear it. Be prepared to discuss your perceptions in class and hand in your listings.

3. Using album covers, record jackets, encyclopedias, or other sources, prepare introductions for specific pieces of music in two different formats. Lengths should be either 30 or 60 seconds for purposes of this assignment. (11-50 space lines = 30 seconds)

4. Read the copy at the end of the chapter for each format onto your cassette tape, using a style as close as possible to that used by the station or stations of that format in your area.

5. Be prepared to pronounce and write phonetics for the correct pronunciation of the list of classical composers at the end of this chapter.

6. Learn the pronunciations of the musical terms list that follows the list of composers. Be prepared to match the terms with their definitions when presented with a list of each.

VOCABULARY WORD LIST   COMPOSERS   Unit 11-A

Name	Pronunciation	Birth/Death	Nationality/Claim to Fame
Bach, Johann, Sebastian	bok'	1685–1750	German; organist, cantatas, Brandenburg concertos
Bartók, Bela	baur' tok	1881–1945	Hungarian; five toned scale, Hungarian folk music
Beethoven, Ludwig van	bay' toh vun	1770–1827	German; nine symphonies, Moonlight Sonata
Bellini, Vincenzo	bel leen' ee	1801–1835	Italian; operatic composer
Berlioz, Hector	bair' lee ohs	1803–1869	French; operatic composer: Carmen
Bizet, Georges	bee zay'	1838–1875	French; operatic, composer: Carmen
Brahms, Johannes	brawmz'	1833–1897	German; Hungarian dances, Cradle Song
Buxtehude, Dietrich	bewks tu hew' du	1637–1707	Swedish; composer of fugues and suites
Chabrier, Alexis Emmanuel	shaw bree ay'	1841–1894	French; composer: Rhapsody Espana
Chopin Frederic	shoh' pa(n)	1810–1856	Polish; pianist-composer: concertos, polonaises
Copland, Aaron	kohp' lund	1900–	American; symphonies, opera, ballet: Appalachian Spring

Debussy, Claude	deb' yew see (or any syllable)	1862–1918	French; Clair de lune, The Afternoon of a Faun
Dvořák, Antonin	du vor' zhauk	1841–1904	Bohemian; Humoresque, symphony: From the New World
Glazonov, Alexander	glau' zu nof	1865–1936	Russian; symphonies, ballet
Gounod, Chas Francois	gew' noh	1818–1893	French; opera: Faust
Grieg, Edvard	greeg'	1843–1907	Norwegian; Peer Gynt Suites
Grofe, Ferdi	groh fay'	1892–1972	American; Grand Canyon Suite
Handel, Geo. Frederick	haun' dul	1685–1759	German-English; oratorio: The Messiah
Haydn, Franz Joseph	high' dun	1732–1809	Austrian; "Surprise" Symphony
Hindemith, Paul	hin' du mit	1895–1968	German; "atonal" music
Khachaturiean, Aram	koch u too' ree un	1903–1978	Armenian; symphonies, concertos, "Sabre Dance" from ballet: Gayne
Liszt, Franz	list'	1811–1886	Hungarian; pianist-composer, Hungarian Rhapsodies
Mahler, Gustav	maul' ur	1860–1911	Austrian; Eight symphonies
Mendelssohn, Felix	men' dul sohn	1809–1847	German; Overture to A Midsummer Night's Dream
Menotti Gian-Carlo	mu not' ee	1911–	Italian-American; Opera: The Medium
Monteverdi Claudio	mon tu ver' dee	1567–1643	Italian; Operas and Madrigals

Mozart Wolfgang Amadeus	mohts′ art	1756–1791	German; Operatic, Symphonic, Chamber, and Sacred Music
Mussorgsky Modest	mu zorg′ skee	1839–1881	Russian; opera: Boris Gudunov tone poem: Night on Bald Mtn.
Offenbach Jacques	of′ un bok	1819–1880	French; The Tales of Hoffmann
Paganini Nicolo	pag u nee′ nee	1782–1840	Italian; Violin Virtuoso
Palestrina Giovanni	pal es tree′ nu	1524–1594	Italian; Madrigals
Prokofiev Serge	proh koh′ fee ef	1891–1953	Russian; Peter and the Wolf, opera: The Love for Three Oranges
Puccini Giacomo	pew chee′ nee	1858–1924	Italian; Operas: Tosca, La Boheme, Madame Butterfly
Rachmaninoff Sergei	rok mon′ i nof	1873–1943	Russian; Piano Concerto
Ravel Maurice	ru vel′	1875–1937	French; Bolero, ballet; Daphnis et Chloe
Rimsky-Korsakov Nicolas	rim′skee kor′su kof	1844–1908	Russian; Operas, symphonies, Flight of the Bumble Bee
Rossini Gioacchino	roh see′ nee	1792–1868	Italian; operas: Wm. Tell, The Barber of Seville
Saint-Saens Charles	sa(n) sau(n)z′	1835–1921	French; Danse Macabre, opera: Sampson and Delilah
Scarlatti Alessandro	skaur lot′ ee	1659–1725	Italian; 115 Operas, 600 Cantatas, and more
Schoenberg Arnold	shoh′ en bairg	1874–1951	German; composition with 12 tones
Schubert Franz	shew′ bert	1797–1828	German; Oratorios, Symphonies, Piano Music

Schumann Robert	shew' mon	1810–1856	German; songs, chamber music, piano works
Scriabin, Alexander	skree aw' bin	1872–1915	Russian; 6 sonatas for piano
Shostakovitch, Dmitri	shos tu koh' vich	1906–1975	Russian; symphonies, opera and music for film
Sibelius, Jean	su bay' lee us	1865–1957	Finnish; symphon, Valse Triste & Finlandia
Smetana, Frederick	smet' u nu	1824–1884	Czech; opera: The Bartered Bride
Strauss, Richard	strows'	1864–1949	German; opera: Der Rosenkavalier
Stravinsky, Igor	stru vin' skee	1882–1971	Russian; composed symphonies and jazz
Tchaikovsky Peter Ilich	chigh kov' skee	1840–1893	Russian; 1812 Overture, Nutcracker Suite
Thomas, Ambroise	toh maw'	1811–1896	French operatic composer
Verdi, Giuseppe	vair' dee	1813–1901	Italian; operas: Aida, Rigoletto, La Traviata
Vivaldi, Antonio	vi vaul' dee	1677–1741	Italian; 50 operas, sonatas, concertos
Wagner Richard	vaug' nur	1813–1883	German; operas: Lohengrin, Tannhauser, the Ring Cycle

BROADCAST VOCABULARY WORD LIST: MUSICAL TERMS   Unit 11-B

a cappella (aw ku pel' u)   without accompaniment
accompanist (u kum' pan ist)   one (as a pianist) who plays the accompaniment for a vocalist
                             or instrumentalist
adagio (u daw' zhee oh)   slow (not as slow as largo)
agitato (aw ji taw' toh)   restless or excited
allegretto (al u gret' toh)   brisk and light—not as fast as allegro
allegro (u lay' groh)   fast and lively

andante (awn dawn' tee)   smooth and flowing at moderate speed
andantino (awn dawn tee' noh)   not quite andante
animato (aw nee maw' toh)   lively or animated
appassionata (aw paw shee u naw' ta)   with great feeling
arpeggio (awr pej' ee oh)   a series of quickly played notes
ballet (bal ay')   a classical dance form
brillante (breel yawn' tay)   bright or sparkling
cadenza (ku den' zu)   a showy passage requiring virtuosity
cantabile (kawn taw' bi lay)   songlike
cantata (kawn taw' tu)   a short oratorio with soloists and chorus
coda (koh' da)   ending passage of a movement or work
concerto (kun chair' toh)   a form of serious instrumental music
con brio (kohn bree' oh)   with great spirit
con moto (kohn moh' toh)   with strong feeling
contralto (kun tral' toh)   voice in the range between soprano and tenor
contrapuntal (kon tru punt' ul)   having related simultaneous melodies
crescendo (kru shen' doh)   growing louder
decrescendo (day kru shen' doh)   growing softer
diminuendo (du min yew en' doh)   gradually growing softer
espressivo (es pres ee' voh)   with expression
fantasia (fan tay' zhu)   a fantasy—in free form
finale (fu nawl' ee)   the ending—last section of a work
forte (for' tay)   strong, loud
fortissimo (for tis' i moh)   as loud as possible
glissando (gli sawn' doh)   sliding on a rapid scale, as with a harp
larghetto (lawr get' oh)   slower than adagio, not as slow as largo
largo (lawr' go)   extremely slow
legato (le gaw' toh)   gracefully and smoothly
maestoso (migh es toh' zoh)   majestic
maestro (migh es' troh)   honorary title for conductor
melodic (mu lau' dik)   having a melody
mezzo (met' zoh)   medium
moderato (maw du raw' toh)   at a moderate tempo
molto (mohl' toh)   a great deal or very much
musicology (myew zi kol' u jee)   the study of music
non troppo (nohn troh' poh)   not too much
obbligato (aw blu gaw' toh)   an accompanying part
opus (oh' pus)   number indicating order of a composer's works
oratorio (or u tor' ee oh)   musical telling of a religious story
pianissimo (pee u nis' i moh)   as soft as possible
piano (pee aw' noh)   soft
piu (pyew)   more (as *piu presto*)
pizzicato (pit su kaw' toh)   plucking the strings of a bowed instrument
poco (poh' koh)   little
polyphony (pu lif' u nee)   several melodies at the same time
prestissimo (pres tis' i moh)   as fast as possible
presto (pres' toh)   very fast
recitative (re su taw teev')   speechlike narrative in operas, etc.
scherzando (skairt sawn' doh)   in playful manner
sforzando (sfor tsawn' doh)   with a sudden, strong accent
sonorous (su nor' us)   impressive (often deep, rich) sound
sostenuto (sos tu new' toh)   sustaining the tone
sotto voce (soh toh voh' chay)   in a low, soft voice, almost a whisper
staccato (stu kaw' toh)   with clearly distinct, separated tones

tremolo (trem′ u low)   quivering or trembling
triad (trigh′ ad)   specific type of three-note chord
vibrato (vi brau′ toh)   minute and rapid variations in pitch
virtuosity (vur chew aus′ u tee)   skill or style of a brilliant performer
vivace (vee vaw′ chay)   lively, played with great speed

CASSETTE ASSIGNMENT COPY
HANDEL'S MESSIAH

In 1703, George Frederick Handel went to Hamburg to play violin in the opera orchestra, succeeding to the directorship after filling the place at the harpsichord in an emergency. Here he formed important friendships with the composers Telemann and Mattheson. With the latter he once went to Lubeck to try for the position of organist left vacant by the retirement of the great Buxtehude. Both refused to compete when they learned that the winner was expected to marry the former organist's elderly daughter. Handel never did marry; in fact, there is no evidence that he ever fell deeply in love.

A tradition in many communities at Christmas or at Easter is performing the oratorio of Handel that tells the story of the Christ from birth to crucifixion and resurrection, with special emphasis on these particular events. Perhaps the most famous of the many familiar pieces that make up the oratorio *The Messiah* is the "Hallelujah Chorus."

We now hear the 101 Strings as they perform for our inspiration the "Hallelujah Chorus" from Handel's *Messiah*.

MOZART—OVERTURE TO *THE MARRIAGE OF FIGARO*

TIME: 55

Wolfgang Amadeus (am u day′ us) Mozart continued to build on the heritage of Bach and his contrapuntal style—to add to Handel's powerful oratorio offerings—to enhance the sonata as developed by Haydn and Scarlatti.

The greatest musical genius the world has known, Mozart could compose symphonic movements in his mind, complete to the most minute detail. His operas were written primarily while he was court composer following the death of Gluck in 1787. *The Marriage of Figaro,* however, was composed a year earlier. It contains melodic and harmonic content that has won it wide acceptance to this day—a deserved popularity that may be expected to continue for centuries to come.

We hear now the London Philharmonic, conducted by Edward Downes, as it re-creates the overture from the Mozart opera, *The Marriage of Figaro.*

RACHMANINOFF
PIANO CONCERTO NO. 2

A disciple of Tchaikovsky, Sergei (ser' gay) Rachmaninoff was 20 when Tchaikovsky passed from the scene. Rachmaninoff presented his first symphony at the age of 22 in 1895. The opening of the twentieth century saw the creation of Rachmaninoff's second piano concerto.

Rachmaninoff came to the United States in 1909 and won immediate acclaim. Though during World War I he returned to Russia to entertain the troops, he eventually returned to make his home in the United States.

Rachmaninoff's style is rich and sonorous, often rhythmically vigorous, but also frequently turning on itself in its inner searching and probing.

On this evening's program we will hear the third movement of Rachmaninoff's Piano Concerto No. 2 in C Minor, Opus 18. The melodic core is as lovely and well-loved a theme as was ever written by a Russian composer. The work is marked by staccato passages of throbbing intensity, which lend themselves to piano virtuosity.

Here is Rachmaninoff's Piano Concerto No. 2, marked allegro scherzando.

TCHAIKOVSKY

Peter Ilich Tchaikovsky was probably the most intensely melodic composer of all time. It has been said that no other composer has poured so much personal feeling into his work, and certainly no other has attained general popularity on such widely divergent musical levels.

Tchaikovsky's first job was as a clerk in the Russian Ministry of Justice. But after three years he entered the St. Petersburg Conservatory and attained high honors as a music student. He began teaching harmony at the Moscow Conservatory in 1866, but the salary was so small that he was forced to serve as a music critic as well. It was during this period that such works as *Romeo and Juliet* and *Swan Lake* were written. Also, this time saw creation of the ever-popular Piano Concerto No. 1 in B-flat Minor.

For this evening's concert we have selected (INSERT NAME OF THE WORK).

COPY FOR COUNTRY FORMAT

There can be no doubt that Hank Williams Jr. is one of the truly great country stars of our day. He had number one best sellers in 1979, 1980, and 1981. Bet you remember "Whiskey Bent and Hell Bound," "Dixie on My Mind," and "Texas Women." They're classics. To top it off, all of these hits were composed by Hank Williams Jr., himself.

Surrounded by music all of his life, Hank Williams Jr. began his musical training as soon as he was old enough to hold a guitar, making his first public appearance when he was eight-years-old. Williams was only 14 when he completed the sound track for the movie biography of his father, country idol, the senior Hank Williams. The junior Williams received two Grammy nominations for an album of his father's songs, and was nominated one year later, in 1975, for another Grammy award.

An avid sportsman, Hank Williams Jr. spends his spare time hunting and fishing when he isn't recording or on tour. In 1975, M-G-M Records released "Hank Williams Junior and Friends," a record which has been described as one of country music's most influential records.

Part of Hank Williams Jr.'s popularity comes from the fact that his style incorporates both country and rock, giving it wide appeal. He had nine hits on the Billboard top 100 Country Albums list in 1982.

But, enough of the history lesson. Get ready to rock with Hank Williams Junior as he gives us his number one best seller, ''Dixie on My Mind.''

GOSPEL COPY

The one hundredth psalm proclaims ''Make a joyful noise unto the Lord.'' This Biblical proclamation has been said to characterize the life and singing of one of America's truly great singers, Mahalia Jackson. Miss Jackson is by far the most famous of America's gospel singers, and for good reason. Making a joyful noise unto the Lord has been a way of life for Mahalia Jackson through the many years of her reign.

Gospel music commands interest today far beyond the sanctuaries of the Black church. The broad interest in gospel music has raised Mahalia Jackson to new heights of popularity. Not only is gospel appreciated for its deep emotion and surging rhythms, but its style has sent converts into the popular music field. Gospel singers have used the music as nightclub entertainment with remarkable success. Black church music's influence has been widely felt in the jazz world as performers have turned back to gospel, the roots of ''soul'' music.

After a Mahalia Jackson concert in New York City's Philharmonic Hall, Robert Shelton wrote in the New York Times on October 12, 1962—

''From its humble origins in the store front churches of the negro communities, gospel music was transported last night to the elegant setting of Philharmonic Hall. No singer was better equipped to make the transition than Mahalia Jackson.

This daughter of a New Orleans preacher . . . transformed religious fervor in song into a moving esthetic experience.

. . . When Miss Jackson rolls out her great and flexible contralto, who can question the dignity, artistry and religious sincerity of her singing? . . . She managed to convert even the simplest statement into something purposeful.''

Here is the gospel according to Mahalia. Miss Jackson sings ''Sign of the Judgment.''

OLDIES COPY

One million is the magic number in records as in dollar bills. The million-selling record is something every artist strives to achieve. It's now known as the "platinum record"—and often can be found encased in clear plastic, hanging on the wall for all to see.

Today is million-seller day. How many of the million sellers we're featuring today do you remember? One that has particular interest to folks in Louisiana and custodians of the Cajun culture is the record that first exposed many Americans to life in Southern Louisiana. It was made popular by Jo Stafford. Jo has sung the blues and ballads, hillbilly tunes and rock. It is no surprise then that this ballad won great popularity.

Jo first gained fame in the swing era, as featured vocalist with one of America's great dance bands of the time. She was most successful, however, when she struck out on her own. Dubbed "America's most versatile singer," Jo proved just that with her 1952 recording of "Jambalaya."

Much of the French based culture of southern Louisiana was transplanted from our northern neighbors. So the upcoming music of Percy Faith fits well into our million-seller presentation.

Toronto-born Percy Faith first appeared at a young age as a concert pianist of outstanding talent. When Percy was still in his teens, he suffered an accident to his hands and was forced to abandon his keyboard career. Turning his talents to composing, arranging, and conducting, Faith became even more successful. He is noted for the rich sound of the strings in his work. Another million-seller was his 1953 recording of "Song from Moulin Rouge."

Listen now to "Jambalaya" with a bit of Cajun French influence, followed by "Song from Moulin Rouge," a melody reminiscent of the Parisian French style of music.

URBAN CONTEMPORARY

We're going back a ways to find this cut. It's called "Bustin' Outta the Ghetto." . . . and appears on the A-J-P (Ahmad Jamal production) label. Eddie O'Jay, who fills in the background for us on the album cover, says that he took the pressing home and played it at intervals for two days. After a while he became hung up on side B, track 1, "Play It for the World." Then he says, "It hit like a tornado—side A, track 1, "Bustin' Outta the Ghetto" had in it what is now punk, underground, and a slight taste of calypso, mixed with some soft but demanding-to-be-heard brass." You can do little else but move in rhythm to the music. It's hard not to at least snap your fingers to the beat. Listen for the flair of harmonica that seems to haunt the refrains.

O'Jay later learned that Carlos A. Malcolm, who wrote "Bustin' Outta the Ghetto," was educated at Rainbow City Occupational School, Cristobal Canal Zone and Calabar College, in Kingston, Jamaica. This accounts for the West Indian flavor that permeates much of the music.

The tropical music for the first James Bond film, *Dr. No,* was written by Carlos Malcolm. In addition, Malcolm conducted and arranged all of the music for the Jamaican sequences of the film.

Carlos Malcolm has an album of solid instrumentals that will keep you movin'. Here is the title cut from Carlos Malcolm's "Bustin' Outta the Ghetto."

12

A Look Ahead

OBJECTIVES

Upon completion of this chapter the student should be able to:

1. Explain economic factors that can have an important effect on the future of broadcast announcers.
2. Discuss demographic changes that will be a factor in the future of broadcast announcers.
3. List six technological advances that may have far-reaching effects on broadcasting's future form.
4. Explain programming trends that can be expected to continue into the twenty-first century.
5. Discuss career opportunities for announcers as they exist in four media.
6. Explain six factors that influence your future employment.
7. Discuss five considerations when preparing a résumé.

THE CHANGING SCENE

The only inevitable change is change itself. The technology of broadcasting is changing as you read this. The needs of the audience continue to change. Because of the demands of change, the needs for broadcasting professional talent will also change.

A growing population and an expanding electronic technology will both contribute to what is expected by the public of the broadcasting systems. Underlying all of these factors are the economic conditions of the United States and the world.

ECONOMIC FACTORS

It is a bit presumptuous for a text on announcing to predict the economic future, yet it is possible to recap some of the points that were made by a National Association of Broadcasters publication[1] as they relate to broadcasting. Over the long run, a healthily (though not explosively) growing economy is predicted for the United States well into the twenty-first century. Some of the factors that are expected to lead to this include the following:

1. The American manufacturing segment will be more competitive. For example, lower inventories will be in effect for manufacturers and retailers as American companies utilize computers efficiently with the Japanese-style "just-in-time" inventory acquisition.
2. The lower value of the U.S. dollar is also expected to continue the increase in U.S. exports.
3. Inflation can be expected to be moderate, assuming that Middle Eastern political problems can be held in check and the price of oil held stable.
4. As the baby boom generation grows older, savings are expected to increase, helping to hold down interest rates and making funds available for capital expansion in the economy.

Part of the compensation of the broadcasting field has to be that it is an exciting, challenging—and often fun—career. However, one study has also shown that the average pay is 15 percent to 31 percent greater than other non-agricultural private employment,[2] which is nice to know. As with most careers, wages are based on one's experience, formal training, ability, and enthusiasm for the work, as well as supply and demand. The need for broadcasters, compared with the total number of skilled personnel available, is perhaps the most important factor in determining salary.

As the nation's economy regains strength and remains strong, broadcast-

---

[1] Austin J. McLean, ed., *RadiOutlook II: New Forces Shaping the Industry,* (Washington, D.C.: National Association of Broadcasters, 1991), pp. 8, 19.
[2] Kenneth Harwood, " ' Premium' Pay in Broadcasting," *Feedback, 31:1,* Winter 1991, p. 5.

ing's prosperity, and therefore attractive careers in broadcasting, seem reasonably well assured, as projected by economic experts in the early 1990s.

DEMOGRAPHIC CHANGES

Two reasons stand out as important in the continued awareness of audience demographics: (1) programming must keep pace with changes in audience composition, and (2) broadcasters need to be aware of changes in the potential advertisers as products aimed at changing demographic segments become increasingly important.

Some of the most important population changes will probably be:

- Continued population growth and an expected increase by approximatedly 18 million persons [to 268 million] by the year 2000.
- A rising birth rate, expected through the 1990s.
- A declining youth population, with as many as 38 percent of these being minority youth.
- Aging baby boomers, who change consumption patterns.
- Regional population growth, greatest in the South and West regions, with over 80 percent of the nation's growth occurring in these areas.
- The percentage of minority and ethnic U.S. citizens growing at a faster rate than the overall population, with Asian-Americans the fastest-growing ethnic segment in the U.S. percentage-wise (80 percent). As America enters the twenty-first century, Hispanics are increasing at a 44 percent per decade rate, leading to a nation in which minorities become the majority.
- Two wage-earner couples becoming the norm, with well over 60 percent of American women in the labor force.
- The fastest growing segment of the population age-wise will be people 85 years of age and older.
- The youth population will decline . . . [to the year 2010].[3]

As demographics change, programming will change, making different demands as to skills and areas of expertise for broadcast announcers who wish to be able to adjust to the constantly changing environment. Another important area of change to which announcers must adjust is the changing technology.

CHANGING TECHNOLOGY

It is really not possible to project what the future holds. If someone had tried to tell Herbert Hoover in 1927 that there would be 12,000 commercial and public radio stations operating in the United States in 50 years and that signals would be

---

[3] Austin J. McLean, *RadiOutlook*, pp. 21–38.

retransmitted from satellites orbiting the planet at 22,300 miles above the earth's surface, would he have believed it? Probably not.

Sometimes what appears to be a momentous technical advancement fails to win the favor of the public for some reason. Just because it's possible does not necessarily mean that a particular advancement will become part of the standard system of broadcasting in the United States or anywhere else in the world.

The direction of technology going into the twenty-first century seems obvious, though some simple, unforeseen technological advance could well change technology's directon.

Digital Services

The technology of computers is not only affecting the transmission of printed data, but the "on-off" theory of computer operation is being applied to the way radio and television are transmitted as well.

One unstoppable movement of broadcast technology is the conversion of almost every aspect to digital reproduction. "In every aspect of TV broadcasting, the equipment is going digital."[4] While the first impressive impact of digital technology in broadcasting was probably in the form of compact discs (CD), this is just the first of the systems where digital can be expected to replace analog technologies. Digital produces better sound and better pictures, allowing almost infinite reproduction of a signal without degradation. Digital audio tape (DAT) is one of the advances seen in radio stations. Such traditional production devices as the cart machine can well be expected to give way to computers' hard disks.

Radio Delivery Systems

Conversion of all U.S. radio broadcasting stations to digital audio broadcasting (DAB) has been proposed. In addition to the broad spectrum of sound reproduction, as in the compact discs,

> digital signals are essentially *immune* to noise . . . . In essence, digital receivers are able to ignore and/or correct for any interfering noise radio signals may have picked up in traveling from a station transmitter to listeners' home, car or portable radio.[5]

Satellite transmission promises radio stations that can cover all of the United States by direct broadcast satellite (DBS). Would this mean that local terrestrial radio (the current earthbound transmission) will disappear? No, chances are that traditional AM and FM radio will continue for quite a few years, even when DBS radio is inaugurated.

[4] Randall M. Sukow, "Digital: Choice of a New Generation," *Broadcasting,* October 15, 1990, p. 48.

[5] Austin J. McLean, *RadiOutlook,* p. 40.

Television Delivery Systems

There can be little doubt that television technology will be taking some giant strides forward in coming years, though what the ultimate system will be may be many years away from being determined—if such a determination ever can be expected in the foreseeable future.

High-definition television (HDTV), originally proposed in an analog configuration, is now seen as being realized using digital technology.

Scalability

Delaying the realization of HDTV was the recognition that any system not incorporating digital principles would be obsolete before it became operable. In 1992, another potentially delaying concept burst upon the scene: scalability. Andrew Lippman, associate director of the Media Lab, provided *TV Technology* with a plain language definition. He explained that scalability is

> a digital system in which the aspect ratio, the number of frames per second, and the number of scan lines can be adjusted on-the-fly to the requirements of the individual picture or TV receiver of the viewer's choice.[6]

Aspect ratio, the number of frames per second, and the number of scan lines have been fixed in previous television systems. The benefits of scalability are many. Among them are international compatibility of systems, the ability to adjust the number of lines per screen as the screen increases in size (thus retaining definition), and adaptability to new higher resolution pictures as these become available. The differentiation between film, video, and computers is tending to disappear as the technologies become integrated.

Satellites

High-power broadcast satellite transmission of both radio and television directly to the home seems to be inevitable. Proposed direct broadcast satellite (DBS) systems can send signals directly into the home without the use of a cable system or local television or radio station. This, of course, offers increased competition to cable and to local broadcasting stations, and means that local cable systems as well as broadcasting stations must feature what only they can produce, such as local news. Satellite signals are not the only new transmission medium. "Throughout the developed world, fiber optics will be the transmission medium of choice"[7] for cable and relatively short information links.

As the technology continues to expand beyond the imagination of most

[6] Frank Beacham, "Defining Terms of Scalability," *TV Technology*, 10, no. 4, (April 1992), 13.

[7] Martin Nisenholtz, "New Tool for Marketers," *Viewpoint*, in *Advertising Age*, July 22, 1991, p. 18.

laypersons, video compression is allowing the placement of 100 or more high-power (television) transponders on one satellite, and for much smaller dishes to receive these signals for direct viewing in homes without a cable television link.[8]

Computers

As the technologies merge, the home computer will perform functions on its CRT (cathode ray tube, or television screen), with the individualization of information "empowering the individual to find and use the information he needs when he needs it."[9]

PROGRAMMING DIRECTIONS

More stations, more specialized formats, more specialized information, and entertainment designed for the needs of specific viewers/listeners can be expected to mean a continuing proliferation of formats as well as delivery systems.

CAREER OPPORTUNITIES

New technologies may reduce the number of persons needed to do some untrained jobs, but these technologies can be expected to continue to require increasing numbers of experienced and adaptable people with solid theoretical backgrounds.

Where might there be career opportunities for persons trained as broadcasters, especially announcers? Commercial and public radio and broadcast television stations—both local and network—are the most obvious places. Also worthy of consideration are corporate television; shortwave radio; syndication companies producing both entertainment and news materials; and international, national, and regional cable origination facilities.

Radio

More specialized "narrowcasting" is going to mean the previously suggested continuing increase of broadcast formats and a growing number of program suppliers and networks. Increasingly, network organizations provide multiple-format choices. In addition to seven radio networks run by ABC in 1991, there were some 300 program suppliers and networks listed in *Radio and Records Ratings Report and Directory*.[10] Specialization seems important to announcers, producers, and advertisers as they aim at increasingly narrower audiences. Thus,

---

[8] Peter D. Lambert, "Sky Cable at Crossroads," *Broadcasting*, October 15, 1990.
[9] Steve Coe, "Technology to Change Communications Landscape," *Broadcasting*, October 22, 1990, p. 36.
[10] "Program Suppliers and Networks," *Radio and Records Special Supplement*, Vol. 1/ 1991, pp. 86–99.

adaptability, more than ever, is critical. It continues to be important that students have a broad educational background and learn the basic applicable skills, such as writing and oral language use, rather than just the operation of specific pieces of equipment, which soon become obsolete.

Broadcast Television

In the late 1980s and the early 1990s, enhancing the bottom line had become the primary function of station managers. Many of the family and local station ownerships had been sold to interests that tried to provide the same services as previously at lower cost (and therefore with fewer employees, in many cases). The number of stations has continued to increase at a slower rate than in former years. One of the broadcast systems expected to continue expansion is low-power television, which had just barely begun to be a factor in the early 1990s. Much of the "action" could be said to be in the newer media, media which require many of the same basic announcing and production skills discussed in this text.

Cable

Where once there were three major television networks, there are now about 50, if you count the cable networks. While much of the programming is recycled, there continues to be an expansion as new niches for specialization continue to be found. As competition increases, cable systems and local television stations are cooperating. "Across the country, TV stations and cable systems are increasingly developing joint ventures to provide local news."[11]

Corporate Television

Television that the general public never sees exists to further the objectives of many businesses within their own organizations. One rapidly expanding corporation has said that it

> relies on television for three basic applications: product knowledge, management communication, and merchandising. Although product knowledge and merchandising are priorities, the evolution of . . . management communications programs best illustrates its [management's] use of television.[12]

Some of the specific functions that television might be expected to do are to orient new employees, to train workers, to explain new product lines and selling techniques, to provide intraorganizational management-personnel communica-

---

[11] Matt Stump and Sharon D. Moshavi, "Broadcast Cable: Local TV's Newest Anchor Team," *Broadcasting,* November 19, 1990, p. 19.

[12] Carl Levine, "HDTV Promotes Corporate Culture," *Video Systems,* 17:7, July 1991, p. 52.

tion, and to provide public relations releases to the mass media. Major corporations often produce more hours per week of television programs than do local broadcasting stations. Different companies continue to find different uses for corporate (or industrial or business) television, thus creating new jobs.

GETTING A JOB

There is no one best way to get a job. Each employer has different priorities, but some of the important things employers look for are a good résumé, a broad academic background, college study, professional experience, personal recommendations, a good audition tape, and often a reasonably good live audition.

The Résumé

You probably do not need a résumé prepared by someone else if you have a typewriter or computer available. You should be able to prepare a neat, meaningful résumé yourself. After all, you soon will be a college graduate. It is helpful to have a model to follow, though your résumé will be different from that of anyone else. Here is a format you can follow.

Gerald R. Smyth

597 Rightway Drive
Spokane, WA 99204
(509) 555-1515

Job Objective
To become a television reporter dealing with political affairs and/or sports.

Personal
Born: September 2, 1971
Recreational Interests: reading, athletics, politics

Education
Bachelor of Arts, University of Washington
Associate of Arts, Spokane Community College
Elementary & Secondary education, Spokane Public Schools

Related College Studies
survey of broadcasting; audio production; television production; broadcast announcing; journalism; broadcast news writing; field production and editing; television news production; American national government; local and state government; international affairs; presidential politics

College Activities

Member, Sigma Pi fraternity
Member, Alpha Epsilon Rho, broadcast honor society
Secretary, Political Science Club
News Director, KHUS Campus Radio

Work Experience

Summer Camp Counselor, 1990
Clerk, Robyn's Camera Shop, 1989–1991
Internship, KIRO-TV, 1991–1992

References

Dr. Richard R. Lasso   The Reverend Carl Upstead
Associate Professor Communication   Holy Name Lutheran Church
P. O. Box 34555   4313 Manitou Blvd.
Seattle, WA 98191   Spokane, WA 99207

Mr. George P. Hutton
Robyn's Camera Shop
304 Broadmoor Plaza
Seattle, WA 98199

Your résumé needs to highlight your strengths. You may always add or eliminate categories to fit your experience and accomplishments. Put in a category where you have excelled, such as "broadcasting classes taken." You may want to make a special résumé for each job for which you apply, pointing out those things in your background that you think will appeal to that employer or conform to that job description.

When students are seeking entry-level positions, most employers seem to prefer a résumé all on one page so that it can be evaluated rapidly and they can quickly have an idea of your experience and education.

Academic Background

A college degree is important in getting almost any good job. Yes, there are lots of successful people out there who do not have one, but they are essentially from another generation. Today's employers are looking for educated people who want to advance in the organization by being dependable, punctual, knowledgeable, and quick and eager to learn.

Just being able to run some electronic equipment is not enough. The student who is going to advance in an organization needs communication skills: writing as well as speaking. An employee is expected to bring a broad background of knowledge and probably several areas of some expertise. What are you minoring in? Do you have a hobby in which you can display a proficiency? Have you been active in some campus or church organization?

Professional Experience

Many who are successful in broadcasting start by hanging out at their hometown radio station, learning all they can. They may get a chance to spin a record or read a news brief. This can lead to a weekend or graveyard shift. By the time they are ready for college, these students already have some experience. Working at a campus radio station can help you learn skills you need to get a job, too. A weekend job at a commercial station while in college is an excellent experience and looks good on the résumé. Radio experience can lead to a television job, if that is the way you want to go.

Internships in radio and television can also lead to entry-level positions. An internship for credit from your college is an excellent way to show that you are a rapid learner, that you are proficient at whatever task may be assigned, and that you get along well with people. Television, particularly, requires a team effort. Most employers want to know what professional experience you have had. Getting that first job may not be easy, but an internship is one type of experience that really helps get your foot in the door.

Recommendations

You have no doubt heard the expression, "It's not *what* you know, it's *who* you know." Unfortunately, this is sometimes true. If you can network through the alumni of your college or department, this may be a good way to get an interview. Recommendations on your résumé may have a similar effect. Many résumés list three recommendations. If you can list names that the employer will recognize, by either name or title, so much the better.

Most students have found a professor or adviser for whom they have done particularly well. Being dependable, always striving to improve, being cooperative, and proving your academic ability are the kinds of things professors remember. Sometimes professors have to write rather lukewarm recommendations because they do not really remember much (except what is in the grade book) about a former student. Try to look ahead. What professor are you going to ask for a recommendation? Do some outstanding work in that class. Really put forth extra effort. It will probably pay off in a good recommendation.

Other kinds of persons who might be listed under recommendations are former employers (even if it was not a broadcasting job), a high school teacher, a church pastor, a coach or adviser, or any established adult with whom you have had a longstanding acquaintance. (Obviously, close family relations are not usually considered unbiased.) Try for three references, preferably of different backgrounds, and always ask their permission before using people's names.

Audition Tape

If you are applying for an announcing or news job, you will want to prepare an audition tape. Probably before you leave school you should put together a 15-

minute audio tape demonstrating your skills doing various kinds of announcing: record introductions in various formats, news, interviewing, ad libbing, commercials, and possibly sports. Some employers like an *air-check*. This is a short, recorded collection of an assortment of your performances while actually broadcasting. Cue records, introduce music, and come out of songs, but cut out most of the music. The potential employer does not want to listen to music; he or she wants to hear you.

If you are applying at a television station to work in news, you will want to demonstrate your ability as a news reporter, preferably with some stories you have shot, edited, and narrated on video tape. You can also include a demonstration of your anchoring ability. Other television materials might include commercials or other spots you have prepared or shows you have produced, hosted, or directed, especially if news is not your forte.

Sending out quantities of unsolicited tapes in general is a waste of time. Save your tapes and your efforts for answering ads, when applying in person, or when you have an interview appointment.

In addition to wanting to hear taped materials, most employers will be interested in your writing. You should be saving broadcast advertising copy, news stories, and features or other scripts you have written. These show to their best advantage if they are neatly collected in a portfolio. Bring them with you to an interview.

**QUESTIONS A JOB APPLICANT
SHOULD BE ABLE TO ANSWER**

1. Why do you want to work for this company?
2. What can you do for this organization?
3. What would you like to be doing five or ten years from now?
4. Why should we hire you?

**QUESTIONS YOU MAY WANT
TO ASK WHEN APPLYING FOR
A JOB**

1. What are the prospects for advancement?
2. What would the specific duties be?
3. What are you looking for in a candidate for this position?
4. What kinds of problems do people usually have on this job?

The Job Interview

Contact the proposed employer ahead of time for an appointment. Be on time. Dress as if this is an important event; it is. (As the Head and Shoulders shampoo ads say, "You never get a second chance to make a first impression.") Being relaxed becomes easier as you get acquainted with your prospective employer. You'll find that most job interviewers try to put you at ease. Be informal, but on your best grammar-behavior. Nothing demonstrates your education and communication skills like your speech habits.

You will probably be given some copy to read, perhaps to write or edit. Depending on what the position is, you may be asked to write, to ad lib, to perform any of the skills you have been expected to learn in school.

Very seldom will an employer hire you on the spot. There are usually other applicants also being considered who probably have not been interviewed yet.

QUALITIES MOST EMPLOYERS ARE LOOKING FOR AT ENTRY-LEVEL POSITIONS

honesty	interest in the company
sincerity	research of the company
eagerness to learn	willingness to start at the bottom
enthusiasm	tolerance of others
initiative	interpersonal communication skills
job skills	pleasant to be around
neat appearance	maturity

LOOKING AHEAD

The twenty-first century holds many challenges, and many opportunities. As someone once said, "You succeed because you are lucky, but the wise people create their own 'luck' by being prepared when opportunities arise."

EXERCISES

1. Make a list of various organizations in your area that might employ someone with your training.
2. Bring an article from a periodical discussing some new technological advancement not extensively discussed in this chapter.
3. Prepare a paper outlining new technology described in current periodicals, confirming or modifying projections made in this chapter.
4. Prepare a résumé of your experience and classwork up to this time.
5. Prepare an audition tape demonstrating your announcing abilities.

BROADCAST VOCABULARY WORD LIST   Unit 12-A

1. junta (n)—a military ruling group (usually in South America), often after a coup d'etat

   _____   *hoon' tu*   or   *jun' tu*

2. leprechaun (n)—race of Irish folklore elves

   _____   *lep' ru kon*

3. jocular (adj)—full of gaity and good cheer

   _____   *jok' yew lur*

4. Spokane (n)—city in eastern Washington

   _____   *spoh kan'*

5. quaalude (n)—a ''downers'' drug

   _____   *kway' lewd*

6. spurious (adj)—false, not genuine or true

   _____   *spyoor' ee us*

7. larynx (n)—the voice box, vocal chords

   _____   *lar' ingks*

8. lethargic (adj)—sleepy, slow

   _____   *le thar' jik*

9. macabre (adj)—gruesome; having a deathlike quality

   _____   *mu kaub' (ru)*

10. mischievous (adj)—prone to innocent misbehavior

    _____   *mis' chu vus*

11. proviso (n)—the condition of an action

    _____   *proh vigh' zoh*

12. proletariat (n)—the lower class; working people

    _____   *proh lu tair' ee ut*

13. rancor (n)—disagreement; unpleasantness

    _____   *rang' kor*

14. relevant (adj)—appropriate to the situation

    _____   *rel'   u   vunt*

15. salmon (n)—a fish with pink meat

    _____   *sa'   mun*

16. quay (n)—a jetty or pier extending into a body of water

    _____   *kay'*

17. queue (n)—a line of people or computer jobs waiting for service or processing

    _____   *kyew*

18. algae (n)—aquatic plants

    _____   *al'   jee*

19. disparate (adj)—different, distinct, dissimilar

    _____   *dis'   pur   ut* or *dis   par'   ut*

20. disparaging (adj)—belittling, downgrading in importance

    _____   *dis   pair'   ij   ing*

BROADCAST VOCABULARY WORD LIST   Unit 12-B

1. anecdote (n)—a short (often humorous) story

    _____   *an'   ek   doht*

2. antidote (n)—something that counteracts a poison

    _____   *an'   ti   doht*

3. invertebrate (adj)—having no spinal column or backbone

    _____   *in   vur'   tu   brayt*

4. inveterate (adj)—longstanding, ingrained

    _____   *in   vet'   ur   it*

5. Judaic (adj)—pertaining to the Jewish faith or people

    _____   *jew   day'   ik*

6. risqué (adj)—bordering on impropriety

   ————————————————   *ris   kay′*

7. double-entendre (n)—a second implied meaning (often risqué)

   ————————————————   *dub′   ul - on   ton′   dru*

8. bona fide (adj)—in good faith; genuine

   ————————————————   *bohn′   u   fighd*

9. inviolate (adj)—not violated, intact

   ————————————————   *in   vigh′   u   lit*

10. permeate (v)—to penetrate, spread, or diffuse

    ————————————————   *pur′   mee   ayt*

11. litigious (adj)—having to do with a lawsuit or litigation

    ————————————————   *li   tij′   us*

12. disingenuous (adj)—devious, not straightforward

    ————————————————   *dis   in   jen′   yew   us*

13. incredulous (adj)—not credible, disbelieving

    ————————————————   *in   kred′   yew   lus*

14. debacle (n)—defeat, downfall

    ————————————————   *di   bau′   kul*

15. assuage (v)—to reduce in severity; soften; satisfy

    ————————————————   *u   swayj′*

16. miscreant (n)—an evildoer, scoundrel

    ————————————————   *mis′   kree   unt*

17. contiguous (adj)—immediately adjoining

    ————————————————   *kun   tig′   yew   us*

18. gila monster (n)—a lizard that grows to about 12 inches long

    ————————————————   *hee′   lu   mon′   stur*

19. conscientious (adj)—honest, painstaking

    ————————————————   *kon   shee′   en   shus*

20. hegemony (n)—domination of one state over another

_____   *hi   jem'   u   nee*

WORD LIST PARAGRAPH   **Word List 12-A**

You may talk about spurious reports, but the clamor was real. The junta that took over had jocular leprechauns proclaiming victory for the proletariat from the tops of buildings. It sounded as if the mischievous wee people were on quaaludes as the rancor erupted.

On the other hand, the old guard seemed lethargic, almost to the point of being macabre. Was this relevant to the fishermen on the shiny new quay, fishing for salmon? There was even a queue to mount the disparate, algae-covered dock to take part in the salmon run, and disparaging remarks seemed to permeate the fall air. A fisherman from Spokane tried to strengthen his larynx with loud shouts, yet the demeanor of the town was little changed. Chaos ruled.

WORD LIST PARAGRAPH   **Word List 12-B**

The Judaic gentleman liked to relate an anecdote about the invertebrates on the ark. He was an inveterate storyteller. Some of his stories were a little risqué and rife with double-entendres. Some bona fide, inviolate religious objects he would often hold up to ridicule.

The litigious society in which he lived thought his disingenuous attitude incredulous. It seemed obvious that a debacle would result. The acknowledged miscreant tried to use an antidote he said came from the gila monster to assuage the conscientious, contiguous prelates, but the hegemony of the church was unswayed.

Glossary

Abdomen   the lower portion of the body separated from the thorax by the diaphragm

AC   (see Adult contemporary)

Acid rock   the rock music style that was originally associated with the drug culture: harsh, loud, and raucous

Acronym   the use of initials that are pronounced as a word, such as NASA or AIDS; unlike initials written with hyphens in between (in broadcast style), that are intended to be pronounced as single letters, such as U-S-A or F-C-C

Action news   a TV news format that features news stories displaying physical action that can be reduced to short segments

Actuality   a radio news recorded interview, often part of a voice wrap or other story, which can be used on several newscasts; comparable to a sound bite on television

Ad libs   literally, voiced segments that have not been practiced or written out; stories or dee-jay patter that appears unrehearsed

Adult contemporary (AC)   the adult contemporary radio format; consisting primarily of currently popular and recently popular hits, without extremes such as acid rock

Air check   a recorded sample of on-air performance by an announcer

Album-oriented rock (AOR)   a radio format featuring lesser-known and often longer record album cuts, sometimes of artists who become popular

All news   a format that focuses on news; may be found in both radio and television

All talk   a radio format that includes generous amounts of news programming, but also features various other types of talk shows

AM   (see amplitude modulation)

Ambient noise level   the background sounds that are found in an environment

American Meteorological Society   an organization of professional weather personnel that sets standards of performance

Amplify   to increase a signal strength

Amplitude modulation (AM)   the original system of voice radio transmission, in which intensity of energy transmitted determines the information received

Analog   refers to information transmitted or recorded in a medium using variations in signal similar to the original information (compare to Digital)

Anchor   the primary newscaster(s) on a news show

AOR   (see Album-oriented rock)

Art   "the transmission of feelings" (Tolstoy)

Articles   the adjectives "a," "an," and "the"; *a* and *an* refer to one of a group, *the* refers to a specific item or idea

Articulation   using mouth parts to enunciate speech sounds

Aspect ratio   the width and height of a picture; the standard television picture as established by the FCC in the 1940s was three units high by four units wide

Associated Press (AP)   a cooperative newsgathering organization that serves newspapers, radio, and television

Attenuation   the reduction of an electronic signal

Attenuator   a device that reduces signal strength

Attribution   giving credit for information or a quotation

Audio console (or board)   the central point at which audio signals are selected, processed, mixed, amplified, and routed

Audition   to listen to a signal prior to transmission; to demonstrate performance abilities

Audition side   a second series of circuits in an audio board that provide audio board functions while the board's primary signal is being sent elsewhere, probably to the transmitter

Automatic volume control (AVC)   a feature of some audio equipment that automatically tries to boost any perceived sound to 100 percent modulation

Automation   equipment that plays multiple prerecorded materials in a previously selected order

Backtiming   the process of computing starting time of a segment based on counting back from when it should end

Bass roll-off switch   switch on a microphone that makes possible the elimination of certain lower frequencies

Beautiful music   a radio format featuring lush instrumental music and recognizable themes of the past

Bedlam   (from the name of a former insane asylum in England) complete disorder and cacophony

Bi-directional pickup   a microphone pickup pattern that has maximum sensitivity from two sides

Billboard   a wire service listing of upcoming audio or video segments

Board announcer   the announcer assigned to voice copy during a specific assigned period

Board operator   the person to whom the on-air shift is assigned; in radio, usually includes both announcing and engineering duties

Board shift   the time assigned a board operator or announcer who is responsible for the on-air operation of the station

Boom microphone   a microphone suspended from a mechanism that allows audio pickup without intervention of the performers; in television, the out-of-camera-range microphone may be aimed by a boom operator

Bulk eraser   an electromagnet that degauses (erases) information on magnetic tape; used especially on carts, since cart machines have no erase head

Call-in talk show   a radio or TV program in which listeners telephone in with questions and comments

Camcorder   a video camera and recorder in a single unit

Cardiod microphone   a microphone with a heart-shaped pickup pattern

Cart   an endless loop magnetic tape in a container designed for use on a cart machine

Cart machine   a tape player–recorder designed to play continuous loop, automatic cueing tapes

Cassette   a plastic case containing two reels upon which magnetic tape may be wound

Catch-all question   an interview question (usually at the end of the interview) in which the interviewee is asked if there is anything he or she would like to add

CCD   (see Charge coupled device)

CD   (see Compact disc)

Character generator   a computer designed specifically to print information directly onto a television screen

Charge coupled device (CCD)   the solid-state component that has replaced the picture tube in many cameras

CHR   (see Contemporary hit radio)

Chroma key   a process in which a second video source is inserted into a television picture by replacing all spaces of a specific color, usually blue

Classical music   a radio format specializing in serious music, usually of the European formal tradition

Clip-on mikes   a small microphone that can be clipped on television talent, much like a tie clip

Closed question   an interview question that can be answered with a single word or short phrase

Color person   in sports, an announcer who supplements the play-by-play call with descriptions of the environment and with statistics relating to the game

Commercial   an announcement intended to promote a product or organization for which compensation is received

Common carrier   a third party that serves to transfer information or goods

Compact disc (CD)   a plastic disc played with a laser from digitally coded impressions on the disc

Computer editing   editing of magnetic tape, through use of a computer, to complete a previously determined list of edits

Computerized newsroom   a radio or television news facility that stores all stories on computer for editing and assembling into a newscast

Condenser microphone   a microphone that uses a capacitor as the transducer

Console (audio board)   the electronic control center where audio signals are selected, amplified, mixed, monitored, and routed

Contemporary hit radio (CHR)   a radio format that plays the current top hits

Contractions   shortened forms of combinations of words, usually recommended for oral English (I'll, you're)

Copyright   laws that protect the rights of authors, musicians, and publishers

Country   a radio and cable TV format that features country music and country music stars

Cross over   when a music star from one format records a hit in a different format style, often creating a hit in more than one format

Cross fade   in audio, to fade in one element as another is faded out

C-SPAN   two cable television networks set up by the U.S. cable companies to transmit legislative events and related happenings to affiliated cable companies from Washington, D.C.

Cue   on an audio board, a circuit used to cue records and tapes; also refers to hand or other signals given to a performer while on the air

Cue cards   cards held up for a performer, indicating what is to be said or done

Cue tone   a magnetic tape-recorded signal that stops an audio cart; can also activate other electronic equipment

Cutting block   a piece of metal with grooves to hold tape and to designate the proper cutting angles for physical audio editing

Dash   a punctuation mark made with two hyphens (--), indicating a pause longer than a comma

Database   a series of computer files containing information that can be made readily available

Dead air   in radio, a period of silence

Decibel (dB)   a unit used to measure audio strength

De-emphasis   treatment given to words requiring less than normal stress; e.g., prepositions, articles

Delegation switch   a switch that selects input for an audio board channel

Demographics   composition of an audience in terms of age, income, sex, etc.

Diacritical markings   marks/letters used by dictionaries to indicate correct pronunciation

Dialect   a speech pattern and vocabulary typical of a social class, ethnic group, or region

Diaphragm   the muscle separating the abdomen and the thorax; also, the element in a microphone that vibrates in response to sound waves

Diaphragmatic breathing   deep breathing controlled by the diaphragm and the abdominal muscles

Digital   an electronic system using a computer theory of operation (compare to Analog)

Digital audio tape   audio tape recorded using digital processing

Digital effects   the extremely diverse television picture manipulation possible with digital processing

Digital timing device   a timer that translates directly to numbers, as opposed to clock face and sweep second hand

Diodes   miniature lighting elements activated by electronic impulses

Disco   a music style with a distinctive and unvarying dance beat

Dissolve   in television, a simultaneous fading of one picture as another picture is faded in to replace it

DJ (dee-jay)   a disk jockey; one who hosts a popular record show

Dolly   movement of a video camera toward or away from a subject; also, the wheeled platform upon which a tripod rests

Doughnut   a spot with a beginning and an end that has a hole in the middle to insert additional (usually local) copy

Downstream keying   insertion of an additional video source over the regular output of a video switcher

Dramatic pause   a pause taken before a key idea to give it emphasis

Drive time   top listening time in radio, when people are going to or from work

Dub   to copy to audio or video tape

Dynamic microphone   a microphone with a moving coil transducer

Easy listening   a relaxed-paced radio format consisting of a large number of familiar songs played as instrumentals

Edit   to select (or possibly modify) material to be used

EFP   (see Electronic field production)

Electronic field production (EFP)   on-location video production

Electronic news gathering (ENG)   using video and/or audio recorders to record news as it happens, or interviews from the scene sent directly to the station for airing

Electronic prompter   a one-way mirror over a video camera lens that reflects a script to be read by a news anchor or other person on television

Ellipsis   a series of three periods indicating a pause or that material has been left out which should be implied by the announcer from the context of the script

ENG   (see Electronic news gathering)

Erase head   on a tape recorder, a component that erases magnetic tape before it is to be recorded on by the record head

Ethics   behavior of high integrity

Ethnic   having to do with materials of a given culture

Ethos   persuasion through the use of source credibility

Fact sheet   a listing of information from which to ad lib a commercial, news story, etc.

Fade-in (or Fade on-mike)   speaker moves into the mike's primary pickup pattern

Fade-out (or Fade off-mike)   speaker fades out of the mike's primary pickup pattern

Fader arm (or Bar)   the lever on a TV switcher that fades pictures in or out

Fairness doctrine   a policy requiring equal electronic access on controversial issues

Fair use   the limited use of certain materials under copyright law

FCC   (see Federal Communications Commission)

Federal Communications Commission (FCC)   the U.S. federal agency that governs the use of radio, television, and telephone

Federal Radio Commission (FRC)   the federal agency originally set up to regulate radio

Feedback   the retransmission of a transducer's own signal

Fiber optics   the use of glass strands and laser technology for transmission of audio or video signals

FM   (see Frequency modulation)

Follow-up question   question asked by an interviewer in response to a previous statement by the interviewee

Format   the style of programming, including music, announcers, commercial clustering, etc.

Format clock (see also Play wheel)   a circle divided into pie-shaped segments to indicate an hour's radio format

Formula radio   a radio format stated as a set of rules to be strictly followed

FRC   (see Federal Radio Commission)

Free lancer   an independent writer or producer who sells his or her work to whomever will buy it or to the highest bidder

Freedom of speech   the right of U.S. citizens to speak out on issues within limits as decreed by the Supreme Court

Freedom of the press   a right granted to the press to print or air all material within the restrictions of slander and decency as decreed by the Supreme Court

Frequency modulation (FM)   a system of radio wave transmission that changes broadcast frequency within a given range to transmit information

Frequency range   the limits of an electronic unit to reproduce the full frequencies of the original sound

Frequency response   the range of Hertz that an audio system can reproduce

Fringe reception area   a weak broadcast pickup area beyond the normal range of a radio or television station's signal

Gannett   a chain of broadcast and newspaper properties noted for their support of press freedom

General research source   a source of information that catalogs materials from "all" categories; e.g., an encyclopedia

Generic still frame   a news story visual covering a broad category so that it can be used for many different stories

Government documents   materials published by an agency of the federal government and often found in a library section called Government Documents

Happy talk   lighthearted conversation between news anchors and reporters to create a feeling of neighborliness

Hard news   current events that affect or are of interest to people in the area served

Hard rock   rock music with an extremely heavy beat; variation of acid rock

Head phones   earphones mounted on a headband, used in radio to maintain balance between dee-jay and the music

Headsets   earphones with microphones on a headband, used in TV for intercom systems during production; in radio and TV, for sportscasting

Hertz   (after the German physicist) cycles per second

Hidden agenda   list of objectives to be achieved that are not disclosed (e.g., by an interviewee)

High-definition television (HDTV)   a system of television that produces greater definition and higher-resolution pictures than the original FCC standard

Hits clock   (see Play wheel)

ID (station ID)   station identification; the call letters of a station and the name of the community to which it is licensed

Imagery   pictures or other sense manifestations recalled or imagined, creating theatre of the mind

Infomercial   an extended commercial that may appear to be information programming, demonstration, or lecture

Inoculation theory (Hypodermic injection)   an early communication theory that held that constant repetition of an idea in the media would change people's attitudes

Input   the signal or information flowing into an electronic component or system

Instant replay   in sports television, replay of crucial sports actions, often from a different perspective, to examine technique or rules violations

Intercom   a system for private audio intercommunication, particularly for TV production

International phonetic alphabet   symbols used to interpret and reproduce language sounds

Invasion of privacy   a charge often made against news organizations; infringement on physical solitude is closely related to libel laws, access to private property, unauthorized use of one's name or image, etc.

KDKA Pittsburgh   considered the first commercially licensed radio station

Key   in TV, a special effect that combines two images (see Chroma key and Downstream keying)

Larynx   the voice box; vocal folds where voice sounds originate

Laser   an acronym for light amplification by stimulated emission of radiation; a concentrated light beam used to read the imprints on a CD or "laser" disc

Lavalier   an ornament hung around the neck; applied to a small microphone suspended around the neck on a cord

Lead   the first lines that introduce a news story

Leading or loaded question   a question that may force an interviewee to unintentionally disclose private or previously secret information

Lexis and Nexis databases   vast information resources indexing and recalling important news periodicals via computer

Libel   an untrue statement about a person made in the media that can harm that person's reputation or financial status

Light rock   soft, popular music with a rock beat

Limiter   a device that cuts off extremely high volume and boosts low-level signals

Line level   the proper signal level for processing an audio signal

Lip-sync   the synchronization of lip movement with the sound of a person's speech

Logos   a persuasion technique based on logic

Low-cut filter   a device that filters out low audio frequencies to avoid electric fan noises, bass drums, etc.

Media event   a news happening that would not have occurred had the media not been there to cover it; e.g., a news conference

Microphone   a device that changes sound waves to electrical impulses

Middle of the road (MOR)   a music format for radio that includes no extremes in music style, no hard rock, no opera or symphonies, "not too much of anything"

Mimicry   the replication of another's voice or mannerisms

Mix-effect busses   a row of buttons representing video sources on a video switcher, providing capabilities of fading and special effects

Mnemonic device   a memory aid; often a group of letters or numbers

Moiré effect   the apparent dancing of figures on the video screen as a result of the small size and proximity of the figures

Monaural   transmission or production of an audio signal with only one channel

Monitoring   listening to or watching a signal to make adjustments to the signal as necessary

Monitor speaker   a speaker that reproduces the outgoing audio signal

MOR   (see Middle of the road)

Moving coil   a microphone transducer using a coil of wire in a magnetic field to generate an electrical impulse

Muting relay   an electronic switch that turns off the control room monitor when a mike is opened

Nasality   a voice quality resulting from placing the voice in the head

National Association of Broadcasters (NAB)   an organization of broadcasters that negotiates for the industry and lobbies Congress, etc.

Network feed   programming distributed by a network for airing by affiliates

News consultants   organizations that monitor news formats around the country and make recommendations to stations as to successful techniques

News plus   a modification of the all-news format that may include some music programming, sports, and talk shows, especially outside of normal drive time

News/talk a radio format that consists of news and various kinds of talk shows, many of which deal with current events

Nondirectional mike a microphone that picks up in all directions (no one direction)

Objective in news, an unbiased report; in camera shots, viewing action as if with the room's fourth wall removed

Oldies a music format featuring music that was tops in popularity during some past decade

Omni-directional a microphone that picks up in all directions

Open question a question requiring a statement or series of statements to answer

Oscilloscope a specialized video screen that shows several types of electronic signals

Out cue the ending statement or phrase in a package or other broadcast segment

Output the signal that emanates from a given audio or video source

Overlining lines drawn over certain words in a script to indicate to the reader the pitch or style of reading to be used

Over-the-shoulder shot taken over the shoulder of another person, showing approximately what that person would see; often the head-on view of a person being interviewed

Pace the speed of a presentation; often related to the way cues are picked up by the announcers or actors

Pacer a short musical bridge, or sound effects that keep a rapid-fire pace on certain radio formats

Package a complete video or audio news story, usually recorded in the field and edited for presentation as part of a newscast

Pantomime acting with expression, gestures, etc.—without words

Parentheses curved brackets–( )–used in punctuation and in marking copy to denote a lesser idea or a comment; also sets off phonetic pronunciations in copy

Patch bay or Patch panel a series of jacks that allow routing options for program signals

Patch cord an electrical cable that has proper connectors to function in a patch panel or patch bay

Pathos an appeal to the emotions to attempt to change an attitude

Peak program meter a device used to measure the intensity of an audio signal

Periodical index any of several bound or computerized indexes that list the contents of current magazines and journals

Perspective an illusion of depth created by lines to a vanishing point in illustrations, or by the use of fade-in, fade-out, and off-mike techniques in audio production

Phantom power supply power for a condenser mike from the audio console's power supply instead of from a battery

Physical editing audio tape editing done by cutting and splicing

Picking up cues beginning one's line before the previous speaker, without stepping on that person's utterance

Pickup pattern the area adjacent to a microphone where on-mike quality is achievable

Pinning the needle loudness so sustained as to keep the VU meter needle at the maximum point of its swing for an extended period

Play-by-play reporting and description of sports action as it happens

Play list in format radio, the list of musical selections that are currently to be used, following the play wheel's formula

Play wheel a circle divided into time segments indicating what kind, sequence, and length of music, talk, and commercials to be aired

Plosives sounds that may "pop" when uttered on certain mikes; e.g., "b" and "p"

Point-of-view camera positioning to show what an important character is seeing

Ports holes in the sides of certain microphones to give directional qualities

Potentiometer (Pot) volume control; also known as gain or fader

Pre-amplifier (Pre-amp) a device that provides additional amplification necessary for a microphone input to bring it to line level

Presentational a speech style specifically directed to the audience

Preview monitor in television, a video screen controlled from the video switcher that displays the picture in line to be aired next

Privilege a favor granted to the recipient (as opposed to a right)

Privileged speech statements not subject to libel litigation; made on the floor of a legislature, in court, etc.

Probing question an interview question that follows up on a previously asked question, seeking greater detail or further background

Processing various electronic modification or enhancement that audio or video signals undergo before being output

Production spots audio or video spots that require production elements other than an announcer; e.g., sound effects, music, additional voices

Program on the audio board, the output of the board usually directed to the transmitter or a recorder; also, a coherent unit of speech and/or music usually designed to entertain or inform

Progressive rock music selections designed as an alternative to hit radio rock

Promo a radio or television spot designed to promote the station or the network's programming

Proximity effect added bass perceived usually by a dynamic microphone when the speaker is extra close

Psychedelic rock music alternative for which it was implied that listeners should be stoned to properly enjoy it

Public figures persons who are in the public eye because of their professions or because of something they have done or that has happened to them

Public service announcement (PSA) a spot announcement aired without charge at the behest of a socially responsible, nonprofit organization

Radio and Television News Directors Association an electronic media news directors' organization that encourages quality performance and ethical standards for news reporting

Reel-to-reel (or open reel) a configuration for tape recorders using nonencased reels of tape that pass before erase, recording, and playback heads to achieve these functions

Religious a format that features religious music and programming

Resonance cavities chambers in the head that help give the voice fullness

Résumé a summary of past experience and accomplishments presented to show job qualifications

Revised wire service phonetics a logical, consistent modification of the phonetic system used by AP and UPI

Ribbon microphone a microphone that uses a thin metal ribbon in a magnetic field to serve as a transducer

Riding gain to carefully monitor audio levels

Right as differentiated from a privilege, a legal guarantee granted by the U.S. Constitution

Rip and read the practice of tearing news from the teletype and reading it without first proofing or editing the copy

Rock music (rock 'n' roll) a popular music form with a heavy beat that tends to feature electric and acoustic guitars, drums, keyboard, and other instruments as well as vocalists; said to combine rhythm and blues with country

Routing to send an audio or video signal to a specific destination

Routing switcher a means of sending an electronic signal without patching, by activating a push button to determine a signal's destination

Satellite an object that orbits around a body in space; when manmade, used to collect and retransmit electronic signals

Satellite dish a curved surface that can aim microwave signals to be sent or received by satellites

Sense of timing a feel for the effects of pauses in adding emphasis

Shotgun mike a highly directional microphone with a long barrel (like a shotgun)

Sibilance emphasis of the sound of the letter ''s''

Slate   labeling of a recorded audio or video segment with the name of the material and a countdown for cueing on the beginning of the tape

Soft news   feature or human-interest stories in which timeliness is not a critical factor

Soft rock   rock music that avoids an extremely intense beat and raucous sound

Soft sell   a sales technique that stresses quality, logic, and a noncommanding presentation

Sound bite   a section of audio or video tape that includes sound shot at the scene

Special effects wipes   on a video switcher, various patterns that may be used in changing from one picture to another

Sports information   the publicity department of an athletic organization, such as a college team

Sports psychology   a course offered at some schools that highlights the effects of psychology on an athlete

Spot   a timed segment or copy for a segment of broadcast time devoted to a commercial message, PSA, or promo

Spot set   a period in a musical format in which commercials and other spots are aired

Standard American speech   the English language as spoken by educated Americans without regionalisms

Standup   a section, usually at the end of a news package, in which reporters are seen on the television screen, concluding a story and identifying themselves

Statement of inquiry   a statement requesting information; has the effect of an open question

Stereo   sound that has various elements separated into two or more channels, giving a perception of depth or surround sound

Still store   a device that records frames of video for rapid recall

Straight copy   presentational material intended to be aired without the addition of music, sound effects, or more than one voice

Studio prompter   a device that projects copy on a mirror over the video camera lens

Subjective camera (point-of-view)   a camera perspective that is the view through the eyes of a given character

Subtext   the rationale and emotions behind a character's speech and actions

Sweep   on radio, a period of sustained music; also, the calendar dates when ratings are taken (as in sweep period)

Switcher   the control system device that selects, mixes, routes, and processes a television signal before distribution

TelePrompTer   registered trademark name for a studio prompter

Theatre of the mind   the images created in the listener's mind by words, sound effects, and music on radio, especially during its golden age

Thoracic breathing   shallow breathing in which the speaker attempts to control speech by using the upper parts of the lungs to provide breath support

Thorax   the upper two-thirds of the trunk of the body, from the shoulders to the diaphragm

Time code   a system of numbering each frame of a video tape to allow accurate and rapid editing

Time cues   hand signals, printed cards, various clock forms, etc., indicating to the performer the time remaining in the current program segment

Timeliness   in reference to news material, currently happening or of immediate import

Tone   quality of sound

Track   a pathway created by a record head on video or audio tape

Transducer   any device that changes energy form; e.g., a microphone changes sound wave energy to electrical impulses

Transistor   a device that supplanted vacuum tubes in broadcasting and computing hardware

Tripod   a three-legged mount for a camera

Turntable   a circular platform used to retrieve audio signals from records

Underlining   the most common way of marking a script to indicate emphasis in reading

Uni-directional   a pickup pattern of a microphone that is sensitive primarily on one side only

United Press International (UPI)   a U.S. news service that is privately owned and offers an alternative to the Associated Press

Urban contemporary   a radio format featuring popular, danceable music based primarily on black music types; in heavily Latino population areas, the format may also feature Latin music

Vectorscope   a wave form monitor, usually monitored by an engineer, that shows the color components of a television picture

Verbal crutches   unnecessary interjections in ad lib broadcasting or in speech; e.g., and-uh, yu-know, etc.

Vibrator   the larynx; vocal cords that vibrate to create speech sounds

Video cassette   a plastic container with two reels of tape designed for recording and playback of television programming

Video disc   the video counterpart of the compact disc; any section is easily retrievable, making it ideal for individualized instruction

Vocal cords   folds of the larynx, where voice sounds originate

Voice-over (VO)   narration by an announcer over music, sound, or video

Voice pattern   a tendency for beginning announcers to use a repetitive pitch or pace

Voice placement   a mentally created voice projection focal point

Voicer   in radio, a news story recorded by reporters for use on newscasts; may or may not include an actuality

Voice wrap   a recorded segment in which the reporter presents the introduction and close around an actuality

Volume control   (see Potentiometer)

VU Meter (Volume unit meter)   a device that visually monitors audio levels

Wave form monitor   a video monitor that graphically displays the form of a video or audio signal

Wild sound   sound recorded at a news event; may be used when delivering the copy

Wind screen   a foam rubber cover placed over a microphone to cut down wind noises

Wire service phonetics   a system used to translate words into sounds, using symbols found on a teletype machine

Wow-in   the sound of a record getting up to speed, or the sound made by a record that is cued too tightly

Zoom lens   a lens that allows an infinite number of picture magnification options within the lens's range; can also be used to rapidly magnify an object (zoom in) or rapidly pull back to view a wider area (zoom out)

Photo Credits

Index